MY CROSS TO BEAR

Gregg Allman

WITH ALAN LIGHT

WILLIAM MORROW
An Imprint of HarperCollins*Publishers*

A hardcover edition of this book was published in 2012 by William Morrow, an imprint of HarperCollins Publishers.

FIRST WILLIAM MORROW PAPERBACK EDITION PUBLISHED 2013.

Designed by Jamie Lynn Kerner

Library of Congress Cataloging-in-Publication Data has been applied for.

ISBN 978-0-06-211205-7

16 17   OV/RRD   10 9 8 7

Named One of the 25 Greatest Rock Memoirs of All Time by *Rolling Stone*

"Essential reading for ABB fans . . . the book's detail-rich examination of key events in his music career gives *Cross* its dramatic momentum and value. . . . The book's tone is so open and engaging, *My Cross to Bear* could appeal even to readers whose knowledge of the band begins and ends with 'Ramblin' Man.'"
—*Miami Herald*

"This book is everything you could hope for: in a grizzled, laconic drawl, Allman provides a rambling backstage account of his five decades with the Allman Brothers Band."
—*New York Times Book Review*

"There are . . . finally answers to trivia that has been subject to years of rumors and incorrectly repeated stories."
—Associated Press

"Allman avoids glamorizing or sanitizing to produce a rich, three-dimensional representation of a person with deep musical talent and fragile emotions. . . . As much as his book is about music, Allman essentially writes about the power of relationships. . . . The best of the Allman Brothers Band music resonates with a raw, genuine honesty; Gregg Allman manages to capture that same spirit in *My Cross to Bear*."
—*Boston Globe*

"A soul-searching rumination on a hard-lived life."
—*USA Today*

"Allman . . . offers up larger-than-life scenes from his career in music. He divulges the tension and chaos that eventually led the Allman Brothers to split."
—*Entertainment Weekly*

"Allman beautifully re-creates the rock scene of the mid-60s."
—*Hollywood Reporter*

"A story about musical brotherhood. With gentlemanly charm and compassion, the author vividly recounts how a guitar first transformed the lives of two restless boys. . . . Rich and moving. . . . Nothing less than profound. . . . As his many-faceted memoir so effectively demonstrates, the road does, indeed, go on forever for the Allman Brothers Band."
—*Kirkus Reviews*

"Gregg Allman has long been sitting on one of the great untold stories in the history of rock 'n' roll music."
—*Courier Press*

"A fiercely honest memoir."
—*Publishers Weekly*

"Fans of the Allman Brothers Band are certain to relish the revelations. . . . He presents himself as a man cracked and flawed, yet somehow intact."
—*Birmingham News*

"Sometimes laugh-out-loud funny and other times heart breaking, Gregg's down-to-earth narrative is endearing from beginning to end."
—*American Blues Scene*

"He describes his complex relationship with his brother Duane and his tragic death in 1971, something he's rarely addressed."
—*Detroit News*

"A gut-wrenching, brutally honest self-reflection of a true rock-and-roll survivor."
—*Los Angeles Daily News*

"Gregg presents a story as honest as it is fascinating, providing a glimpse inside one of the most beloved and notorious bands in the history of rock music. . . ."
—*Book Reporter*

To my mom and Duane

My sincere appreciation goes to contributing author John Lynskey, whose insight, knowledge, and experience with the Allman Brothers Band and my career helped to bring this project together. Thanks, bro.
—G.A.

CONTENTS

SEPTEMBER 2011

I was sitting up talking, and I just kind of nodded off. But I didn't nod off; I was Code Blue. I was bleeding inside, and I was drowning in my own blood.

What I remember is that I went to sleep and I had the most incredible dream. It was almost like a still life, and the air smelled so good and music was playing. I always have music in my dreams, and whatever type of music it is, it sets the whole mood for whatever's happening. If it's a nightmare, it's some nasty music. But this music was beautiful.

I was standing at a bridge and it was twilight, and somebody was on the other side. They weren't motioning, they were just looking at me, but the message got through: don't come across this bridge. It was all so beautiful, I wanted to go over there and see who it was. All I could see was a silhouette of the person, with hair down to their shoulders. It appeared to be my brother. Maybe it was just somebody standing in my room, I don't know. But somebody was there, telling me not to come across that bridge. It's not my time yet.

PROLOGUE

January 1995

It should have been the greatest week of my life, but instead I hit an all-time low. The Allman Brothers Band, the band my brother started, the band with our name on it, was inducted into the Rock and Roll Hall of Fame, and I flat-out missed it. I was physically there, but otherwise I was out of it—mentally, emotionally, and spiritually. You might say that I had the experience but missed the meaning. Why? The answer is plain and simple—alcohol. I was drunk, man, just shitfaced drunk, the entire time.

I arrived in New York on a Sunday, got drunk, and stayed drunk for five days, including the induction ceremony itself. My memory is a bit hazy, thanks to the booze, but I remember little bits, flashes of this and that, of the week that ultimately changed my life. On that Monday we taped a segment for the *Late Show with David Letterman,* and when I look at a tape of that night, I don't even recognize the guy singing "Midnight Rider." My face was puffy and bloated from the booze, and my skin had taken on this gray, sickly pallor, which was accented by the fact that I had shaved my beard. With sunglasses and a top hat to round things out, I was really looking rough.

My voice was suffering as well, but I managed to get through the taping. I spent a lot of time making it up and down the stairs that went from the studio to the green room, where there was a bar. After *Letterman* it was back to the bar at the Waldorf-Astoria for vodka and cranberry the rest of the night.

On Tuesday I had to go get fitted for my tux, and after the fitting we had lunch at a Chinese restaurant. My team had the idea to hold an intervention. They were there to tell me that I needed to go into treatment, and I needed to do it now. There was a plan in place, and treatment had been arranged for me at a center in eastern Pennsylvania. They all stressed how badly I needed to do this, because they told me I was dying, and they couldn't sit by and watch me slowly kill myself any longer.

It was a speech I'd heard before, but this was different. A little voice told me that enough was enough, and this time I listened. I gave in and told them I would go. I resigned myself to going at the end of the week, but until then I just kept right on drinking, man—I drank constantly. I couldn't *not* drink, you know? Sad but true: I could not not drink.

Later in the day, we headed over to Sony Studios on West 54th to do some vocal overdubs for the Allman Brothers record *Second Set*. Tommy Dowd, our beloved producer, was there, and what should have been real simple became an ordeal. I couldn't get the fucking words to come out right. The alcohol had tied my tongue in knots, and the guys in the booth were literally cutting one word at a time. I was spitting and sputtering; we finally got it done, but it was torturous.

We had another TV appearance scheduled for Wednesday, this time on *Late Night with Conan O'Brien*. We did *Conan* during the day, and played a couple of songs, including an extended version of "Statesboro Blues" that just went on and on. Dickey Betts and Warren Haynes really were unbelievable, but I was just trying to hold on. I was a scary-looking sight—my eyes were hollow, empty, and so yellow that they looked like a couple of lemon slices.

After that, we were scheduled to rehearse for the induction ceremony over at the Waldorf, where the band was going to work up a shorter version of "One Way Out." I just couldn't make it. Sorry, but I was worn out, and I couldn't do it.

Thursday was the ceremony, in the ballroom of the Waldorf. That morning, I took some shot glasses, and I measured them out just right. I didn't wanna get drunk. So I lined up the glasses, took the shots, and I was doing all right. Back then, I didn't have the shakes—I had the hydraulic jerks. I had to keep a half-pint up under the bed in case I sobered up in my sleep. I could hardly walk, I was shaking so bad.

One of my old buddies called me from downstairs, and I went down and saw everybody I ain't seen for a hundred years. Next thing you know, I was at the lobby bar. "C'mon, man, let me buy you a drink." They started collecting in front of me, from people all around the bar. Needless to say, I sat there and got shitfaced. Believe it or not, this turned out to be a good thing.

My dear mother, Geraldine, was there, and she was very worried about me, as were a lot of people by this point. I found out later that Jaimoe, my bandmate and a sweet man, was upstairs in his room, and he was actually crying because he thought I was dying—literally dying.

I managed to introduce my mother to Ahmet Ertegun, the founder of Atlantic Records and someone who had meant so much to my brother and me. I was trying to pace myself, but when it was time for me to go onstage, I was in bad shape. Willie Nelson presented the band with our award, and when I got up there he asked me, "You all right, Gregory?"

"Willie, I am *not* all right," I replied. I tried every trick I knew to keep people from knowing I was drunk, but I couldn't stand up straight; I was kind of weaving.

One thing I'd been concerned about beforehand was my acceptance speech. I had to say something, so I wrote several ideas down on this little notepad—little phrases and what have you, things I had said in the past. I'd organized them onto one sheet of paper, and that became the speech I was going to give. There were a lot of things I wanted to say—about my mother, about the fans, about Bill Graham—but instead I just got up there and said, "This is for my brother. He was always the first to face the fire. Thank you." That's about all I could get out, and it was one of the most embarrassing moments of my life. I had to get the hell off that stage, because I was getting a little woozy.

After the band performed "One Way Out," I got out of there as fast as I could. I went up to my room, changed into my jeans and leather jacket, and headed back to the bar, still clutching my Hall of Fame award. People were surrounding my table, telling me how great I was, buying me drinks, but I felt nothing. I had just won the highest award there is in my profession, and I didn't give a damn—I just wanted another drink. People would ask to hold my award, and I'd let 'em; somebody probably could have run off with it, you know?

The agreement that I had made was that the next morning, a Lincoln Town Car would take me to a treatment center, which was actually a farm in east-central Pennsylvania. It was about a four-hour ride, and we left around noon. I emptied the minibar in my hotel room for the drive, and I had some Valium as well. I had all these little airplane bottles of booze in my coat pocket, and we got in the car and started driving. I spent the ride taking pills and washing them down with those mini-bottles. Somewhere in Pennsylvania, we stopped at a little Italian restaurant to get something to eat, but of course my meal ended up being four double vodka and cranberry—I never touched my veal marsala.

We got back in the car, and we finally arrived at the center, which is in a little town by a river. I had two mini-bottles of vodka left in my jacket, so I put them in my fist, took the lids off of both of them, upended them like a double-barreled shotgun, and emptied them both as we pulled into the driveway. It was so pathetic, but I remember thinking, "You are better than this, and it's time for this crap to stop." I knew it was time for a change.

Welcome to the story of my life.

A day at the beach with my brother

CHAPTER ONE

Brothers

I WAS BORN ON DECEMBER 8, 1947, AT 3:23 IN THE MORNING, AT the old St. Thomas Hospital in Nashville. It was a beautiful building, all marble and brownstone. Now they've moved to the outskirts of town, but like everybody I've ever known in Nashville—"Where were you born?" "St. Thomas."

My brother, Duane, was born on November 20, 1946, one year and eighteen days before me. Same hospital, same doctor.

In late 1949, when I was two years old and my brother was three, my father, who was about thirty at the time and a lieutenant in the army, was assigned to Ft. Story in Virginia Beach, Virginia, as a recruiter. My father had fought in the last part of World War II and had landed on the beaches at Normandy on D-Day. He'd been a gunnery sergeant and a lieutenant, and he'd just gotten promoted to captain. He was getting the pay, but he hadn't gotten the bars yet.

The day after Christmas, he and a friend of his, who was a

master sergeant, went out to a tavern that they always went to, just shooting pool and drinking beer. The year before, when he was overseas, my father had ordered a brand-new Ford, so he'd gotten one of the first '49 Fords that came off the line. That night, he and his friend took his new car, and they were definitely celebrating being back home.

After they'd been there for a bit, this dude at the bar started asking them, "Tell me about the war." He was buying them beers and all this stuff. It got late into the night and the guy asked them if he could get a ride home, and they said sure. They got up the highway, and my father asked the guy where he lived. He said, "You turn right up here on this dirt road." Of course, back then the roads in that part of Virginia barely had asphalt, especially out in the cornfields. They turned and started going on one of those roads through the corn, and when they got to a place where the corn stopped, the dude pulled out an army .45. He told my daddy to stop and get out, so they did. They're talking and talking, and he thought they had a bunch of money because of the new car and their uniforms and everything.

My dad said, "You can have everything—take the car, take everything."

His friend, the sergeant, said, "Listen, buddy, we don't mean ya no harm."

And the guy goes, "Oh, you know my name. Now I gotta kill ya."

It turned out the guy's name was Buddy Green—first name Buddy, or maybe that was his nickname. Either way, he misunderstood what my daddy's friend had said, and they were in trouble. My father gave some kind of signal and he and his friend took off running, but the guy got my father three times in the back. He missed the sergeant, I think.

At that time in the state of Virginia, they had a sentence called

"99+1," and you couldn't serve the one until you served the ninety-nine. So it was a hundred-year sentence, and Buddy Green got that. He recently died in prison, but at one point I started getting these letters from him. I guess one day one of his partners in prison must have said, "Hey, look whose papa you killed, asshole." And, oh, they were these mournful letters, like "I'm sorry to the 16th power," over and over. But I never wrote back. Matter of fact, I think I might've done away with the letters.

My two uncles, Sam and Dave—sounds like a band to me—they always drummed it into my head not to ever hitchhike or pick up a hitchhiker. And I listened to them. The only time I ever did bum a ride was after my brother called me in March 1969 to come join him and these other four guys to play some music.

My dad was named Willis Turner Allman, and they called him Bill, mostly. When he was younger they called him Billy. His family was from White Bluff, Tennessee—actually, they were from Vanleer, Tennessee, which is a small suburb of Dickson, which is a small suburb of White Bluff, which is a small suburb of Nashville.

Growing up, I spent a lot of time at my grandmother's house, and I still remember the address—703 Eighteenth Avenue South. My grandmother's name was Myrtle Allman, and my grandfather was named Alfred. They were my dad's folks, and they were married back in the days when the family kind of appointed who your spouse was going to be. You see those old oval pictures, where the ladies were all buttoned up, with their ankles covered up and everything—those were the times when they'd met each other. They stayed married long enough to have three boys in four years, and then they divorced—goodbye, end of story, I hate your fucking ass.

My mother is named Geraldine, but they called her Jerry. She was from Rocky Mount, North Carolina, and her maiden name is Robbins. She had a sister, Janie, and two brothers. Her oldest brother was Robbie, whose real name was Swindale, which was a popular name in parts of North Carolina back then. He built the Atlantic City Pier basically by himself. He had another guy help him pour the cement, but he put all them pilings in. He was a tough old bird who died of cancer, and he died slow. His last few days, he was just pissed off, man. My mother was the youngest sister, but she wasn't the baby. The youngest was my uncle Erskin, who died a long time ago of testicular cancer. He died a very young man, and he was kind of a groove.

As I remember it, my parents met in Raleigh, North Carolina, during World War II, when my father was home on leave from the army and my mother was working in Raleigh. Eventually they moved to Tennessee, and the first home my mom and dad had didn't have plumbing, and all my mother wanted to do was get the hell out of Vanleer. My mother didn't get along with the Allman family worth a damn—she didn't back then, and now, hell, there's not many left on either side. I love them all, but they don't talk to each other. There's no love lost there. After my father died, she was gone, out of there.

I don't have the slightest memory of my father, nothing. As far as I was concerned, it was always the three of us—my mom, Duane, and me. I wondered about it in the first and second grade, but you're so damn young you can't understand it. When I was in the fifth grade, I went over to a friend's house, and I thought, "Who is this big son of a bitch kicking my friend around? I sure am glad that I ain't got one!" I thought it was quite a bonus not to have a father.

One day I was sitting with my mother, watching this speech by John F. Kennedy. He said, "Ask not what your country can do for you—ask what you can do for your country." My mother said, "God, your father used to say that years ago. That's how he snaked all them young boys into joining up."

After my dad died, we moved to Nashville, and my mother went to work for NAPA—National Auto Parts Association. One day, a delivery boy named Elvis Presley came by with some car parts. My mother came home and said, "This deliveryman came in, and he looked funny. He had one of them riverboat haircuts, and his name was Elvis." Sure enough, he came on the TV, and Mom said, "That's him—that's Elvis!"

My mother must have really loved my father a lot, because she never remarried and she had no social life when I was growing up. She only had one boyfriend, a guy from Greece. He was a terrible driver—it took him like six tries to get his driver's license. He was some kind of master chef, and he had to drive to Orlando to pick something up. On the way back, he had a head-on crash with a tractor-trailer, and I can remember how hard that hit her. She never went out on a date again.

Later on in life—when I was old enough not to get smacked for asking something like this—I asked her about it. She said, "I was so afraid that some belligerent guy would come around here and knock you boys around, and I'd have to kill him, and I didn't want that to happen." At first I didn't believe her. I thought that maybe she just didn't want the confusion, but I didn't know that much about life and love, I guess.

Still, my mother knew how to wield a switch, but that was a real rare thing. One time, she caught me playing with matches. We had these big hedges that went around the house, and there was this space in between 'em. Me and one of my little school chums were in there and we were lighting model airplanes with a can of lighter fluid—I'm sure every kid did it.

Well, the house was built of wood, and the wrong spray and

the right match . . . I don't know if it would've gone up or not, but there's always that chance. My mother came out of those hedges—she just appeared there—and she grabbed me up by the wrist and I was just kinda dangling. And pow! I knew not to squirm either, because it would last twice as long.

We lived at 214 Scotland Place. I've been by there since, and they've built onto the house, because when we were there we had a huge yard. My mother couldn't stand the neighbors, because they built this huge treehouse that she said looked like the "damn shanty Irish." I didn't know what that was, but I thought it must be a bad thing to be from Ireland.

In our house, you'd go down the hall and my mother's office was there, which would have been another bedroom. The bathroom was right there, and then there was the two bedrooms, Mom's and ours. In between was a closet—*the* closet. See, my mother had to work every day, and the year that Duane started school, she hired this young black lady named Gladys to come in and watch me. Gladys would lock me in the closet, and she told me that she was a personal friend of the boogieman, and even though I couldn't see him, he was in there with me. If I did anything that she didn't like, or if I tried to get out of there, he would jump on me and eat me. I was four years old and, man, I was scared to death.

I can still remember the sound of the hair coming out of Gladys's head when my mother pulled it out. She asked me to go get something out of the closet one night, and I tried to be as cool as I possibly could be. I was like, "I got to do something right now. I'll get to it later." She tried it two or three times, and she was watching me, and finally she said, "Come on in here and sit on my lap. Why don't you tell me what's in that closet?"

I told her the whole story, and I begged her not to tell Gladys. Boy, my mama's face was getting red—she was like a locomotive.

So I kind of put it out of my mind, but the next day Mama came home early from work, and oh man! The door busted open and she came in, and Gladys was laying there with a fifth in her hand, with one of my mother's dresses on, watching TV. My mother grabbed her by the hair, saying, "Don't you never come back here again," and every time she said something, she pulled some hair out. I thought she was gonna kill her, man.

Back then money was tight, and we didn't have much, but my mother did have a home entertainment center—the big floor model, with a big TV. You slid something back and it had the changer there, the speakers were all over the place, and you had your big storage space. It was mahogany, and it was set up right by the front door. She had *Johnny's Greatest Hits*, by Johnny Mathis. I always thought that was a beautiful record, with all the strings and everything. On the other hand, she listened to this other guy, Vaughn Monroe. Vaughn would be on the radio when she took us to school in the morning—every morning, man.

The first person I knew who really loved music was David Allman, my uncle. When you're real young, if something really moves you, you spend a lot of time on it. Uncle David had this old radio—it was a Philco, kind of roundish, and it had a big dial with all these bands of different colors on it. Every now and then, he would let me monkey with it, but if Grandma caught me, she'd tell me to leave it alone. "That's David's, and you know he brought it back from Okinawa." She was a terror sometimes, but a sweet terror.

Late at night, he'd put that radio on and I'd listen for hours. I loved to sleep over with David, because I knew we'd listen to music. Uncle David just loved his music, and he could really sing. He'd walk around the house just singing. He could sing a low note and rattle everything in the room. He had a hell of a throat, and if he'd ever put it to use, he could have been something. Sadly, he passed away in 2010.

WHEN I WAS IN THIRD GRADE, EIGHT YEARS OLD, MY MOTHER packed Duane and me off to military school. Having my older brother with me was the only thing that saved me, because back then I knew—I didn't think, I knew—deep in my heart that my mother hated me. I just couldn't figure out *why*. I thought she just didn't want us around, but I look back at it today, and I was so wrong. She was actually sacrificing everything she possibly could—she was working around the clock, getting by just by a hair, so as to not send us to an orphanage, which would have been a living hell.

The real reason we went was so my mother could go to school to become a CPA. They had all these strange laws back then, and I think you had to go to an on-campus college for that degree, had to stay there on campus, something like that. It seems ridiculous to me, but that's what I was told. All I know is that she worked her ass off so that we could go to Castle Heights Military Academy in Lebanon, Tennessee.

Castle Heights was a real mix of kids. Some came from broken homes, some came from South American countries like Venezuela, Colombia, and Brazil, and some came from wealthy parents who just wanted to get rid of them and were all too happy to just let the kids grow up at school. We had a lot of people who were kind of unruly. I remember this one boy named Gonzalez. I'll never forget how they kept hazing him and hazing him. I was in the junior school at this point, and he was up in the senior school. He went home for Christmas vacation, and he got a .22 rifle for a gift. When the boys started messing with him, he turned around and shot and killed some son of a bitch. He shot him right through the heart, man. When my grandmother heard that, she kept going on about it, saying, "I told you it was a hellhole," and telling my mother how she messed up again, how we were going to turn out to be hoodlums.

A typical day at Castle Heights would start with the bugler blowing that damn reveille at six o'clock sharp. You'd get up, get dressed, go outside, and hit formation. You'd march to breakfast, and after that was over, you could go down to this little area called the "butt hole," which was the only place you were allowed to smoke. People did everything there, man—they chewed tobacco, and there was one guy who would go the drugstore and get oil of cinnamon, and take toothpicks and soak them in it and sell those sons of bitches. This guy was a real go-getter. By the time he left that school, I don't know how much money he'd racked up, but he had it going.

After breakfast, you'd go back to your room. You'd have about an hour to shower and clean up your room, then you would have a quick inspection. There were two guys to a room, and me and my brother were roommates. There was no air-conditioning, and the mattress was only about two inches thick, over a thing of tightly wound springs, so it was like the valley of fatigue, because you never slept well.

After break, the bell would ring for your first class. We'd have three classes, then break for lunch. After lunch, we had an hour break, so you could go read your mail or whatnot. Then another class or two, and then you'd go to drill instruction. You'd go down this huge field, and you'd see big old groups of kids getting ready for war, and that was a dismal sight. We'd carry a damn M1 rifle that weighed nine pounds. It was terrible.

The instructors were retired army personnel, and a lot of times we would talk behind their backs, saying, "These guys couldn't make it in the army, so they sent them to us." Some of them were really rough, man—they'd scream at you, and you'd have to answer with all that "Sir, yes, sir" bullshit. That's probably where I developed some of my voice, because when I had earned a little rank, they gave me the "Sir, yes, sir" right back.

If you look at pictures of me and my brother while we were there, I look sad and depressed while Duane has this look of defiance. That's how he was—he was probably feeling the same way as me, but that's just the way he came across. Me, I just hated the whole idea. I hated being away from home. I was just too young. I learned how to cuss, and in the third grade I knew every word there was.

One good thing was that I didn't get hazed too much, because I had my big brother there, and he wouldn't let nobody fuck with me. He made friends with some of the bigger guys, so that helped too. Then later, when we came back, we had them guitars, and they saved us. Still, you could plan on a scuffle or two at least once a month. Sooner or later, there was going to be an all-out fight, especially after Christmas, because nobody wanted to be there, and it had turned cold—that's when all the fights usually started.

But Duane couldn't do anything about the instructors. If your grades weren't good enough, they would beat you with rifle straps or a canoe paddle, which is pretty heavy. They would drill holes in it to make it hurt more. The worst one was the coat hanger— they'd pull it out straight, and start at the back of your legs and end up at your shoulders. Oh man, that was a beating. The one thing you did not want to hear was "Bend over and grab that table, boy."

It sounds like a sob story, but I have to say that it did make me stronger in certain ways and weaker in others. I spent a lot of time alone there, and to this day I don't like to be alone. The thing was, I really dove into my studies. I was first in my class two years in a row. There was nothing else to do but study. I had a real interest in medicine, and I often wonder how it would have been if I had kept on with my interest in medicine or gone to dental school and come out an oral surgeon.

My brother also tried to get something out of it. He read a lot, and I should have followed his example. When he died, he was reading the *Lord of the Rings* trilogy for the fifth time. He was crazy about J. R. R. Tolkien. He also was a big Kurt Vonnegut fan. That came later on in his life, but his love of reading started at Castle Heights, because it took you away from what was going on around you.

My biggest cross to bear, my biggest worry, during the first part of my life was school, and all the changes that came with it. Life for me was not knowing what was going to happen the next day. It seemed like nothing would happen for a long time, and all of a sudden a great change would come down. I was always kind of afraid of that, because change hadn't always been a good thing.

For years I held my mother responsible for that. I wanted to hurt her, because I felt that she hurt me. I cried myself to sleep at night for a week after I first got to that place. I know it sounds like I was a real pussy when I was a kid, but at that age, half a hundred miles away from home might as well be ten thousand miles. I would sneak off someplace, find a phone, and call home, collect, about eight times a day. I did it just to mess up her day, because I was so angry at her.

I said to her one day, "Mama, people step on ants, because they just didn't see them. They didn't mean to kill them, and that's kinda like the situation we got here, with you stepping on me." I said shit like that to her all the time—I just wanted to fuck with her. Underneath it all, I wanted her to understand how badly I wanted to come home, but it didn't work.

I can only imagine how she must have felt when she hung up that phone, because there was nothing she could do about it.

There were times when she would have enough of it, and she'd go into a rage and try to explain it to me, and she'd be yelling and crying at the same time. She tried to beat it into my thick head that she was doing this for me, not to me. In later years, I came to understand that, but it took me a long time to get over it.

AFTER FOURTH GRADE, MY MOM HAD HER CPA LICENSE, SO WE could come back and be with her. For a long time after coming out of Castle Heights, I was still kinda shell-shocked, like these ghosts were around me. I was so afraid of having to go back to that damn place that it lingered with me. After being in military school, public school seemed really loose and jive. I thought, "Shit, how does anybody learn anything around here? Everybody is talking to this person or that person and throwing spitballs." In military school, you walked into class in single file and stood at the chair until the instructor told us we could sit down. Adjusting took a long time.

Back in Nashville, I had to deal with this girl who sat behind me in the fifth grade. Fifth grade was kind of rough for me—I only did half of it in Nashville. I was starting to get into clothes, and I loved cowboys. I'm not sure if it was my mother or my grandmother or one of my uncles who got it for me, but I got a Gene Autry shirt for my birthday. It was one of those shirts that buttons around, and it was black. That was my favorite shirt.

Remember those little round things with sticky stuff on the back that you would put on notebook paper? If you accidentally ripped the paper out, you would get one of these things, and just lick 'em and stick 'em, and it would heal up the hole in the paper. Well, this girl had a little box of those, and she was licking them bad boys and sticking them on the back of my favorite shirt. I could feel every time her little hand would just barely touch me, and I knew what she was doing. She wasn't trying to do anything malicious. She was just flirting with me, but I didn't realize that.

I turned around to her and said, "If you stick one more of those things on the back of my shirt, I'm gonna knock the hell out of you."

Well, the fact that I said the word "hell" really took her aback. She couldn't wait, she couldn't *wait,* to stick another one in the center of my back. I came around real quick, and bap! I gave her a haymaker that knocked the shit out of her. I turned back around, and the teacher hadn't seen anything. Oh God, was that a mistake. I put it out of my mind and forgot about it—and was that another mistake. I didn't know about vengeance and shit, you know?

These other two guys and I kinda hung together. One guy's name was Win Dixon, and the other guy was Lee Craft, who actually came to one of my gigs not too long ago. We walked around the side of the school to the bike rack, and when we got there, all the spokes were kicked out of my wheels. Everybody else's were fine, and one of them guys said, "Man, looks like somebody's got it in for you." And right then, bang! It felt like a hammer had hit me in the temple. But it wasn't a hammer, it was that girl's pocketbook—I don't know what she had in there.

For what seemed like the next three or four hours, she just danced on my head, man. All I could see was shoes and petticoats. I was getting my ass whipped for the first time in my life—by a girl. My partners were sitting there, and they couldn't do nothing, so they were laughing and clapping. I mean, she was hurting me, man—she was banging on my head, and she wouldn't stop. She would jump in, do a number on me, and jump back out. So my bloody ass pushes my bike home, and my mother asks, "Honey, what happened?" I said, "Oh . . . never mind." God knows if my brother had found out—oh boy!

Now, my brother did kick my ass pretty much every day for the first few years. There were times that me and Duane just hated each other's guts. You know how it is with brothers. He got me to do what he wanted, and if that required a beating, then I got one. As a matter of fact, when we were really little and they took him off the bottle, I was still in the crib, and if one of my extremities, say a finger or a toe, was poking out where he could get to it, he would grab it; even though he only had a few little teeth coming in, he would bite down to the bone. I still have a few little scars on my hands from him. From that time on, little by little, he was toughening me up.

My brother had a great sense of timing, and he used to pull shit on me all the time. We were sitting down at the table one night, and my mother was already a little bit pissed at me. I think I had gotten some bad grades, and she was on my ass about it. I was remaining silent, hoping that if I didn't think about it, it would go away.

So we're all eating in silence, and we're sitting on these hard, flat chairs. My brother was wearing a bathing suit, and it was still a little bit wet. All of a sudden, he farted like a fucking moose, and that wet bathing suit on that hard chair amplified it even more.

The thing is, Duane was able to keep a straight face, and he went, "Gregory—at the table?"

My mother gave me one look and said, "Get up from the table and go to your room."

All I could get out was "But, but . . ." as I tried to tell her that his butt did it, but my mother was like, "Shut up."

So I go without supper because he farted! It's a wonder that I didn't get the belt as well. He had the devil in him, boy.

Duane actually hung me one time. My brother had light skin—people with red hair should not get out in the sun. Every time he got a sunburn, he'd get big bubble blisters. One day when we were real young, he had one of those blisters on his shoulder, and he had his shirt off. He didn't want it to pop, because the skin underneath was raw. We were climbing a tree, and I put my foot down on what I thought was a limb, but it was his shoulder. That blister popped, and he was screaming. All I thought was "Oh shit"—I knew he was going to whip my ass.

He went in the house for a minute, and then he came back outside. He had this long rope, and he could tie a knot, man—Duane loved rope. He made a perfect hangman's noose, and he told me, "Try this on, man." He put it around my neck, and it was real rough rope, real stiff. He tied the other end around a limb of the tree that he could reach, and he said, "I'll be right back."

He went inside the house, and then came out and said, "Bro, they made some cookies. C'mon inside!" I come running after him, and I got to the end of that rope and—bam!—it jerked me right off the ground and tightened around my neck. My mother came out, and I'm choking, because I can't get a breath of air. She got it off my neck, and she wore his ass out for that. "What do you mean by hanging your little brother? Where did you learn to tie a knot like that? What is wrong with you?"

Duane was only a year older than me, but in his mind it might as well have been twenty years. He was a world traveler compared to me, even at age five. I was a bigger kid than he was, and when we got older, I was a bigger man than he was. His chest had no definition at all, and had one little patch of hair on it, while I had a whole chest full. He hated that. Later on in life, when everybody found out that the girls loved hair on the chest—like Sean Connery as James Bond—he was not happy with me.

But the thing was, I respected him and I loved him, and he didn't have to beat me to get that. He was my hero, even while he was beating me. That sounds a little sick, but I knew that he wouldn't let nobody else mess with me. Most of the time, he'd only give me one lick, just to let me know who was boss. I'm not holding a whole lot of scars from it, just a few—some inside, and some outside.

I suppose it could have gone the other way, and I could have believed that he didn't love me or care for me, and we could have grown up just hating each other's ass. Who knows, though, because the guitar might have solved that.

WE MOVED TO DAYTONA BEACH, FLORIDA, IN 1959, RIGHT SMACK dab in the middle of the fifth grade. My mother loved Daytona Beach. I guess she'd been there when she was a teenager, and she always wanted to go back and live there. It's funny: to this day, my mother doesn't ever complain of pain, except for her sinuses; she's always had sinus problems. Later on in life, I said to her, "Mama, you moved from Nashville to Daytona Beach, Florida— hell, you should have gone to Arizona! You moved to the damn humidity capital of the world."

At first, I hated the fucking place aside from the beach and the warm weather. One thing that saved me from running away and going God knows where is that I rode my bike down to the beach where they were having the last NASCAR beach race. It was scary, because after you came out of the south turn, you had two straightaways, one paved and one beach. Toward the end of it, you had nothing but soft sand, and the whole thing was like a demolition derby. They would stop the race every now and then and get these half-ass little steamrollers out there and pat the sand down a little bit, but those guys were doing 80 to 100 miles an hour, in those big old swaying Pontiacs. It was something to behold, and I wouldn't trade it for nothing.

Because they shaved my head at Castle Heights, I wouldn't cut my hair anymore. I didn't grow out my hair because everybody else did. I grew it out because I remember them taking it down to my scalp, and with the light color of my hair, it looked like I was bald-headed. I don't have the best-shaped head in the world—I mean, bald is beautiful, but not if your head looks like an old basketball with no air in it.

When I went back to Nashville the summer after we moved to Florida, my grandma had been moved into a housing community, which was a big change. She'd always seemed pretty independent. My grandmother read her Bible every day, she smoked three packs of Tareytons a day, and she was one of the finest cooks I have ever witnessed, to this day. She had her ups and downs, man. She loved her gossip, and she talked to herself when she was mopping the floor. She'd start every sentence with "Well, gentlemen . . ." That was an old country way of talking. "Well, gentlemen . . ." is definitely the country side of the Allman family.

Seeing her in that housing was tough, you know? Didn't seem right. I think my uncle Sam was footing the whole bill, and my uncle Dave was on the police force, but I don't know who was paying for what.

My grandmother and my father's brothers were all we had left back in Nashville. A few years before, my grandfather had passed away, but because he and my grandmother were divorced it hadn't impacted her much. Though my grandmother didn't much like Alf, his sons loved him and us grandsons were crazy about him. He brought us firecrackers and barbecue—he bought me a Wham-O slingshot with a sight on it, and a whole bag of ball bearings. I thought, "This old man is the hippest son of a bitch I've ever seen!" What kid didn't want a slingshot like that one? You could take down a pretty good-sized alley cat with one of them!

My grandfather made whiskey all his life and sold it to the state police. I think he worked in a sawmill, because I remember him always having coveralls on and dust all over him. He taught me lots of good things—just hitting me with random bits of wisdom. He told me one time, "Gregory, there's two things that gets you in trouble and one of 'em's your mouth." I was way too young to understand, but later on it hit me.

I was playing with one of those fly-backs one day—the paddle with the ball on a string. He was watching me, and he came up and took the ball in his hand and let the paddle drop.

"Gregory," he said, "I'm gonna tell you something about love."

I'm thinking, "Oh no, here he goes"—'cause I was like five or six.

"If I squeeze and squeeze and squeeze tighter and tighter on this ball," he said, "it might pop out of my hand. But if I just keep a nice, easy grip on it, it'll stay with me forever." I really loved that old man.

The truth is, my uncles and mother tried to keep him away from me as much as possible. Sam and David would take us to see him, in moderation. Nothing really bad ever happened, even though I got a fishhook in my hand one time. My uncles were very good about letting my mother know where we were, and calling ahead and asking to see us. That's why I looked forward to summertime, because I finally had a couple of dads. Though one of them was in this thing called the army, and it dragged him off sometimes, I could always count on the other one being there.

Every time Alf's name came up though, my grandmother would go, "Shi . . ." She wouldn't say "Shit," but we knew what she meant. He was a drunk, a saloon rat—he was a lot of things, man, and she hated him.

I think back now to all the questions I wanted to ask her.

"Why don't you love him, Grandma? Look at me and tell me why you don't love this man, who I love so much? Have you given him a chance? What happened between you all? Why can't you just part as friends?" I don't understand that about divorce. I've had a few, and it's not like I want to have a big reunion, but I don't hardly ever hear from any of them. There's no "Hi, how you doing?" We did once say that we loved each other, and I did pay them all a fair amount of money.

About fifteen years ago, I was in a session, cutting my record *Searching for Simplicity.* I remember somebody talking about this whorehouse, and somebody said, "Gregory, have you ever paid for it?"

I said, "Pay for pussy? There's too much of it." Then I thought, "What am I talking about?" I told them, "Correction—I have paid, and paid, and paid, and I'm still paying for something I ain't getting!"

Seabreeze High School

CHAPTER TWO

Dreams

THERE ARE VERY FEW THINGS THAT JUST TOTALLY ALTER YOUR life. It's like you hear a voice yelling, "Come about, because we are changing course."

One night, my mother dropped me and my brother off at the Nashville Municipal Auditorium, and we spent a buck and a quarter to sit in the cheap seats. The show was called a "revue" because there were a whole bunch of different acts, and they were given maybe five songs each.

Jackie Wilson was the headliner. He closed with "Lonely Teardrops," of course, but he put his coat on the stage floor before he got down on his knees, so he wouldn't get his pants dirty, and that was disappointing. They had the orchestra down in the pit, and I can still see the natural starburst that came off this horn player's instrument when he stood up to take a solo. I guess that was my first taste of live music, much like it must be for our fans who hear us live for the first time. Cheap seats or no cheap seats, it was amazing.

Next to Jackie was Otis Redding, and Otis just took it, man. It was a huge stage, at least twenty-five yards wide, and Otis just ran back and forth across it. He got the whole place singing, and moving faster and faster. Otis was a big old son of a gun, and when he came back out to take a bow, I could see that he had big old stumps for feet. He was a big man, and I mean *big*—Otis was Mean Joe Greene big, that's how large he was. He could really sing, and that band could take it down low.

The girls up in the front row were melting in their seats, and we were watching the whole thing unfold. My brother was just mesmerized—he was frozen, and he looked stuffed, like a taxidermist had gotten through with him. Nothing on his body moved during the whole concert. I had to poke him a couple of times to make sure he was still there with us. He had a time, man, I'm telling you.

That music hit Duane, and it stuck like a spaghetti noodle against the wall. That music was in his heart, and it was in mine too. Then we got to playing it, and we realized how important it really was.

That Otis show was the start, but I didn't have to wait long for more. By August 1960, toward the end of our visit with our grandmother, I was kinda wanting to go home. It was hot as a bitch, and there was no air-conditioning back then, and no sea breeze in Nashville. One day, I looked over across the way, and I saw this mentally challenged guy named Jimmy Banes, who lived over there with his mama and another man, who I don't think was his father. I hope he's doing all right, if he's still alive. He was outside, and he had an old beat-up Packard, and it looked like it was flat black, or else it had never been touched by wax—one or the other. The car ran, and he drove it around, poor guy. He was painting it with a paintbrush, like a house paintbrush.

I had been taught not to ridicule people who were different, so I just went over there and said, "Hey, partner, how you doing?" More than I was looking at him or his situation, I was looking at him painting this car—tires, grille, over the lights, everything. He was painting it black, and it already was black, and he was painting it so it would shine.

In the projects, they always have the front porch—the stoop, they call it. Sometimes there would be walkways going off of both sides, depending on the size of the place. There's usually a swing that hangs there, and they had one of those. There was a bunch of stuff—a ball glove, odds and ends—out on the porch, but one thing in particular caught my eye.

"What do you got up there?" I asked.

"What?" Jimmy asked back.

"That thing, leaning against the house," I said.

"Oh, that's a guitar."

"Okay" was all I said back, and he went on about his business. I waited until he got through painting, and said, "You know how to play this thing?"

"I sure do," he replied. Jimmy picked it up and started playing "She'll Be Coming 'Round the Mountain," and, I mean, he was playing it with a vigor. I thought he was gonna bang the damn strings off of that son of a bitch.

This guitar was a Beltone, and those things are almost impossible to play. This guy might have been autistic, you know? He had filed down the bridge on this old funky-ass twenty-two-dollar guitar, and the thing had enough action to where it wouldn't be too hard for a kid to pick it up and, if done correctly, it could be played. Now, a barre chord was kind of a bitch.

He got through the song, and it was a hell of a lot better than I could do it, so I asked him to play something else, and he showed me a chord. He told me, "Look, you gotta keep these fingers inside"—he was teaching me an E chord. "You gotta keep these three fingers inside these outside strings, because if they touch your finger—oh boy."

"Why?" I asked.

"Well, it will just be bad," he said all cryptically, as if the boo-gieman would come get you.

I'll tell you, my life changed that day. It did. Jimmy and I sat up on that porch until he had to put the top back on his damn paint so it wouldn't dry out. We talked and talked about that guitar, and I went over the next day, and the next day, and I was so thankful for him. Later on, I was at a party, and I picked up a guitar, played maybe three chords, and my brother just about shit himself.

When I came back to Daytona after seeing Jimmy Banes in Nashville, there was still a little bit left of summer, about five weeks or so. We went back to school after Labor Day, much later than they do now. So I went down to the newspaper looking for a job, because I wanted to get a guitar real bad, and I found one at Sears for twenty-one dollars. I knew a guy who had a paper route, and I used to help him with it, and there was nothing to it. All you had to do was remember the damn houses—this was back when people used to put their address on the mailbox.

I had some rough times: a few dog bites and acute ingrown toenails, which two of my children suffer from today. The nail would just dive right down into my toe, the whole thing, both sides. I went to the podiatrist time and time again, and he would take the scalpel and start at the top and go in about a half-inch and cut all the way down. One time I went down and missed the pedal, and I pulled my pant legs up and pus was just sprayed all over the place. That was brutal, man.

But I never thought, "This ain't worth it." I knew I was gonna get that guitar.

Finally, I had saved the twenty-one dollars, and I went down to Sears on my bicycle. I walked up to the counter and told the guy I wanted that Silvertone, and I handed him the money. He told me, "Son, with tax, that'll be $21.95," and he wasn't about to let that ninety-five cents slide. Man, I was just crushed, totally crushed.

I got home and told my mother what had happened, and she could see the hurt and disappointment in my eyes. Well, you know mothers—I didn't even have to ask her. She gave me a dollar, and the next day I rode back down there and got me that guitar.

I didn't want anybody knowing about it, because I didn't want to hear them saying, "Oh, you think you're a star?" People always have something to say. Of course, I didn't have enough money to buy a case, not that that finger-bleeder was worth a case anyway.

About the time I bought my guitar, a motorcycle of Duane's had just fallen apart. It was an old used bike, and Duane had got it off some guy for like seventy bucks, which was still a lot of money for a teenage kid. Of course, Duane started playing my guitar, and I told him to go out and play with his motorcycle parts. He snatched it from me a couple of times, and my mother caught us fighting over it—and thank God, because my fingers were about to go.

There's no question that music brought me and Duane closer together. When we first started learning, it was competitive as hell, almost to the point of me saying, "Fuck you, go find another goddamn band." I had been practicing all this time while he was out motorcycling, and then all of a sudden his bike breaks and he wants to horn in. Eventually we made peace, because that was the only way it was going to work, and he could see that—the only way that we were going to sit down and have me teach him the map of that damn guitar was if we could get along.

If he was to walk into the room right now, and you asked him, "Did this guy teach you how to play the guitar?" he would tell you, "Yeah, I guess he did." But it wasn't like, "For today's lesson . . ." or anything like that. He just watched me, but he watched me like a hawk. If I did something just a little bit different, he'd be, "Why? What's that?" He didn't miss a thing.

Long after he could play circles around me, he'd still say, "You ought to hear my little brother play," and "little brother" pretty much stuck right up to the end of his life. Either that or "bay-brah," as he said it, which is something he got from our old friend Floyd Miles, because that's how Floyd would say "baby brother."

I played that guitar constantly, every day and night. I'd stop for a while and do my homework, but by the end of the year my mother was getting frustrated. My brother was worse, because he would play all day long, while my mother was at work. Duane passed me up in a flash—he got real good. My brother was born with the passion to play, that serious passion that he had for the guitar. That passion was second only to a woman, and it was one of them definite loves, because your guitar ain't gonna leave ya, just like your dog ain't gonna leave ya. He had a real love affair with that guitar.

The first gig I ever played was when I was in the seventh grade. It was me, my little Fender guitar, and a Champ amp. This was at R. J. Longstreet Elementary, right down the street from my mother's house in Daytona. These two guys were supposed to play with me: one of them played drums, and the other one played another guitar—we weren't hip to a bass yet. We were going to play three or four songs in the lunchroom, and we borrowed a set of drums from my English teacher, Mr. Anderson. He was such a nice guy—very tall and skinny, very cool. We had a couple of Ventures songs that we were going to play, instrumentals only, no singing. Forget singing, man.

Right at the last minute, them two boys chickened out on my ass. They just didn't show. There I was, with my little tiny amp and my little guitar. I'm up there by myself, the lights were on, and I turned red as a fucking barn, and I stayed that color throughout the whole performance. Mr. Anderson got up and played the drums, which was really nice of him, but it made me look like I was sucking up to a teacher. Right at the end, I played a Jimmy Reed song, and that went over pretty well.

I didn't know what the outcome was going to be, but in the days that followed, a lot of people came up to me and asked, "When are you going to play again?" That was cool, because a lot of them had never even seen anybody play music like that, and they liked it. And when I came back the next time, I came back full force.

As WE GOT OLDER, THERE WERE TIMES THAT MY BROTHER LEFT ME behind, and I didn't understand it. I even went and asked my mother, "Duane doesn't like me anymore?" That just crushed my mother, and she told me, "No, no. Your brother loves you. He's just growing up, that's all." She really tried to explain that to me.

There was this pretty little girl named Sherry, who looked like Meg Ryan, and she was my brother's first girlfriend. Boy, she was gorgeous. She had this leopard-skin hat, and I guess it was real. She'd wear that hat, and it was the sexiest thing in the whole world. That's when I started to notice girls—this would have been right around the time we moved to Daytona. Duane started going to these parties, with boys and girls, and the boys would eventually go home and the girls would sleep over.

My brother loved women, and they loved him. He was real,

real private about it, even with me—he'd just give me a wink or a nod and walk on. Of course, he'd have to have a blow-by-blow description from me about my women. "Tell me everything, Gregory," he'd say. "Don't you hold back shit."

I had two real heavy crushes when I was in high school. The longest one was this lady named Dee Dee Cornelius. Her father was a math teacher of mine. I took her to the prom and what have you. She was a sweetheart.

Then there was the first heartbreak I can ever remember—I mean Shatteredsville. Vicky Fulton, Victoria Lynn Fulton. I had spent the whole summer before tenth grade with this babe, and I went further with her than I had gone with anybody before. I was infatuated with her—we had the school rings and all that. Then my mother came to me around mid-August and said, "Your grades are so bad, you're going back to military school." I was crushed.

Just as I was preparing to leave, I found out that the school was full. My brother could get in, but I couldn't go until January. My brother's grades didn't get him in as a junior, though, but as a sophomore. Pissed him off, man. He was back in little brother's grade, back with the hired help, so to speak. Believe me, it wasn't because he didn't know the shit. He could learn it just like that. It was just that now he had a guitar under his arm constantly. He was learning that guitar, but they didn't notice things like that. No grades for that—not back then, anyway.

So Vicky and I stayed together that fall, and right around Christmas I got the news that I was going back to Castle Heights in January with my brother. My hair was just getting right. I had a kinda half-Elvis, half-Beatles haircut, I guess. It was nice and poofy, and the sun had bleached it out. I'd been on the beach every day, and my skin was so dark that I looked like a negative that hadn't been developed. I had some freckles—it was the darkest tan I ever had.

So I went back to Castle Heights in tenth grade, and it was terrible. I got through the year, and I came back to Florida. I went to see Vicky, and her house had this long dock that went out over the water. She said, "Well, it's nice that you're back." Then she grabbed my hand and put the ring in it.

I said, "What's this?"

She said, "I'm so sorry." I was gone for five months, and she had fallen in love with the captain of the football team.

Oh man—I found out what the blues was. Every morning, I'd stop by this one restaurant and have breakfast. They had "Dark End of the Street" on the jukebox, and I'd play it and sit there and cry. The waitress got to know me. I would sit in a booth, way in the back, and every morning I'd have me a cry.

Boy, it hurt so bad, because I knew I was gonna see her. She dressed prettier every day, and her little ass got tighter every day. I didn't want nobody else—if Raquel Welch had fallen out of the sky, I would have tripped over her and not noticed it. It felt like I had a hole right in the middle of my soul. I didn't even want to play guitar no more. I sold my guitar, I sold my amp. I just said, "Fuck it," and I got back into the books. My brother thought I was crazy, and he just mocked me. He said, "Fuck you," and went off to play with someone else.

I don't know how much time passed. It seemed like forever, but it was probably like three months, just long enough for an infatuation to get over with. In other words, until some other chick speaks to ya. I was no great shakes back then, I was pretty quiet, but when we started playing that music, here they come!

Years later, I went up to Vicky's high-rise one night, and we were feeling pretty good. She was so glad to see me, and she wanted to show me what it was that I had missed. Let me tell ya—that was one special night. I might as well have been Gene Kelly coming out of that place, and it had been raining! We caught up, and then some.

Duane's first true love was a girl named Patty Chanley. He had a daughter by her, who's deaf, and who now lives in Daytona Beach. In my eyes, that relationship was very legit, because he really loved Patty. He went through many changes during high school, juggling this here and that there, and her old man absolutely hated him, to the point of saying, "I've got a shotgun loaded with rock salt, and I'll shoot you in the ass if you come around here anymore." I've got to hand it to my brother, because he just said, "Fuck you, old man. Me and this girl, we care about each other."

I remember Duane doing strange things, man. One day in the summertime, he was in our room, and he was doing all this math work. He's working all these numbers, so I asked him, "Duane, what the fuck are you doing?"

"Well," he tells me, "I just measured my dick, and from the day we got out of school until today"—which was the last day of summer vacation—"I've given her nineteen miles, four hundred seventy-two feet, and three inches of dick!"

"Where in the hell did you come up with that figure?" I asked.

"Well," he said. "I counted a few times, and I got me an average of how many strokes it took me before I finished. I took that and multiplied it all out, and came up with that figure."

WE HAD A FRIEND OF THE FAMILY NAMED MAX GATEWOOD, WHO also moved down to Daytona from Nashville. Max had no wife or children, and he was just a cool guy. He'd come and get us sometimes when we would go on leave at Castle Heights. He would take us to this place called the Copia Club in Nashville.

Max had a brand-new 1960 Thunderbird—God, that car was beautiful. He'd come get us at that wretched school because he knew how much we hated it. He bought us BB guns, but he wasn't weird or anything. When he died, he was buried with a diamond ring that I bought him with some of the first money I ever made. The first thing I bought was a pair of snakeskin boots, and then I went and got him this ring. It looked like a saddle, and it had sixteen diamonds in it. Max Burton Gatewood Jr.—let him not be forgotten.

We'd take four or five of the guys from school and come back to Nashville, because he'd give us his car. We'd all sleep over at his house, and if we wanted to drink, we had to do it there. He was just a hell of a guy. Somebody once asked me, "So what does he get out of all this?"—trying to make something of it. I just said, "Man, get out of here, put that shit away." It was so great to have that outlet, and it helped me to get through that school.

When we first started playing, Max brought this guy that he knew up to see us, and he played guitar. We'd play and sing, and I'm learning all these chords, and I'm certainly paying attention. And my brother, he just had it inside of him. The music just flowed from his brain to his fingers. He just knew.

We actually formed a band at Castle Heights called the Misfits. The great thing about it was that when we played after one of the football games, or the prom—we played all that shit—we got to wear our civilian clothes. I had this pair of jeans that was skintight, and I loved it.

That was a big deal, because we had to wear uniforms all the time, every day. White shirt and a tie, man. We had drills and inspections every day, and on Sundays we had a pass-and-review, which was when all the folks came out to watch—unless it rained, and we used to pray for rain. We're talking wool uniforms, heavy-gauge wool. Believe me, you didn't want to run out of drawers, because you didn't want to wear no pair of wool pants without no drawers on. It takes a hell of a dude to do that. In the spring, you got to change the wool pants for white pants, but everything else would stay the same, no matter how hot it was.

They had a great shop class there, and I learned a lot about measuring stuff, building things, woodworking and all that. That was good, because you were moving around and working with your hands, and that took your mind off of stuff. I also joined the school band, playing cornet, and earned a sharpshooter's medal, because I got forty-eight out of fifty bull's-eyes. That was from the prone position, which really isn't that hard. They took us down to the range, with live ammunition and everything. When you got up to the high school, they had Browning Automatic Rifles and a lot of that heavy shit. ROTC was one of your classes, and they had incendiary grenades, Bouncing Bettys, claymore mines—all that shit. They taught you how to defuse them, how to wrap a bandage and treat a wound.

In the fall, we had something called bivouacs that would last a week. Behind the school there were woods, and I mean the thick woods. We'd go when the leaves were turning nice colors and it was cooling off. We'd have the blue team and the red team, and it wasn't really nothing but a paintball game. They called them "blood bullets" back then, but they were just paintballs. One time, my brother got lost, and he stayed out there overnight with a couple of other guys. They just found a cave and hid out for the night.

In the end, despite the few good things, I was totally lonesome and out of place—a ship drifting and drifting. I didn't make a lot of friends because I didn't want nothing to do with the place. I didn't want to go there, I didn't want to be there. Everything you did, they told you how to do it. They told you how to do everything but take a shit, man. They put saltpeter in the potatoes so nobody would get horny, and they put laxative in the coffee so everybody would crap at the same time. You'd walk into the bathroom, and up on this big concrete slab was a row of about ten toilets, and everybody would sit together. I mean, Jesus Christ, that was terrible.

Every day, I'd wake up and see the springs on the bunk above me, and I'd think, "Oh no, it's not a bad dream." But I never realized that it just came down to me saying, "By God, all you got to do is get the fuck up and walk out."

After a little while, my brother did just that. He just took off, and when he got home, he called me, saying, "Come on, man, the band is together!"

"I'll be right there," I said.

That's when I realized that, all this time, these people had me buffaloed into thinking that if I didn't do exactly what they said, something real bad was going to happen. Bullshit. Now that I was leaving, they were kissing my ass.

I went in there and said to the guy in charge, "Sir, I'm leaving."

He told me, "If you stick around here a little while, you'd get yourself some rank, maybe a captain or a major."

"Sir, no disrespect, but a captain of what?" I asked.

"That will be all, Mr. Allman." He'd heard all he needed to.

I about-faced, man, and I had that uniform off by the time I got to my barracks.

I was never the same student in public school that I was in military school. I got so far into music, and it had gotten so far into my soul, that it totally pulled me off my studies. When I got back to the big green high school in Daytona, Seabreeze High, my discipline didn't stick. I'd had dental or medical school in mind, but once I'd gotten music in me, there wasn't a chance in the world of that. Well, if I had fallen on my ass, maybe I would have gone back to school—but music would have always been in the back of my mind. I went to my first football game, and girls were there, cheerleaders were there. Between the women and the music, school wasn't a priority anymore.

MUSICIANS FIND MUSICIANS, AND I MET EVERY ONE OF THEM IN Daytona—black, white, and everything in between. Stealing licks—somebody would show you a lick, and that would open up a whole can of worms of licks. I was really studying them, and by this time, Duane was too. I don't know who was playing guitar on Little Walter's records, but it seemed like after Duane got a hold of that record, he just got a fire inside.

After Duane and I left Castle Heights for good, he started hanging out with a guy named James Shepley. They let me in to their crowd every now and then, because for some reason I wasn't shy to play whatever I knew to anybody. We went to one party, and we took all our shit, because we were going to impress the girls, but then Duane and Shepley chickened out. So I picked up Duane's guitar, which was a Les Paul Jr., and I played it real well. I even sang along with it a little bit. It got real silent in there, and that kind of scared me, but afterwards some little girls were asking me, "So what is this?" Suddenly here come Shepley and Duane, grabbing their guitars, because of course now they want to play, and it turned to bedlam.

I thought Shepley was the coolest thing that ever walked. He was the one who taught me how to play Jimmy Reed, and he was so good about it. I'd be struggling, and he would tell me, "Man, you're trying too hard. Feel how stiff your hand is? Feel my hand," and it was like his hand was asleep—it was just laying there, no pressure at all.

Jim was a strange little guy. Today, whenever the Brothers play around Hartford, Connecticut, where he lives, I always put him on the list, but he never shows. I think that's why he didn't end up in the band, because he very well could—and perhaps should—have been in the Allman Joys, and probably in the Allman Brothers. I don't know if he had a stage-fright thing, maybe that was it. We would ask him to come play, and he'd always back out.

Shepley tapered his own pants, and he must have had a hundred pairs of pants. I thought, "What a groove, to have every pair of pants you own tailor-made," and that's why I've still got this thing about my pants being right. Stovepipe pants is what we wore. That means they're tapered like hell—I mean tight, tight—to the knee. Then it's the same size as your knee, all the way down, so you can wear boots with them. That's what I've always worn, but back then I had to do it myself on the damn sewing machine. I went to school one day, and one whole side came undone.

If a musician could play, we didn't look at his skin color, but unfortunately we were in the minority back then, since when it came to racism the shit was boiling up in in the South. In Nashville, there were always two water fountains and four bathrooms: men and women white, men and women colored. I would always think, "What's wrong with those people? Are we going to get sick if we go near them? I mean, they come over and clean the house." I remember Little Rock and the lunch counter boycotts and the signs, "No Niggers Allowed." My grandmother would take my head and turn it away, saying, "Son, don't even worry about it. You're too young to worry or understand."

I was just confused about the whole black-white thing, but I became quite unconfused in later years. I don't know if my mother had a racial thing per se. It was just the way she was brought up. That kind of thing is just passed on and passed on from one generation to the next, and it's still happening today. I can't stand it, I can't stand it at all. There are good and bad people, there are heartful and heartless people, and they come in any color, any size that you want.

When my brother and I were young, we were always around white people. Our elementary school was white, and Castle Heights was the same way. The only black people we had in our lives when we were growing up were our babysitters, and two guys named Johnny Walker and Claude, who were the custodians at our grade school.

As Duane and I were playing our way through high school in Daytona, we met this guy Hank Moore who had the Hank Moore Orchestra, and Hank Ballard and the Midnighters were his backup singers. We pooled our money and Hank Moore came down to our house, and we had the whole garage band together. It was my brother, me, a friend of ours named Van Harrison on bass, and a kid named Tommy Anderson playing drums. Tommy was something. That skinny little kid could go, man. We called him "Slick."

So Hank comes down to my mother's house at 100 Van Avenue (which is still there now, with her still in it, at ninety-four years old), and he's sitting on a barstool in the middle of the room ready to teach us. When we played in our garage band, no one ever wanted to play the bass, so Hank explained to us about the bottom end. He sat there and took us through "Done Somebody Wrong," and that changed my whole life. I saw the structure of music, and we all got it. I was like, "Take all my money—I win."

Then my mama came home, and she'd never grabbed me by the ear or pushed me from behind, but this time she did. She said, "Come in the kitchen. I want to talk to you right now." She didn't grab Duane, she grabbed me, and she said, "I want to know what you're doing with that nigger in the front room."

"Nigger?" I asked, confused. "Ma, that ain't no nigger. That's Hank Moore."

"So what's he doing here?" she asked me again.

"Well, so far, he's taught us all kinds of good music."

"I want him out of here as soon as you can do it." She said it in a voice that meant business, but I forgot about that as soon as I got back in there. I just picked up my guitar and started playing, and by now, man, we had it. My mother went back there to get dressed, and she noticed that we were all playing together—it was the first time we ever sounded like a band. It didn't change her mind about a black man being in the house, but it changed her mind about the music.

Those summers back then were just priceless. They were the formative years. The great thing was that we had two guys to do it with. Duane and I could play off each other, and if one of us missed something, then the other one would pick it up.

It wasn't too long after that that I met Floyd Miles through my brother. Duane went down to this place under the Ocean Pier Casino called the Surf Bar. Floyd's band was called the Houserockers, and they played a lot at the Surf Bar, which was owned by a real rich guy named Nick Masters, who also owned the casino.

This guy Daps was the piano player, and he taught piano over at Bethune-Cookman College. His real name was Lindsey Morris—we called him Daps because he was such a dapper dresser—and he also had the Lindsey Morris Trio. I played with him, my brother played with him—shit, everyone played with him. Floyd always played with him. He played drums and sang, and they played all these Otis Redding songs.

I don't know why Floyd took an interest in me, because he and Duane were real tight, but for whatever reason I started to hang with them too. As I started playing, I noticed that the more I played, the better I played, and the more I seemed like I was into it, the more they let me into that older circle. I was the youngest one there, and I would just sit there and study Floyd. I wouldn't take my eyes off of him. I watched his every single move. I studied how he phrased his songs, how he got the words out, and how the other guys sang along with him.

He noticed all this, and I guess he saw the hunger in my eyes to be a part of this thing. Me and my brother both finally joined Floyd's band, but they only needed one guitar player, so we'd switch off every other night. In the beginning, I played lead guitar, my brother played rhythm, and he sang. Now, he damn sure couldn't sing, as you can tell by some of the recordings he made. But the more I played, the better I got, and when I started singing, that was the best me and Duane ever got along during my whole damn childhood.

I became a singer out of necessity, not by choice. My brother came to me and said, "Hey, man, we gotta do something."

I thought, "Oh fuck, here it comes. He's gonna push me out of the band and get Shepley in."

Instead, he said, "Obviously, I've been playing a little more lead."

"Yeah, because you quit school and have had nothing to do for a whole year but sit home every day and play."

To sing properly, you have to get into a mind-set where you don't give a damn if somebody doesn't like it. You couldn't care less, you're singing for the gods—because they gave you the ability to sing, or at least what sounds like singing to you. You're putting your whole soul into it, all the happiness you ever had, every tear you've ever shed—all of that goes into your singing.

It was once said that the blues is nothing more than a good man feeling bad, and that's what it is. Believe me, singing a blues song makes you feel better afterwards. Singing the blues doesn't mean that you have them at that minute—the blues usually crawl up on you late at night or early in the morning. You get the blues when someone close to you dies or has an accident or gets sick, or when your dog passes away, and singing is a way of letting go of it.

Me and my brother had this friend in Daytona Beach who was like the audiovisual dude in school. I wouldn't really call him a geek—he didn't wear glasses or button his shirt all the way up. He would come to our gigs and make recordings on one of those old suitcase Ampexes. They sounded so crispy and rich. Even back then they sounded great, and they still do.

He sent me a recording of the third or fourth night that I ever sang. My brother comes up to the mic and says, "Now little Gregory Allman's gonna come up here and sing you a song."

"Man," I said to Duane, "if you wouldn't do that, I wouldn't be so damn scared"—because I was petrified, I was just catatonic.

When you hear it, ooh, you know talent isn't something inborn. That tape is atrocious, man. It sounds like some country bastard that's trying to sing James Brown songs, but he doesn't have any lips. It's terrible—I don't know, you might not think it's terrible, but I do. I've never played it for anybody.

But I stuck it out. And the more I did, the more I learned. Early on, Floyd gave me a tip about singing that I later heard from some other people: don't sing from your chest. If I sang more than a couple of songs, my voice would be gone, because I was singing from my chest. You don't want to do that, because then you're blowing wind past your vocal cords, and they'll get pretty tattered if you keep doing that.

Floyd pulled me over to the side and said, "Listen, Gregory. If I may, can I give you a little word of advice? Let's say I was going to count to three, and haul and hit you in the stomach as hard as I could. What would you do?"

I told him, "I'd tighten up my tummy."

He put my hand on my stomach and said, "You see how

hard that is? That's where you sing from. That's where the power comes from. When you know you're going to scream, you lay your head back, which spreads your vocal cords real wide, and when the scream comes out, it barely nicks your vocal cords. You don't want to do too much of that, because there's soft, tender meat down there."

It took me forever to figure it out. Floyd said, "You'll get it when you don't think about it," but I kept thinking about it and thinking about it. I don't know what day it happened, but once I got it, then I didn't think about it. Now I don't know how to do it any other way. Starting then, many nights I'd be coming off the stage and all the band, my brother especially, started saying, "Man, you're sounding better every night." Of course, I didn't believe them.

Coming up, I sang a lot of Otis Redding, a little James Brown. That would always tear my throat up. You have to find out your range, so you won't get up there and encounter a note that there ain't no way in hell you're gonna hit. You know to lower the key or change the phrasing. I learned all about phrasing.

The more different songs I tried, the more I learned, and I must say I had some great teachers. Half of them didn't know they were teaching me. I would just go somewhere and stand and watch. I'd be so focused, the ice in my drink would melt.

"Little Milton" Campbell had the strongest set of pipes I ever heard on a human being. That man inspired me all my life to get my voice crisper, get my diaphragm harder, use less air, and just spit it out. He taught me to be absolutely sure of every note you hit, and to hit it solid. Little Milton taught me to know what you're going to sing, to know what ladder you're going to climb, and to know how many turns it's going to take. I learned from him to understand which part needs to be soft and which part needs to be delivered with force, what I call "throat busters." On those, you just harden up your tummy, and you let that boy out real quick, you kinda let it escape. Milton could do that better than anybody, and his voice was strong as ever, right up until the day he passed.

I had a lot of respect for my throat and my ears, although I did smoke cigarettes. I used earplugs, I drank hot tea and honey, I gargled in the shower, and I let the hot water run down my throat. But the one thing that brings your throat back completely is sleep—lovely, peaceful sleep, and lots of it.

I think I'm singing better than ever, but I can't do as much as I used to. I can't sing as long and as hard, song after song. Still, when we play our annual shows at the Beacon Theatre in New York City every year, I get stronger as the run goes on. I'm not sure why that is, but I think opening night is so tough on my voice because I'm so nervous. It's opening night, and you've got those butterflies.

THE ESCORTS WAS OUR FIRST REAL BAND. WE DID A WHOLE BUNCH of old R&B love songs, stuff like "Pretty Woman," "I've Been Trying," "Hi-Heel Sneakers," and "You've Lost That Lovin' Feeling," which we butchered. "Are You Sincere," by Lenny Welch, was one of my brother's choices, and we did "This Boy" by the Beatles, because we had to play enough Beatles songs. We did some instrumentals as well, including "Memphis" and our version of the theme from *Goldfinger.* We'd also do "Wild Thing," which got us real close to getting fired several times.

Most clubs just wanted us to be a jukebox onstage, and we were a great one. They wanted you to play this many Top 40 songs and this many Beatles songs, or you shouldn't even bother calling them because they wouldn't hire you. And we could do both. We played so many of 'em. I remember every Motown song was like that, with that great guitar sound they got. I will never know why they stopped recording in that studio in Detroit.

The songs we played were a collection of tunes that we all happened to know; if me and Duane and one of the other two guys in the band knew it, that song was in the bag. If there was a song that only one of us knew, that sometimes got learned and sometimes not. It was like taking a song apart and putting it back together like a model airplane, finding out what goes here and what goes there.

I tried my best to sound like Aaron Neville on "Tell It Like It Is." If that man knew how many 45s I wore out trying to get his inflections down, and his emotion—but I never, ever came close to sounding like Aaron Neville. We were doing "Turn On Your Love Light," because we had heard Bobby "Blue" Bland do it, and, man, you talk about an original talent—there will be, and can be, only one Bobby "Blue" Bland.

We bought as many records as we possibly could. We would save our money, borrow from others, whatever we had to do. Duane would take my dough to buy records, and he would say, "But, bro, we *need* this. Can't you see you're holding back progress?" "But, bro"—when I heard those words, I knew what was coming. "All I need is half of your money," and then the next day he would need half more. But he would come back with something amazing and we would learn eight songs off of that.

We played shows constantly. I didn't go to my high school graduation because I had a gig that night. As a matter of fact, I stood my date up for the prom because I had a gig. But I'll tell you, none of the people I went to school with did a damn thing. At my high school reunions, I find out that this guy's in jail, this guy's dealing dope, some of them died in Nam—hell, there's nobody successful, so I guess missing the prom wasn't that big of a deal.

Around that time, this band called Sweet William and the Stereos came into town. They were headed down to Fort Pierce to play in this big club called the Shamrock, and they wanted to borrow my brother for a bit. Their regular guitarist, a guy named Jimmy Matherly, couldn't leave town with them. He'd had a divorce in Daytona, and my understanding was that the judge made him stay in town to take care of certain financial obligations. Duane said, "Fuck it, I just wanna play," so the switch was made. They took Duane and left Jimmy with us.

This cat could play—holy shit! He was a real country dude and a real nice guy. He played a full-blown Gibson 355, through one of those triangular Gibson amps, and it sounded like a million bucks.

Not long after we temporarily swapped Duane for Jimmy, word got out that I was still a virgin. Girls had never noticed me until I bought a guitar, and for a while I thought, "Well, is it because I play music? What if I sold insurance?" That bothered me for a long time, it really did. I was a pretty shy guy in high school, and I still have a certain amount of shyness today. It's just something that you have. I've worked on it, and I'm much better today than I was. Back then, though, being shy made things difficult with the girls, and everyone had been giving me a hard time about being a virgin.

One day, Matherly pulled me aside and said, "Man, I heard that they've been bugging you about being a virgin?"

"Maybe so—what the fuck is it to you?" I said.

"Wait a minute, don't get huffy," he said. "Dig it, man, I got divorced recently, and I know what it's like. They would bug me about her owning my dick, and the first hundred times it was funny, but then it got unfunny. Look, I got to sign some papers with her, and if you want, I'll set you up with her, and I'll tell her what's happening."

See, he was still friends with his ex, and he was going to tell her that I'd never had my hambone boiled. So he set it up with her and told me we were all set, and she said I should come over for dinner. She lived in one of those one-bedroom studio apartments, with one of those Murphy beds, and it was already down, so I'm thinking that everything is cool. Of course, he ain't said nothing to her and ain't said shit about my "situation."

We had dinner, and she turned the lights down low, and we were sitting there watching TV, got a candle burning. I sort of put my hand on her tummy, then slid it up around her boob, and she said, "Oh, you came for that!"

"Nope—no, no!" was about all I could get out before I jumped up ready to bolt for the door.

"Wait just a minute, honey. Did Jimmy Matherly put you up to this? He did, didn't he?"

And with that, she proceeded to show me what it was all about. I'm telling ya, it pretty much took a stretcher to get my ass out of there. I thought that was the finest thing I'd had since black-eyed peas. I think she later told Jimmy that I got the lay of my life—like he never did!

GIGANTIC
SHOW and DANCE
The Allman Joys

Playing their smash hit "SPOONFUL"

on Dial Records

Fort Brandon Armory
TUSCALOOSA
Friday, November 25

Admission $1.50   8:00 — 12:00 —

Don't Miss the NEW Psychedelic Sound

The Allman Joys, 1966

CHAPTER THREE

The Foot-Shootin' Party

IT WAS ONE OF THOSE DISMAL, COLD, RAINY JACKSONVILLE DAYS in 1965 when I took Duane down to the induction center. He'd been up all night, drunk as shit, and his plan was to try and convince them he was a sissy. He had the swish going, and he had on these panties that ran up his ass. There were all these rednecks there, with that "I wanna get me a gun and kill a Commie for mommy" attitude.

A lot of guys we knew were getting drafted and sent to Vietnam—seemed like more were getting their draft cards every day. The way it worked was, you'd go to this old, terrible three-story army building in Jacksonville, right down the street from the WAPE radio station. You reported in the morning, and then around noon they gave you a break and you got a box lunch. I had taken Duane up there in my mother's car, and he came back out to the car at the break, and he was crying—that was something the average person never saw my brother do. He hardly ever cried, and if he did, he went off somewhere alone to do it.

This day, though, he was really crying, and he told me, "Baybrah, I can't pull it off, man. They ain't buying this shit at all."

"Man, just be as brave as you can," I told him, "and fuck those motherfuckers. No matter what, do not get on that fucking bus."

"I know, I know," he said, adding, "Shut up, you little know-it-all prick."

"Well, I'm just trying to give you some kind of help here," I said. "Just tell them to take their war and stick it in their ass, and we'll deal with tomorrow tomorrow."

He went back in there, and the officer in charge said to Duane, "What's this panties shit?" The guy took them off of him, threw them over in the corner, and told my brother, "Put your fucking pants back on. You're fine," and he stamped my brother 1-A. Then he said, "Now go into the room over there. We're gonna take an oath."

This asshole in a little fucking Smokey the Bear hat tells my brother, "Hey, blondie—raise your right hand," and Duane put his hand in his pocket. That guy started going off on my brother, telling him that he was going to spend the rest of his natural life in Leavenworth, busting rocks. They told him to go on home, and that the marshal would be by to pick him up.

Duane came back down to the car, and he looked drained, man—he wasn't the same person.

"I'm going to jail, man."

Just joking, I said to him, "Knowing you, they'll lose your fucking card."

Well, guess what? They lost his card. They never came after him, never called him, nothing. As far as the United States Army was concerned, my brother was no longer in existence.

A year later, they called me with my "greetings." Things were just going right with the band, and of course, that's when they called me up. Man, the bottom just dropped out for me. I went to my brother, and I said, "What am I going to do?"

"Well," he said, "like you told me—just don't go."

"Man, I don't think that works but once," I said. "And besides, you still might get a letter tomorrow."

Then it came to me: I decided to shoot myself in the foot. It seemed like the thing to do, and when I told my brother, he was in complete agreement.

"Yeah," he said, "that might just work. I'll tell you what we're going to do—we're gonna have a foot-shooting party. We'll get a bunch of whiskey and have a bunch of women come over. We'll get you good and fucked up, and then you can take care of business. You can do it out in the garage, and then we'll take you on down to the hospital, and then over to the induction center. It's gonna work out fine, bro."

The fateful day arrived, and my brother invited a bunch of friends and told them that we were going to have a foot-shooting party. We put a big box full of sawdust out in the garage, and my brother turned to me.

"Are you ready to go?"

"Yeah, I'm ready," I said.

Now, I wasn't slobbering drunk yet, but I wasn't feeling any pain either. Then something occurred to me and I got Duane's attention.

"Hey, genius, we forgot something."

"What?" he asked.

"A fucking pistol, man."

"Oh shit."

There was a silent moment, and all the girls were crying, and I realized, "This really is a foot-shooting party. Somebody is fixing to shoot themselves, and that somebody is me."

Duane, Shepley, and I got in the car and headed over to "Spadetown," as we called it, to get a pistol. It wasn't a racial thing at all, because we loved it there—it was just the name that everybody used back then. They had the best barbecue over there, they had the cheapest gas, and they had the best records, so we loved to go over there.

Now, I know this sounds like a bullshit story, but it's all true, every word of it. We stopped one guy on the street, and he said, "Can I help you?"

One of us asked him, "Hey, man, you know where we can get a Saturday night special?"

"Oh," he responded, "it's a *pistole* he wants! Well, maybe I do."

"How much is it?" I asked.

"Well, how much do you got?" he replied.

"C'mon, man, how much is it?" Meanwhile, I'm thinking, "Man, don't fuck with me—I'm fixing to shoot my own ass."

"It costs however much it is you got in your pocket."

"How far do you got to go to get it?"

"I just got to pull it out of my pocket is all."

"Well, in that case, we got twenty-seven dollars."

"Ain't that strange," he said. "Because that's just how much it is." We collected up all the dough, gave it to the man, and he gave us the pistol, a .22 short, and three bullets, and we took it back to the house.

If you picked that damn pistol up by the butt and shook it, the whole thing would rattle, like somebody had loosened all the screws on it. A precision weapon it wasn't. I mean, that gun had no hope. I asked my brother, "Man, you expect me to fire this fucking thing?" He told me, "Don't worry about it, man. You'll be fine."

I did luck out in one way, because beforehand I had studied a foot chart. The long bone in your foot comes to a V with the bone next to it. I wanted to put the bullet between the two bones, so I'd crack both bones but not break either one. Just take a little off the side, you know? I didn't want a permanent limp or nothing—I was just trying to dodge the draft.

I had on this pair of moccasins, and I dotted that spot on my foot just perfect. I ended up with a big old target on my moccasin. The girls were watching this, and when they saw the target, they really started in with the tears.

I got this big old shaky-ass gun, and I went out to the garage by myself. I sat down, drew a bead on my foot, and all of a sudden, it hit me—I was fixing to shoot my own ass with a fucking gun. At that point, I decided to weigh things out and see what exactly it was that I was going to gain from inflicting pain on myself.

I got up and went back inside and poured myself another stiff drink, and I said to my brother, "Man, this is fucking crazy. I could miss and maim myself for life, and then it wouldn't be so funny." By this point, the girls are crying even harder, so Duane said, "Give me that fucking thing—I'll do it!"

Now, he's pretty loaded because he'd been drinking all day, and when he grabbed the gun, he points it right between my eyes. I'm thinking, "Shit, he's gonna miss and shoot me in the head."

"Give me that fucking thing back, and get the fuck out of here," I said to him.

He left, and I drew down on that target, and boom! The fire came out of both ends of that gun, and it scared me to death.

Man, it felt like a rocket had gone through my foot, and for like three seconds I thought I was going to die. Then it went numb, all the way up to my thigh. Every time my heart would beat, the blood would spurt out the hole in my foot, like a geyser. My brother got a beach towel and wrapped it around my foot, and he and Shepley loaded me into the car. Even though he was good and drunk, Duane insisted on driving, and we headed off to the hospital.

We got to the emergency room, and the doctor asked me what happened, and I told him, "Well, I was cleaning my guns before I had to go off to war, and when I got to one of my Magnums, I forgot I had a round in the chamber. It went off and hit me right in the foot, Doc."

He goes, "My, I wonder how much of your foot is left," and he starts to poke around down there.

Suddenly I had a bad thought: "Oh, fuck me. He's gonna see the target on my damn moccasin, and he's gonna put two and two together. He's gonna call Selective Service, and I'm gonna end up in Leavenworth!"

For some reason, he left the room, and I said to my brother, "Man, there's a fucking problem."

He's like, "What? What is it?"

"The moccasin's got a fucking target on it." I said.

"Oh shit," he said, without seeming all that worried. "Just wait a minute, I'll be right back. I'll fix that."

I'm thinking, "Why don't you just take it off, damn it?" He goes and finds a marker and paints a target on the other moccasin, and I'm like, "Man, what is wrong with you?"

A nurse came in and hit me with a shot of morphine, so I was really rocking now. The doctor returned, grabbed the moccasin, and without even looking at it, snatched that son of a bitch off and threw it over his shoulder. That hurt worse than the bullet going in did, because the damn leather had sunk inside the hole and dried in there, and he just ripped it wide open again.

He asked me what caliber gun it was, and I told him it was a .22 Mag. He said, "Well, you're lucky, because it could have hit one of those bones, traveled down it, and come out the tip end of your toe, and you might have never walked right again. Don't worry, I got just the thing for you."

He pulled out this little tube, which looked just like Blistex, and he stuck it in the hole and filled the wound up with this goo, put a Band-Aid on either side, and told me, "Okay, you're out of here."

"Wait a minute, Doc," I said. "I've been mortally wounded here. I'm fixing to go off to war, you know?"

He said, "You're going to need some papers drawn up," so he wrote up what happened, but I thought, "Fuck that," and just stashed that report—I never took it with me.

We went back to the house, and I put on a bandage so big that I actually sprained the toe next to my big toe. By the time we got to the induction center in Jacksonville, I didn't know where the fuck I was. I'm on these crutches, trying to manipulate them up these steps, and I was struggling, man.

I finally made it into the room, and the officer asked, "What happened to you?"

I told him, "I was cleaning my favorite Magnum, and it went off and shot me through the foot."

He didn't even look up. All he said was, "You're out of here." And that was it for my military service.

BY THE SUMMER OF 1965, WE HAD BECOME A PRETTY GOOD BAND, and we were calling ourselves the Allman Joys. Van Harrison, who'd been at my house that time Hank Moore had been in our living room, was on bass for us. Van also played linebacker on the high school team, and one night before we had a gig, we were listening to the game on the radio. Van was going to meet us at the gig after the game, and we heard on the radio that Van broke his leg. He broke it real bad too—all the way broke. I'll be damned if he didn't go down, have it set, and come straight to the gig and play. He was a little happy, but he made it. Van was a hell of a guy.

We had some changes with our drummer. First we had Maynard Portwood, then Tommy Anderson took over. Tommy, for some reason, couldn't go on the road, so we took Maynard back.

We started out playing anywhere we could, because we just had the fever for it, and they can't turn you down when you tell them, "Man, we'll do it for nothing." There was a place called the Safari Hotel, right on the corner of South Atlantic and the beach, run by a guy named Bud Asher, who later became the mayor of Daytona Beach. I think he still owes us some back pay!

There was this other group of dudes across town who were "the" band in town. That was the Nightcrawlers, who had a regional hit called "The Little Black Egg." Sylvan Wells, the founder of that band, is now a very prominent attorney in Daytona Beach, and he turned out to be a hell of a guy. We had a battle of the bands with them, and all this stuff going on. Then "The Little Black Egg" came out, which was about as bubblegum as you could get—sort of along the lines of "Crimson and Clover," only with half as many chords. There's only two, instead of four. Get the fuck out of here, you little black egg!

They were the hotshots on the other side of town, and then we got called to do our first University of Florida fraternity gig. We killed 'em—I guess we had some butt-bumping rock and roll going down. Van Harrison was good, man. He played with a heavy hand; he didn't play with a pick. We played stuff like "Blue Moon" and "There's a Thrill Upon the Hill," but we did no original songs—at this point, we never even thought about it.

The song list would kind of make itself. We had a hell of a rockin' version of "Walk, Don't Run," and we played "Neighbor, Neighbor," the Eddie Hinton song. We also did a lot of old ethnic stuff, blues and whatnot, that carried over to the Allman

Brothers. An example would be "Trouble No More," which was the first song we worked up with the Brothers. It was a pretty obscure record, but you would take some of those old album cuts, and there would be something on there—a hook that you could change or something—and who gives a damn who wrote it? It just had that old-time feel to it, and we loved it. We also played our own version of "Tobacco Road," and it was psychedelic, man. We came close to losing a couple of jobs after playing that. It amounted to what "Mountain Jam" is now.

We listened a lot to WLAC, the radio station out of Nashville that played all that old blues. You could get that from Miami to New York on a nice clear night, usually in the spring and the fall. When we were going from gig to gig and driving for hours, we would listen. We'd say, "Man, check out that guy blowing that harp," and they'd come on and say it was Sonny Boy Williamson.

That's when I first heard Jimmy Smith, Little Milton, Howlin' Wolf—I thought they were joking, a guy named Howlin' Wolf. Muddy's the first one we really got into, because if you'll notice, there's Muddy Waters songs all through the Allman Brothers records. My brother would play that stuff on acoustic for hours.

For me, it was mostly rhythm and blues. Garnet Mimms, Otis, Patti LaBelle, Jackie Wilson, even B.B. King was on the rhythm and blues chart. My brother was also a big fan of Jimmy Page and Jeff Beck in the Yardbirds, especially Jeff Beck. At this point, Eric Clapton was back in the shadows—we didn't hear about him much. Duane also listened to a lot of the Rolling Stones, while I was still listening to Bobby "Blue" Bland.

Every time a 45 would come out, we'd buy it, jump on it, and learn it. My brother would cop licks off of those records. When "Over Under Sideways Down" came out, it threw my brother into a fit until he learned it. He wouldn't sleep or eat until he had it down. We were also doing "Yesterday" and "Paperback

Writer," because you were always expected to play a lot of Beatles songs. We did a lot of stuff off of *Revolver*. That's still the best Beatles album.

I'm telling you, when the Beatles first came out, I just went, "Okay, it looks like I'm going to med school. Music has been a nice thought!" Everybody and their brother—no pun intended—had a band, and I was thinking, "Man, we're never going to make any headway doing this. There's so much talent, and so much more that's probably going to be found. We've got no chance."

Though we admired the British Invasion, we thought some of the music was kinda funny. I hate to mention any names, because Graham Nash is a really good friend of mine, but we thought the Hollies were silly. Now, I'm just crazy about my man Graham—I did his TV show, *The Inside Track,* in 1990, and it turned out really nice. He let me borrow this black guitar that he had bought for David Crosby. Let me tell you, that guitar was special. If I was going to steal anything, that guitar would be it. For real, I almost left there with that guitar.

No matter what everyone else was doing, though, my brother always believed. He kept that light going. He was like, "Man, you need to do this with me." One night I had a date, but he talked me into canceling it and going to play a gig with him. It was going to be our first date, and I couldn't wait, but he talked me out of it. My brother had the drive, and I couldn't turn him down.

Meanwhile, I'd lay in bed at night wondering if we were ever going to play our own music. Where was it going to come from? Was this whole thing going to blow up in our faces? When things would get down, Duane would just inject some energy into it, and he could always figure something out and know what to do. My brother was a hell of a chess player, actually—not too many people know that.

We would rehearse every day in the club, go have lunch, rehearse some more, go home and take a shower, then go to the gig. Sometimes we would rehearse after we got home from the gig too, just get out the acoustics and play. The next day, we'd go have breakfast, go rehearse, and do it all over again. We rehearsed constantly.

At the time, we were wearing black suits, white shirts, red silk vests, and a white silk tie. That was us, man. The clothes were Duane's idea—he saw them Beatle jackets and he went crazy. It was the look of the time.

That summer of '65, we were the top dogs in town. Hands down, hell yes, we were the best. Our last couple of gigs, we just knocked them dead. We played the Safari, we played the bandshell, and they were just packed. I was amazed by it, man.

We decided to give the road a try, and a guy named Toby Gunn, who had Toby Gunn Enterprises out of Atlanta, booked our first tour as the Allman Joys, and he was booking us for $440 a week—and had the gall to take $44. He was like sixty-nine years old, and he was totally unhip. It was just the four of us, no crew, getting $100 each a week. We traveled in a 1965 beige Chevy station wagon, with a 300-horsepower engine in it, pulling a trailer. It was a big trailer, but that engine pulled it with no problem. We ran that son of a bitch down, man.

We split to go on the road on July 5, 1965. Unfortunately, Van Harrison decided to enroll in college, so we got a guy named Bob Keller to play bass. The gig was at the Stork Club in Mobile, Alabama, and we were booked there for a week. When we arrived, the head of the club greeted us and told us to come back to his office. He unbuttoned his shirt and turned around to show us an army .45.

"Now listen up here," he said. "If you all got any knives or guns, or any shit planned for my club, just remember, I got bigger ones than this in here," patting his big fat belly, holding his .45. "Now, I'll see you tomorrow night, and there ain't gonna be many people in here, because it's a Monday night." Well, we played that first night, and the guy loved us so much, he held us over a few weeks.

We went from the Stork Club to the Sahara Club in Pensacola, where we were booked for a few weeks. At the Sahara Club, they had a big old floodlight, pointed straight at us, but it was recessed into the wall, so we were the only ones who could see it. If we got too loud, or played too many slow ones, they would flash that light. Once for loud, twice for slow. One Sunday we had an off day, and this guy asked us to come over to Dauphin Island, Alabama, down the way from Mobile. I'll always remember the room—it was exactly the size of the original Fillmore West. It looked like it, it felt like it, same ceiling height, and there were a lot of people there, man.

I can remember saying to the crowd, "Boy, we got something for your ass!" And we lit into "Paperback Writer," and them people went crazy. We'd slip a good rocker on them, and we had them going.

That was an amazing day. It's the first time I'd ever seen wall-to-wall people, what they now call "festival seating." You talk about scared—I had some serious stage fright, but once I got up there I was fine. We mesmerized those people. Something deep inside me told me, "Man, everything is going to be all right. You don't have to worry about going back to school." For the first time, I believed it. I felt it.

Pensacola was a real turning point in my life, because I realized that if we did things right, we could grab people with the first eight bars of a song, and we wouldn't have to worry about the rest of the night. The key was getting them right away. You can't pussy around up there, as scared as you might be. I learned to ignore hecklers, because we had a couple of those there. They didn't like it because their girlfriends came to see us, so these guys came to the hotel once and they wanted to kill us. I learned about dealing with that kind of thing as well.

In Pensacola, we were staying at one of those no-tell motels, with little bungalows by the week. Pine Haven or Pine Hurst or something. I had this song written. I was lonely, again, and there was a woman that I had really wished was there, to bring me some happiness and companionship and all that goes with it. I had the song, but I didn't have the title. I'd go, "But back home you'll always run / With sweet . . . Bar-bar-a." It had to have three syllables in it, it just had to. I had tried every damn name. I had almost settled on "Delilah," but I knew inside me that wasn't what I wanted.

It was my turn to get the coffee and juice for everyone, and I went to this twenty-four-hour grocery store, one of the few in town. There were two people at the cash registers, but only one other customer besides myself. She was an older Spanish lady, wearing the colorful shawls, with her hair all stacked up on her head. And she had what seemed to be her granddaughter with her, who was at the age when kids discover they have legs that will run. She was jumping and dancing; she looked like a little puppet.

I went around getting my stuff, and at one point she was the next aisle over, and I heard her little feet run all the way down the aisle. And the woman said, "No, wait, Melissa. Come back—don't run away, Melissa!" I went, "Sweet Melissa." I could've gone over there and kissed that woman.

As a matter of fact, we came down and met each other at the end of the aisle, and I looked at her and said, "Thank you so much." She probably went straight home and said, "I met a crazy man at the fucking grocery." So that's how "Melissa" got finished.

From Pensacola we went on to Savannah, then on to Nashville, at the Briar Patch, where we met John Loudermilk, who wrote "Tobacco Road" and songs for the Everly Brothers and Eddie Cochran and a bunch of other people. He wrote "Then You Can Tell Me Goodbye," which we later recorded. We met John when we were staying at the Anchor Hotel. Right next door to the Anchor was a place called Mario's, a really fine Italian restaurant. John and George Hamilton IV and their two ladies were over there having dinner. The rooms at the Anchor were laid out in such a way that we could actually set up and play, so we're in there, just blowing away, and there's a knock on the door. It's John Loudermilk, and he said, "I'd like you to come out to my house tomorrow, guys."

We had the good fortune of spending a whole summer with Loudermilk, just watching him write. His wife went off to Europe, the three kids went off to camp, so for a month I got to live in his house. He had forty-five gold 45s on the wall. That was impressive, man.

Loudermilk was a generous host and an even better person. Somehow, my brother had acquired a Triumph motorcycle, a T110, and I was having a fit for one. I'd always loved them. I'll be damned if I didn't find one in the paper, a used Triumph Bonneville, but they wanted $1,700 for it. Loudermilk saw how bad I needed it and bought me that bike. When that man looked at you, he looked at all of you.

I learned a lot from that man, really. He and I would sit down to write songs, and I would absolutely film him with my eyes. I guess he saw in me someone who could flat-out pay attention, keep their mouth shut, and watch how the process is done. I will be forever grateful for what he did for my songwriting. John Loudermilk taught me to let the song come to me, not to force it, not to put down a word just because it might rhyme or fit. He taught me to let the feeling come from your heart and go to your head.

You know, it's all been said before. How many different ways are there for people to say "I love you" in a song? Yet every day, they're still coming out with love songs. A long time ago, I was reading this thing about Lauren Bacall, and they asked her what it was like when Humphrey Bogart died, and she said, "Well, one day, I noticed I didn't go up the steps so fast." I thought that was a really good answer—kind of vague, kind of poetic—and it would be a great line for a song.

After Nashville, we headed to St. Louis to play at Gaslight Square, because the money was better. We started going back and forth from St. Louis to Nashville on a regular basis. While were on the road, we would share a room with two double beds, push them together and then sleep on them crossways. When you woke up in the morning, if the beds had rolled, your ass would be on the floor, your head would be on one bed, and your feet on the other bed! We slept like the Three Stooges, man. The first time I got my own room, I was lonely as shit.

We were out on what we called back then the "Chitlin' Circuit." We played in the old roadhouses, places that have chicken wire in front of the band so they won't get hit by the bottles. We'd have Sweaty Betty and her sister dancing like go-go girls. Some of 'em were super fine, until they started talking.

We played five sets a night, forty-five minutes a set, six nights a week. We didn't have any drinks unless somebody bought 'em for us. Every now and then, some dude would waltz up to the stage with his honey, and I don't know who he was trying to impress, but he'd hand us a hundred-dollar bill and say, "Would you play 'Wipe Out' or 'Ticket to Ride' or whatever?" One guy came up and said, "Do you know 'na, nana nana, nana nana'?"

I said, "You mean 'Land of 1,000 Dances' by Wilson Pickett?"

"Oh, is that the name of it?"

Everybody would request whatever was real hot on the charts, and you'd better know how to play that son of a bitch, and if not, you better learn it tomorrow afternoon.

At those shows, it was all people that wanted to unwind from the day's work. There were some nights where we'd be playing to like fourteen people, and that doesn't feel too good. But the places were just jammed on Friday and Saturday nights, and there was always one of the other days of the week that every town had—girls' night out or whatever. I don't know if they had a dudes' night out. But pretty soon, it started being full every night.

After that first run, the station wagon was shot, so damn if my mother didn't up and buy us a 327 Chevy 108, one of them long vans. We met this guy in Birmingham who sold us some Vox equipment and let us pay on it as we could, though I don't think we ever fully paid him for it. When we'd been in Pensacola on that first tour, a dear friend of mine named Barbara Trouncy and her mother had bought me a Vox organ. She cared about me and wanted me to have it.

At first, there wasn't a lot I could do on it. For a while, it sat there on stage left, as I was still playing my Gretsch. People would come by and ask, "What's the matter? Keyboard player sick?" When it came time to play "Wooly Bully," I could do it on the Vox. "When a Man Loves a Woman," no problem—I had it. The organ came with a plastic card that was laminated, and it went A, B, C, D, E, F, G, and major, minor, augmented, third, ninth, fifth, and there was a little picture in each block, with little red dots showing where your fingers go. That's how I learned to play keyboard.

As time went by, I got more and more tunes down with the Vox, and by the time we were in Birmingham the guy there had a used Leslie 147 amp that he sold to me. I hooked it up and ran it through a Beatle Top amp, and that son of bitch sounded real close to a Hammond, which added so many dynamics to the band. Let me tell you, the guys were going, "Jesus, that's a Hammond!"

I saw my first Hammond organ at the Martinique Club in Daytona. A guy named Johnny Ford, who'd died before we hit the road in '65, had played one. He drank himself to death. He was from Knoxville, and he played in this little trio with a guy named William Sauls, who everyone called Sweet William, this big fat white bass player, and another guy named Stallsworth on drums, who played a gorgeous set of black drums. He had his cymbals real high—he was the first real drummer I ever saw.

The first time I actually played a Hammond was at the Bali Restaurant, where my mother was the accountant. They had one there, and sometimes I'd sneak in early in the morning, and I knew how to start it. Nobody would be in there yet, and my mother was way back there in the office, and I'm just having a ball playing that thing.

I loved it, but then I didn't see another Hammond B3 until we played at Gaslight Square in St. Louis. It was this little slice of town, kind of like Bourbon Street. It was just one street, and all the dens of iniquity were there. When we played at Pepe's a Go Go, which was next door to the Whisky a Go Go, I was talking to a guy named Mike Finnegan who played with a band called Mike Finnegan and the Serfs. I asked him what that big piece of wood was on the stage. He said, "Come on up here. I'll show you."

Now, as a rule, nobody let you play their Hammond. "Don't ride my Harley, don't mess with my wife, and no, you can't play my Hammond." That's just it, man. But Mike Finnegan let me sit behind his, which was very cool of him. And, man, when I heard that B3, it just melted me. In the next day or two, he turned me on to Jimmy Smith and Groove Holmes. That Hammond just struck me. It was nice, round, kind of dull-ended instead of sharp, and I thought it blended with a guitar just perfect. I've always been pretty much surrounded by guitar—even if it was just my brother, there was plenty of guitar. The next time I sat down on a Hammond, I would write "Dreams."

We went to New York for the first time in '66, and we played a place called Trude Heller's, which was on 9th Street and Avenue of the Americas. Trude's son, Joel Heller, owned the club around the corner, which was called the Eighth Wonder. New York was something else. We were only there for about a week, and we had to audition, so I'm glad we got the damn job, because we went all the way up there. If we hadn't got the gig—shit, I don't know what would have happened.

Trude's was a strange place. They had go-go boys dancing, and I didn't understand it. The son ran a matinee at the Eighth Wonder, and we'd play that, because we got paid double. On Saturdays and Mondays we'd go in and there wouldn't be a man in sight, not one dude in the place. Then we were like, "Oh, I get it!"

You couldn't play any slow songs, because if you did, Trude would run out in front of the band and jump up and down, waving her hands. One night, the whole damn Rolling Stones filed in, and my brother, being the ballsy son of a bitch that he was, launched into "19th Nervous Breakdown," and we just smoked it, man, smoked it. I sang it, and I did my best. They liked it—they were going, "All right, all right."

We hooked up with the guy who worked as the maître d', and one night after the gig, we were covering everything up with sheets and he said, "You all want to come over to the house, man, and smoke some?"

My brother offered him a cigarette, and the guy goes, "That's not what I'm asking."

Then my brother flat-out said it—and I never thought I'd hear him say this, but he said those magic words: "You mean, 'mar-a-juan-a'?" I'd give anything for a tape of him saying that. That serious, drawn-out "mar-a-juan-a"—classic, man.

None of us—not my brother, not me, not any of the guys—had ever smoked pot before. None of us. So we told him, "Yeah."

We were staying at the Chelsea Hotel, and we went to his house from there. It took us a while to find a place to park because we had a trailer hitched to the back of our car. We went upstairs, and he's got one of those small, cigar-box-sized apartments, but it was full of this good-smelling stuff, and I'm going, "So that's what it looks like."

I thought the whole thing was a sham. We smoke some, and I'm sitting there, waiting to feel something. I'm like, "When's the ball gonna drop?"

The guy was like, "What, you ain't high? Man, we smoked about half a box of this shit." He said, "Why don't you stand up?"

"Okay," I told him. "I gotta go piss anyway."

I stood up, and my brother said something, and I started to laugh, man, and I laughed from that time until we got back to the Chelsea. Maniacal laughter. It took us almost an hour to go two and a half blocks.

When we left New York, I came back home with one of those tall instant iced tea jars full of the brown, which I bought for about forty dollars. We turned on all our buds, like Shepley and them.

By the time we got back home, Maynard wanted to get off the road, so we got Billy Connell, a drummer we knew from

Montgomery, to take over. We came back through Nashville to play the Briar Patch for a second time in the summer of 1966, and that's when we met a songwriter named John Hurley, who was a friend of Buddy Killen, a local producer. John Hurley really liked some of the shit he heard at the Briar Patch, and he liked some of the songs I had written. He told Buddy Killen about us, and Buddy was impressed enough to book us into a studio outside of Nashville called Bradley's Barn, which the famous producer Owen Bradley had built.

The Barn was a great place. They had isolation booths, baffles, Ampegs, MCIs—anything you wanted, they had it. It was a very impressive place, and the sound was really good. It was nice to be in a studio, but I didn't feel like we were lucky or we had made it to the big time, because of one thing: we weren't doing our own songs.

We did stuff like "Spoonful" and "Crossroads," but they changed the arrangements, because they wanted to hear something that sounded like the Rascals. There was an endless supply of Blackbirds—speed—so it's no wonder "Spoonful" sounded like it did.

I spent countless hours, whenever we had time off from the Briar Patch, trying to write some shit with Hurley. Let me tell you something—anyone who thinks that writers are born, bullshit. Writing is hard work and nothing else. Nothing came out of that time, nothing worth a damn, anyway.

So you can imagine how I felt years later, when those half-ass demos came out as an album on Dial Records. We made it clear to them that we never wanted those songs released, that we were way too stretched out on those goddamn pills when we did them, but they proceeded to put that motherfucker out anyway.

It was called *Early Allman,* and it came out in 1973. If you bought it, little did you know that you were buying some songs that weren't even close to being finished, because the time hadn't come for them to be finished. We had to live a little bit longer, experience a little bit more, and just keep playing and playing. I had to get better as a songwriter, and stay at it for a while, and finally some really good songs came out of us. But at that particular time, we didn't have it in us. I'd scribbled the outlines of "Melissa," but I hadn't even played that for the band. We weren't capable of completing any songs worth releasing to the public, and that's why that Dial record should never have come out.

That record had a bunch of songs that I wrote either by myself or with Hurley or Loudermilk. "Gotta Get Away" and "Oh John" were my songs, as was "Bell Bottom Britches," but that's actually a Loudermilk song. Then there's "Dr. Phone Bone" and "Changing of the Guard" and "Forest for the Trees," which were all written by me and John Hurley. They were terrible songs, just awful.

But Loudermilk had inspired me to keep writing. I didn't have much confidence, because so many of my songs had hit the round file. I didn't want to be a jukebox anymore, so I kept writing, even though I didn't have much to show for it by this point. But the first time I showed everybody a song and it jelled, they just forgot all them other tunes. Mass amnesia, I'm telling you.

That was an important day, because I can't tell you how tired I was of singing about tears on my fucking pillow, of using up my throat to sing "Wooly fucking Bully." I was sick of learning parts and making sure that they were right, especially to Byrds songs. I used to hate to see them coming, because they were rough. We did tunes like "The Bells of Rhymney," but I think we only played that once. The club owner came up and told us, "If you play that song again, you're fired!"

After we finished our second run at the Briar Patch, we moved on to Paducah, Kentucky. Duane and I rode our motorcycles there. It was October, and you could feel it on those bikes, man—we just about froze to death. Paducah was a shithouse of a town, and we weren't there but for two weeks. We went straight on to St. Louis for our second run at Gaslight Square and ended up staying the winter in St. Louis. By that point, it was just me and Duane, because the draft took Bob Keller, who we replaced with Michael Alexander. But then Billy Connell got drafted, and that was it.

In the spring of 1967, we were still in St, Louis, and we crossed paths with Johnny Sandlin, Paul Hornsby, Mabron McKinley, and Eddie Hinton. They had a band called the Men-Its, and the draft had gotten their lead singer and their guitar player. We had known them from the club circuit, and it didn't take long for them to get rid of Hinton and form a new band with us. We called it the 5 Men-Its—for about five minutes. Then it turned into the Almanac, and then we went back to the Allman Joys for the rest of the time we were in St. Louis.

The lineup was my brother on guitar, myself on keyboards and guitar, Paul Hornsby on keyboards and guitar, Johnny Sandlin on drums, and Mabron McKinley on bass. Paul and I would float back and forth from guitar to keyboards, depending on the song. Duane and Paul worked up the dual-guitar arrangement for "Dimples" that we later used in the Allman Brothers. We called Johnny "Duck," because he kinda looked like one. His playing gave the band some funk, which is what me and Duane had been looking for.

In March 1967, we started rehearsing our butts off in St. Louis, and the owner of Pepe's a Go Go really had a lot of faith in us. He'd let us stay in the club all night, and leave the heat on and bring in food for us, and we would rehearse. We were doing things like "Stormy Monday," "Tell It Like It Is," and "Neighbor, Neighbor."

About this time, the Nitty Gritty Dirt Band came through town. They had played the Kiel Auditorium and then dropped into Pepe's for a beer, and we were smoking that night. They just sat there stunned—they were knocked out. We had never heard of them, but Bill McEuen, their manager, really talked us up. He was all about us going out to L.A.—"C'mon, let's go to L.A. You guys will be stars"—and he actually gave us the money to drive out there.

Now, I was against going to L.A., because I didn't like the pitch that McEuen gave us. When he told us he was going to make us the next Rolling Stones, I was just howling. It was so fucking lame, man. Johnny Sandlin was against going too, but my brother just told us to shut up. Anybody in their right mind would have said, "Hey, I ain't never heard of the Nitty Gritty Dirt Band, so how the fuck are you going to make us the next Rolling Stones?" Duane bought into it, though. I think in part because he just wanted to get the fuck out of St. Louis.

So we went.

Onstage with the Hour Glass, 1967

CHAPTER FOUR

Hollyweird

WE DROVE OUT TO L.A. BY THE SOUTHERN ROUTE FROM ST. Louis, and we were somewhere in New Mexico or Arizona when we stopped at a drive-in restaurant where they had those girls who would come out and take your order and bring the food out to your car. This little Latina girl comes out, and my brother says to her, "Hey, are you one of them damn Mexicans that we've been hearing about?" We're all telling him to shut the fuck up, because there's this big fat Mexican guy behind the counter who looked pretty pissed. But there was no controlling Duane. My brother would say just about anything he wanted, especially if there started to be too much of a lull. In the end, we didn't care too much. We were having a blast because we were going to Hollyweed.

I didn't know Johnny Sandlin, but he knew me. He knew

everything that I was about, and he wanted to know everything else—that is, after I opened my mouth and started singing. After a couple of road trips with him, and taking a few pills and spilling out our life stories, we started talking about the people who turned us on to music, who our favorite singers were, and it turned out that we were talking about all the same people. Johnny had a good background in production and engineering, so when it came time to run any kind of machinery, like if we were recording ourselves, he would be the one to do it. He had the dexterity, and he knew why shit did what it did. Johnny and I saw eye to eye on just about everything, and he and Duane were real tight too.

So me and Johnny really got along well, but as for me and Hornsby, he stayed out of my way and I stayed out of his. We didn't have a lot in common. I guess he expected me to ask him to show me a bunch of licks, and I didn't do it. It wasn't because of him; I've just never done that with anybody. The licks I've learned, I've just kinda learned them on my own. It's not that I'm above being taught better ways to play music, but I like to watch people and to listen—have it sort of rub off on you.

As for Duane and I, we were getting along pretty well, but we were both tired of just barely making ends meet. He was ready to stop fucking around and make some dough. I kept thinking that if we went back home, we could make some dough there. He sat me down and told me, "Dig it, we are not going home. You got that? I'm not going home, you're not going home. You'll thank me for this one day."

The truth is, we'd almost parted ways in St. Louis before leaving for California. We were freezing to death, and we were filthy. I wanted some pussy, but I was too nasty to get any. I didn't have money, I was as hungry as a son of a bitch, and to top it off, I had to sell the motorcycle that Loudermilk had bought for me. I was in a shit mood, but Duane had so much faith in the two of us. He just knew that if we stuck together, we'd come out on top, but I didn't believe that at all.

Duane would have hung on until the last club owner in Tijuana fired our ass, and then he'd still look for another gig, whereas me, I would have been more like, "Why beat a dead horse?" I probably would have left after a couple of years if the powers that be didn't make things happen as they did. I would have gone back to school, maybe gone that dentist route; Duane would have called me a pussy and hated me for the rest of my days, all while he became a real big star.

When we arrived in L.A., McEuen got us to sign a management contract with him and a record deal with Liberty Records. Pretty much straight away we located an apartment complex called the Mikado, which was right across from the Hollywood Bowl. The whole place was covered in bougainvillea and honeysuckle, and you could smell it everywhere. I met these beautiful women, and I would get them over there to my lair and let them smell that honeysuckle—boy, I'm telling ya.

My brother and I met these two little girls when we first got to Hollywood—God, I look back now and I wonder why we weren't never in jail. One of them had long black hair past her elbows, and the other one had white hair that was the same length. They wore these little dresses, and I swear, their hair was longer than those dresses. I went out with the blonde, and my brother went out with the one with dark hair, and the first night we took them back to our place and took them to our respective bedrooms. There wasn't any hors d'oeuvres, no wine or champagne, just some cold beer. We got them into our rooms, stripped them down, and fucked like you can't believe. Talk about "Welcome to California."

We became really good friends with these girls. Every now

and then, we'd have a case of the hornies, so we'd just give them a call. We never really took them out on dates, because we didn't have the money, but we'd bring them to a few gigs.

The first gig we did when we got out to L.A. was opening for the Doors at the Hullabaloo Club. Of course we knew who they were, because that was the summer of "Light My Fire." Talk about some stage fright—there was like twenty-eight hundred people in that room. The damn Martinique held twenty-eight! There was a round stage in there, and it would turn clockwise when one band was through, and turn back the other way when the next band started up.

I'll never forget it—we were doing "A Change Is Gonna Come," and there was this damn catwalk, and I was going to walk out there. All these record company people were in the crowd, and just as I went, "I was born . . ." my throat cracked something terrible. The place got silent, and I couldn't believe it happened, but we got out of it because I just went back, strapped on my guitar, and we kicked into "I Can't Turn You Loose." Back then, not too many people had heard of Muscle Shoals or Otis Redding or anything like that, so they liked that a lot.

That goddamn Sam Cooke song. Do you know how many times I've relived that moment? Over and over again, man. It's like the kick that was missed to lose the Super Bowl. You just torture yourself over something like that. That's why I don't listen to show tapes—I've never even watched the *Live at the Beacon Theatre* DVD, and it's gone platinum now. I know that's terrible, but all I'll hear are the mistakes. You can pick your own stuff apart so much, so once something is done, it's done. It's easier for me that way.

Liberty brought in Mr. Dallas Smith to produce our first record. It was actually Dallas who came up with the idea to change our band name from the Allman Joys to Hour Glass. Now, here's a guy who was an ex–shoe salesman from Miami—

and as a producer, he was a hell of a shoe salesman. The guy used to wear this damn grease in his hair. He had a bunch of diamond rings and was a little heavy around the waist, but had real skinny legs. He wore leather jackets with long sleeves, silk pants, and the fucking Elvis glasses with the holes in them. Just Hollywooding it up, man.

His other band was the Sunshine Company, and by the name alone, you could tell that they sang about nice and happy things, like skipping through the park. We got packaged together because we had the same manager, the same producer, the same record deal—the same bullshit.

When it came time to record that first Hour Glass record, Dallas came to us with a washtub full of not cassettes but acetates. One of them was signed by Carole King, and I've still got it. It's called "No Easy Way Down," and we recorded that, along with another one of her songs, "So Much Love." They handed us that basket of songs, and said, "Okay, now pick out your album."

I couldn't believe it, and neither could Sandlin. He couldn't understand how he had joined up with such great players, and now here we all were, in Hollyweird, selling out. That's how he felt about it, and let's face it—we were. We *were* fucking selling out, but we were staying alive.

We recorded *The Hour Glass* in about six days during August 1967, and then the mixing started. Of course, Dallas started showing off his stuff, so I think the whole thing took two weeks. Recording that album was a horrific experience. We hated the whole process, because every time we tried to loosen it up a little bit, they would stiffen it right back up. They'd force us back into the pop bullshit that they wanted us to do. Duane would try to get some kind of groove going, and they would shoot him right down.

The music had no life to it—it was poppy, preprogrammed shit. When we played live gigs, we did nothing off the record.

We ignored that shit and played the fucking blues. Boy did that piss them off. People from Liberty would show up at a gig, and we wouldn't play one song off the record.

One night we played the Whisky A Go Go, opening for Paul Butterfield. There was a waitress there who was just drop-dead gorgeous, one of the prettiest women I've ever seen. I thought to myself, "What the hell are you doing slinging drinks in a dive like this?" I asked somebody to go ask her what she was doing after she got off, and I got a note back that said, "Nothing, but I sure would like to do it with you." Let me tell you, I played some music that next set—I got down into the groove.

She had a town house down on Hollywood Boulevard, after it turns into a residential section. We got to her place, and she pulled out a bottle of Tuinals and a big bottle of brandy. We took a Tuinal each, and a couple shots of that brandy, and, man, we fucked like a couple of minks. She was every bit as good as she looked too.

I woke up the next morning, and I put on my drawers and my pants and threw on a T-shirt, and she put on about the same. There was a knock on the door, and she opened it just a bit, looked out, and said, "I think it must be the paper boy." All of a sudden, bam! The door busts in, and it's these three hooligans, and they had guns. I went, "Oh shit," but I was also thinking, "Baby, the pussy was worth it. If I gotta go today, at least I am scrubbed and tubbed." I mean, she fucked me until I was just fucked out, and that was back in my prime. After about seven times, I was begging her to stay away from me and to please just leave me alone.

These guys come in, and one of them started slapping her around. I stood up, and the other two grabbed me, and one of them starts poking me a few times. I didn't want to hit him back, because I didn't want all three of them motherfuckers beating on me. They were just slapping me a little bit, so I just kinda turned the other cheek, but I was afraid for my life. They ended up trashing the place and taking a few things—these motherfuckers were thugs, just street hoods, who must have seen her coming and going.

After they left, you'd think she would be weirded out by something like that, so I started getting ready to go. She stopped me.

"Hey," she said. "Let's take another Tuinal and drink some more brandy, and fuck some more. That'll take our minds off of what happened."

"You're the doc," I told her. "Whatever you say." Hollywood could be a strange place sometimes.

THE RECORDING PROCESS ON THE HOUR GLASS ALBUM MIGHT HAVE been terrible, but what was even worse was that Liberty wouldn't let us play that many gigs. They were "saving" us. For what, who the fuck knows. Maybe they were just pissed off that we played what we wanted to and not anything from that lifeless album. But for whatever reason, we only played about once a month, at rock halls like the Avalon, the Kaleidoscope, the Fillmore, the Vault, the Troubadour, a place called the Magic Mushroom, and a couple of times at the Whisky. They were somewhere between nightclubs and opera houses, so basically they were roadhouses. I never understood why they didn't put us on the whole tour with the Doors, or get us to open for the Rolling Stones. We wanted to play all the time, but they just wouldn't let us.

Back in them days, there were usually three or four bands on the bill. That would give everybody at least an hour to play, and the headliner would get a couple of hours. We would hang around and watch whoever else was playing—Jefferson Airplane, Buddy Guy, Buffalo Springfield—because I wanted to learn all that I could. I was never at home, I was always out. Even if we weren't playing. I'd be checking out other people all the time.

In the L.A. area, there was a group of bands including Spirit, the Seeds, and Love, and we'd all play the same clubs and hang out together. We played down at the Cheetah Club with the Electric Flag when they were in their prime—Mike Bloomfield was in perfect form. We were part of that whole scene, and one of the guys we found was Jackson Browne.

I met Jackson through Jimmie Fadden, who was the harp player for the Nitty Gritty Dirt Band. Jackson had actually been a member of the Dirt Band in their early days. He would crash at my place from time to time, because he was too proud to go back to his parents' house in Long Beach. Jackson knew he wasn't going to do anything else but write songs and play music. He's a hell of a nice guy, incredibly funny, incredibly sarcastic, and him and my brother really hit it off—he was absolutely flabbergasted by Duane's playing. Jackson was our kind of folk, a person that I just liked being around.

I watched Jackson write a lot of stuff, and I mean slave over it. He was so deeply into it that he didn't know I was in the room. Every now and then, he would crawl off with that guitar and you would hear some really beautiful melodies coming from the bedroom. He would come over quite often, and he'd tell you that he was starting to get a little too bluegrassy, a little too country, and we brought him out of that. We took him on some gigs with us from time to time, but of course, none of us were known by anybody at this point. Jackson Browne was just this guy named Jackson Browne—he was just another musician.

We used to rehearse quite a bit at the Troubadour, because we lived close by and the owner, Doug Weston, was pretty cool about letting us use the place. One day we were in there rehearsing, and they were working on the power. Like I said, me and Hornsby would switch off on keyboard or guitar—Paul mostly played organ, and I mostly played piano and guitar.

I was playing guitar on this one thing, and I had my hand resting on the guitar and I went to touch the microphone. I got a couple of inches away from the mic, and it sucked me right to it. That's a bad kind of shock, because a shock usually knocks you away from the mic. I'd never had a shock like that, and it gave me a good jolt. They had flipped the whole circuit. You look back and wonder, "Now, why wouldn't they say something about that?"

We got through with the song, and I went to sit down at the piano. I heard my brother say, "How's he doing that?" I looked around, and Hornsby had one hand on his Tele and the other one around that microphone stand. His hair used to be real long and straight back then, and it was standing straight up in the air. My brother is going, "Damn, man, will you look at that!"

I just did a dive across the stage, hit him, and the plug pulled out and broke the circuit. Paul fell just like a statue, straight down. He got up and said, "What's happening?" He didn't remember anything, but the poor cat probably didn't get a hard-on for three or four weeks.

Because we spent so much time at the Troubadour, I used to see Tim Buckley play there quite a bit, and, my God, there was a man who made beautiful, passionate music. He played a twelve-string, and his voice had a range that was unbelievable. Tim called me right before he died from a heroin overdose. This was 1975, and I was at my home in Macon. The phone rang, and there was a bunch of people at the house, so at first I couldn't tell who it was. Tim told me that he had read an interview with me, and that I had said that one of my wishes was to record an album with him.

I told him, "Absolutely," and said to name the time and place and I would be there.

"Wow," he said. "It just seems like you would be the last person in the world to want to record with me."

"Man, we could do something great together," I told him, but he died before we could. I was so elated by that phone call, you couldn't talk to me for three or four days.

The first time we ran into Buffalo Springfield was when we opened for them at the Fillmore, and they were so good that night. We had been around them for a while, so they showed up early that night and heard some of our set. We stayed, of course, to watch some of theirs, and I thought, "Stills sure is singing kind of bluesy tonight."

Later on, when I got to know Stephen, he told me, "Man, you sure were a tough act to follow, even back then." I was really flattered by that. The two of us have always been pretty tight; we only see each other maybe twice every three years, if that, but he's a great guy.

Moby Grape was another band we really dug. Their bass player, a guy named Bob Mosley, was a big lumberjack-looking dude who played a white bass that hung down real low. He would come and sing this kind of a gospel number, and I'd never really seen anybody play some serious bass and sing their ass off at the same time like he did.

One night we played with Ike and Tina Turner at the Avalon. Buddy Guy was playing that night too, and he had a Fender Twin amp and a cord that had its own carrying case. This cord was so long, he could go out in the crowd and play, and they would have to turn his amp up as he got farther away from the stage.

Seeing all the shows and meeting everyone was all well and good, but what it really did was make us want to play more, which Liberty made increasingly hard. To help pass the time and deal with the boredom of not playing, I got into riding horses. There were a couple of places where you could go and rent a horse, with these huge fields to ride in. As a matter of fact, Dallas Smith used to go out there quite a bit. They had big rocks going sideways into the ground and it was neat—they used to film *The Lone Ranger* and a lot of cowboy movies there, and you could get out there and play, get the horse to do circles and all that.

I finally talked my brother into going out there one Sunday. It was a nice crisp, cool day, and he had on his corduroy jacket. We got the horses, and he was like, "Come on, man. Get on and let's fucking go!" As always, he was ready to hop.

I said, "Look, man, you gotta go across the street to get to the field. That street is asphalt, and your horse is shod."

Duane was like, "What the fuck do you mean, 'shod'?"

"He's got steel shoes on," I started to explain. "And steel shoes and asphalt means take him over him real slow, or he'll slip and bust both your asses."

Duane goes, "Are you through?"

I said, "Yes, but just hold him back until you get to the field, and then you can let him go."

Well, guess what happened? He no more than touched that goddamn asphalt, and the next thing I know, I see that horse rear up in the air, and my brother and the horse go down in a heap. I'm thinking, "God, why? Why didn't you just bring me out here and let me get trampled?" I knew what was coming, and getting trampled would have been better than that.

Duane was pissed off, and of course it was all my fault, no question about that. "See," he said, lighting into me. "You fucking pestered me about this Lone Ranger shit, and now I fuck up my goddamn arm."

He said some really hateful shit because he was so angry, telling me, "Take me home, and do not come around me. You are not welcome—do you understand?" He suffered a pretty bad sprain, and he had to keep his arm in a sling for six weeks, and he didn't speak to me that entire time. He didn't want nothing to do with me. Then on top of everything, he gets a raging cold, so he was ready to put a hit man on my ass.

It was his birthday on November 20, so I went and bought him a bottle of Coricidin, a bottle of pills that said it was for colds. Then I went by the record store and got that first Taj Mahal record, with all the butterflies on the cover and him sitting on a rocking chair. We'd played with Taj before, borrowed an amplifier from him. So I got Duane that record and the pills. Well, I couldn't have picked two better things.

I wrapped them up and put them on his doormat, and I knocked and ran. That was in the morning, and that evening my phone rang.

"Hello?"

"Hey, brother, get over here—get over here, babybrah, quick. Quick, man!"

It was a little chilly out, so as I was putting on my coat, the phone rang again. "Where are you? Where are you? Get over here quick."

"Jesus! All right, I'm coming!" So I hustled it over there.

He said, "Man, thank you," and he grabbed me and kissed me. He always kissed me, on the mouth, anywhere. So he kissed me on the cheek, and he said, "Man, that record you brought me is out of sight. There's a guy called Jesse Ed Davis on there, this Indian dude, and he plays guitar with a damn wine bottle. Dig this."

And then I looked on the table and all these little red pills, the Coricidin pills, were on the table. He had washed the label off that pill bottle, poured all the pills out. He put on that Taj Mahal record, with Jesse Ed Davis playing slide on "Statesboro Blues," and starting playing along with it. When I'd left those pills by his door, he hadn't known how to play slide. From the moment that Duane put that Coricidin bottle on his ring finger, he was just a natural.

Looking back on it, I think that learning to play slide was a changing moment in his life, because it was like he was back in his childhood—or maybe not his childhood, because it never seemed to me like Duane was a child, so it was more like going back to his first days of playing the guitar. He took to the slide instantly, and mastered it very quickly. He practiced for hours and hours at a time, playing that thing with a passion—just like he did when he first learned to play the guitar.

WHEN WE WERE ABLE TO PLAY SHOWS, WE WERE PLAYING A LOT OF R&B and some blues. We always stuck to our guns musically. We were determined to do what we did best and how it was the most comfortable for us, so we did songs like "Leaving Trunk," "I'm Hanging Up My Heart for You," the Solomon Burke tune, and "Dimples," which took on a life of its own. We did "Stormy Monday," "Feel So Bad," and "Love Light"—I remember Johnny Sandlin keeping time on "Love Light" with that big foot of his. Somebody had given him a set of drums, and I'm telling you, it looked like they had barf on them. They were orange and yellow, like a big pile of pizza puke. They looked like shit, but boy did they sound good.

People wanted me to get out there and stand up with a microphone and be a frontman, and I don't know why. We were what we were, and by God, that's what they should have been searching for—a one-of-a-kind thing. As long as it sounds good, why should it matter if someone is standing up or sitting down? Sounding good was what mattered, and my brother really believed that.

We would meet people in the business who would say things like, "Well, if you all turned just a little bit pop . . ." Duane would say back to them, "If you just turn your ass a little bit around, the door is right behind you." His attitude was that if what he was playing wasn't good enough and we had to play somebody else's shit, then fuck that. It's like the difference between owning a car and being a cabdriver.

Neither Dallas Smith nor Bob McEuen could really express what the hell they wanted us to do. If they had just shut their mouths, pushed the right buttons, and let us play, we'd probably still be living on the West Coast.

Mabron McKinley eventually went back home to Alabama, because he took a whole handful of acid and never quite got back, you know? He just got fucking out there. He called a band meeting one day, and we were all there, including Johnny's wife and Paul's wife, who had moved out there by this time. We met in Johnny's room, and Mabron was holding a Bible and said, "Now listen, you all. I know you may be disbelievers, but the end of the world will be upon us real soon." He gave us a date and everything.

We all looked at him and said, "Mabron, now listen, man. You need to think more about playing bass than the end of the world." He was way into UFOs, and after taking all that acid, he saw UFOs all the time. Of course, they were probably birds.

I have no idea why he took all that acid, but I never knew Mabron that well. Either way, we knew he wasn't going to last and we'd have to get a replacement, so we talked about a guy named Pete Carr from back home. We didn't want to use anybody out there, because it was obvious to us that we would have to retrain them. Nothing against West Coast players, but if they ain't from the South, just forget about it. It would be like trying to train an accountant to be a bouncer.

Pete was from Port Orange, Florida, and he was known as a good guitar player. He became kind of a protégé of my brother's, because whenever we would come back home to Daytona to play,

Pete would be right there. He had played guitar with the Men-Its for a while, so when Mabron finally split, we called Pete. We told him that we wanted him in the band—but as a bass player, which he had never played. All that guitar stuff that he had learned, he could forget about it. How's that for a challenge?

We flew him out to L.A., and it worked out so good—he made that transition instantly. Pete put some spark to it, some life to it. You can tell the difference between the two records, and he had a lot to do with that.

Our second Hour Glass record, *Power of Love,* which we recorded in January 1968, had a lot more of my original songs on it. I said to the Liberty guys, "Look, it's going on the record, and that's all there is to it. We ain't putting nothing else on there."

I ended up with seven of my songs on it, including "Changing of the Guard," which dated back to the Allman Joys, and "To Things Before," plus "I'm Not Afraid" and "I Can Stand Alone." We also did "Norwegian Wood" by the Beatles, where Duane played electric sitar, which sounded pretty good. "I'm Hanging Up My Heart for You" was also a hell of a song, and I loved to sing it.

We felt better about *Power of Love* than we did about the first album, but we were still getting really fed up about not having any gigs or cash. Thank God for Pete Carr, because he added much-needed comic relief to the situation. We started calling him "the Beaver," because he looked like one. It got to the point where I couldn't go to lunch with Pete anymore, because I almost died from laughing. He kept us going at a time when the rest of us were ready to quit.

After we put out *Power of Love,* the record company finally paid for us to go on a small tour. We actually flew on that tour, and I thought it was the big time. A limousine would pick us up and take us to the hotel, and all Johnny Sandlin kept saying was,

"Here we are, man, in a big old long black limousine, and I got five dollars to my name! We're going to play with Big Brother and the Holding Company in St. Louis. I'll be damned." We were going to play the Kiel Auditorium, and it was like hometown boys make good, because we used to play in that St. Louis shithole, and now we're playing the big auditorium.

We got there in the early afternoon, and we were setting up our stuff, because there were no technicians, no roadies—and no Hammond yet either. We're sitting there, and these two dudes come in wearing skinny ties and hats with feathers in them. My brother went up to get something to drink, and he came back and told me, "Hey, man, you see that fucker over there in that green suit? He's looking for you, so you'd better go up there and talk to him, because he ain't getting my stash on account of your ass."

I went over and said, "Hello, might I help you?"

"You are Mr. Gregory L. Allman?"

"I am that, sir."

"Do you have a picture ID?"

"Yes, I do." I showed them my ID, and as I held it out, the cuffs went right around my fucking wrist. They told me, "We're from the Health Department," and I told them, "Wait a second, man. You don't need to cuff me," so they took the cuffs off.

They told me, "We have a girl in our clinic, three blocks over, who has a syphilis sore on the back of her uterus that dials out at about five and a half centimeters, and she told us the last person she was with was you."

"That's impossible," I said, "because I just came into town today, and I haven't been here in months." This chick must have heard of us and picked my name at random or something.

They said, "That doesn't matter at all—we have our instructions to inoculate you, and, sir, if you won't come peaceably, we'll be glad to show you the way."

I look up, and there's two more big Italian dudes standing there. So I go down there, and they fill both cheeks of my ass with about five million units of medication. Well, I couldn't get my pants on after that. I had to stand up and play that night with my pants down real low and my drawers showing above them—kinda like the kids wear them now.

My brother laughed at me, but you know that you should never laugh at the misfortunes of others. It wasn't much later that he got on a plane at the request of Atlantic Records, to come and play on the Aretha Franklin song "The Weight." My brother got up there, and the same thing happened to him. On his way out of town, they got him and shot him in the ass with that shit. Whole different girl, whole different story, but the same end result.

Aside from St. Louis, we also played Cleveland, Montgomery, Tuscaloosa, and Jacksonville, and we ended up in Muscle Shoals, Alabama, at Fame Studios, to record a session the way we wanted to. It was a hell of a session—we almost hit the note there, man. It felt so good, because we were back down south, on our own turf. I was never so glad to be in Alabama in my life, and Duck kept saying, "Why did we ever leave, man?"

We were away from that whole pseudo-star shit, and it made a huge difference. At first when it came to stuff like the limousines, I'd thought, "Yeah, we're styling, man," but that didn't last long. We just wanted to get away from California and those fuckers at Liberty. It was a great session at Muscle Shoals, especially the B.B. King medley we did. We knew that was the way we were supposed to be recorded. We had the freedom to dictate those sessions, and it was the way we were meant to sound.

We go back to California all excited about the great music we'd cut, and they didn't want to hear it. The people at Liberty hated it, thought it was garbage. We had gone back there with the attitude that we had had a good tour, and this music was what we were really all about. Dallas Smith was talking while the Muscle Shoals tapes were playing, and I could see my brother sitting over there, getting hotter and hotter.

I'm thinking, "Here it comes," and sure enough, Duane stood up and pointed at the Liberty guys in the room.

"I'll tell you what," he said. "You, you, you, and you and Liberty Records can kiss my fucking ass. Me and the guys are picking up and going the fuck back down south, or anywhere but here. Fuck this place, and all the tinsel, and all the other bullshit. Stick your papers and contracts up your ass, we're outta here."

Of course, it wasn't that simple. Liberty threatened to freeze us, so that we couldn't record for any other label for seven years, unless I stayed and recorded with their studio band. So I stayed. I stayed for our band, and they hated me for it—they did. Duane even told me how he felt on the way out, between all the "fuck you"s. The other guys were like, "Man, we didn't know that you were so easily scared." I wasn't scared—I didn't want nobody to be frozen. What if a contract came up for them and then Liberty was to step in?

The whole thing just sucked, and I couldn't understand why the other guys were so pissed at me. It wasn't my idea to go out there in the first place, and I was just trying to save their ass. I had to believe that Liberty would freeze us, because there you are, standing in their place, right in the middle of Hollywood. So I stayed, but I was there in body, not spirit.

I cut some songs with this whole big band, and after we ran one of them down, I told them that it was in the wrong key. Dallas Smith decided to throw his weight around a little bit. He'd say, "What the fuck are you talking about? I've been working all day, trying to get this thing to work, so I don't need you telling me how things are supposed to sound."

I couldn't believe what they were having me do. I mean,

"D–I–V–O–R–C–E"? It was bullshit, but Dallas Smith and them would come to me and say, "We want you to do this song. Just do it, and don't worry about it. Do it as a favor for me." Bullshit—I was doing it as a favor for somebody's publishing company. That's why they had us do that ridiculous song, "Bells," on the first Hour Glass record. That song has got to be the epitome of hokey, of absolute sellout bullshit. Had I not been hungry, had I had any choice at all, I never would have done those songs.

On those sessions, I put those poor guys through such shit. After that "D–I–V–O–R–C–E" session, I made them not want to do another one. I kept telling them I was sick and couldn't make it, and they kept calling me. I'd show up late, I was just a prick about it. I would have rather been in hell with my back broke than do those sessions.

It was during this time that I started hanging out with the guys who were in Poco. I knew Rusty Young real well, and I knew Richie Furay from Buffalo Springfield, and Jim Messina was there too. Richie came over one night, and he told me, "Look, man, we've got some guys together. We don't have any songs, but we're working on some things."

Richie had been hanging out at the "Heart House," which was where the guys in this band called Heart lived. Heart consisted of John Townsend and Ed Sanford, two Alabama boys. They had two guys with them I really loved playing with: Court Pickett, who played guitar, and Lou Mullenix, who could play the shit out of the drums. He went on to play with Dr. John. They were wonderful people, from Tuscaloosa, but Lou ended up dying from a methadone overdose a few years later. Another Alabama cat named Kim Payne was a roadie for them, so this was the beginning of my relationship with Kim.

I started hanging with Richie and them, and we learned "It's Not My Cross to Bear" and "Dreams," which I had actually written at the Heart House, on Ed Sanford's organ. Everybody had gone out one night, so I was at the house by myself. I had a big fat joint, so I smoked that bad boy down and I started writing.

The words to "Dreams" are completely true. At that time, I was staying up at Julia Brose's place. Julia worked for Dallas Smith as his secretary. She was very pretty, and she lived up off of Laurel Canyon. You'd go up there, and on this little hill was a little tiny shack, just big enough for a very romantic hideaway. Of course, she had an old man, who happened to be in the Doors—she was hanging out with John Densmore, and she eventually married him. Julia's been married to so many musicians; there's no telling what kind of royalties she gets.

When I was staying up there, when I woke up and my eyes would open, I would be looking down the mountain. If it was raining, there would be mudslides and all that. That must have been in my mind when I sat down behind Sanford's Hammond.

Just one more morning, I had to wake up with the blues
Pulled myself out of bed, put on my walking shoes
I went up on the mountain, to see what I could see
The whole world was falling, right down in front of me

That's where the lyrics to "Dreams" came from.

I ended up staying at Julia's a bunch. Sometimes she would be out for stretches of time and I'd stay there. One time Julia was on the road with the Doors, so she asked me to watch her dog, who was going to have puppies. While I was there, her next-door neighbor turned me on to my first tab of Orange Sunshine. I'm tripping out when the dog starts having puppies. It's times like that when I don't like being alone, but God bless that neighbor.

I did my best to help the dog out with the puppies, and it went okay. Then I looked out the window and here come four limousines up the drive. It's them, the fucking Doors. All of them come in—Densmore, Jim Morrison, Robbie Krieger, and Ray Manzarek—because Julia wanted them to meet me. Robbie and Ray split, but Densmore and the Lizard King decided to stay. Julia introduced me, and I'm like, "Hey, how you doing?" and of course, I'm still tripping.

Morrison looks at me and goes, "What you got there on your hand, man?"

"Oh," I said looking up at him, "it's just a little puppy juice." Densmore was looking at me kinda strange, and my man Morrison said, "Oh, boy, this is going to be a good one. I have to stay and hear about this."

He left laughing—and the good thing was, we were all laughing so hard that Densmore wasn't thinking about me banging Julia, because he thought I was just the house sitter.

DUANE HAD BEEN BACK IN FLORIDA FOR A WHILE WHEN I CAME home from California to see what was happening. This guy named Butch Trucks had some kind of an idea about forming a band by combining his group, the 31st of February, with Duane and me, but he was the only one thinking that. I was planning to go back to L.A. to fulfill the deal with Liberty, and Duane was looking for something else to do, and eventually ended up in Muscle Shoals. We did a few tracks down in Miami, around late '68, but that was it. I had to get back to California, so I said, "Fuck it," and went on back out there.

Butch may still hold a bit of a grudge, to this day. He thought that was the beginning of the Allman Brothers Band—in his mind, it would have been David Brown on bass, Scott Boyer on guitar, Duane, me, and Butch on drums. Honestly, I don't know how that would have worked out.

It seems to me that people sometimes have the wrong perception about what going into a studio means. Just because you lay some stuff down in the studio, that doesn't mean it's automatically a finished product. In that particular case, the stuff we did in Miami was an example of going in there, laying it down, and seeing what came out of it, because you never know. A lot of songs have come about doing it that way, but in my mind that wasn't a formal recording session at all. We weren't cutting masters; we were just fishing for ideas.

The right players weren't assembled for those sessions. No offense meant, but Butch and those guys had been playing Dylan, the Byrds, with the twelve-string guitar and Fender bass—the whole folk-rock thing. They sounded very, very good, and live, the 31st of February was real good. I saw them many times, and they were great. But that sound isn't what me and my brother were all about. We were coming from a completely different direction.

So I went back to California, because it just wasn't happening. There was no Jaimoe yet, there was no Berry Oakley or Dickey Betts either. Duane and I knew that nothing was gonna come out of that group, so he wasn't pissed at all when I headed back west.

I needed some money to get to California, so I sold parts of two of my songs to this guy Steve Alaimo, who claims he "produced" those sessions. I sold him half of "Melissa" and "God Rest His Soul" for $600. I gave the band $300 to have some money to eat with, and I took the other $300 to get a plane ticket.

"God Rest His Soul" was a song I wrote in tribute to Martin Luther King, right after his assassination. I never intended to put that song on an album. I thought Martin Luther King was a beautiful man, and he was trying to bring us all together and end the strife in this country. He knew we couldn't do that by fighting each other, and he knew we couldn't do it by bombing other people halfway across the world. He was trying to show us there was another way to go about it, and he died because of that, so "God Rest His Soul" was my personal memorial to him.

So Alaimo ended up owning some of my music that he had nothing to do with for a grand total of $600, even though down the road I was able to gain back half the credit for "Melissa" by paying him $10,000. Alaimo did all right for a guy who didn't write no fucking songs. Personally I could never take credit for something I didn't write, or spend money I didn't earn—I just couldn't do it. Karma does come back around, so I hope he lives to be a hundred and his wife has a baby every day!

After I went back out to L.A., I didn't know what was going on with my brother. I thought he was either in Jacksonville or Miami; I doubted that he was in Daytona, but I didn't really know where he was. I figured that if he hit the big time, I'd read about it in some magazine.

Meanwhile, I got heavy into my songwriting, and I didn't even know why I was doing it. I guess it was because of all the emotions and feelings that were going through me every single day. I was being left out of something that I wanted to be a part of, but that hadn't really come about. I felt pretty much abandoned by my brother and the other guys. They just wrote me off, saying, "Fuck you, man. Stay away from us, you Hollywood motherfucker." They laid some pretty heavy shit on me.

Finally, around Christmas, I got word that my brother had gone to work for Rick Hall at Fame Studios in Muscle Shoals. It was a bad day when I heard that, because I thought that if he was on the damn staff, he was going to get paid a lot of dough, so he'd never have to go out on the fucking road again and we were done playing together.

Still I kept writing. I had access to that Hammond at the Heart House, so I could work some stuff up with it. Half the time

I was walking around and I didn't have enough to eat. Then I met this chick named Stacy, and she was always good for a meal. She lived at home with her mother, who was an amazing cook. I looked forward to going over to her house, because I knew I was going to get to watch a little TV, drink some lemonade, have a few snacks, and then her mama was going to make an incredible fucking meal. Then we'd go into her room, fool around a little bit, and I'd go home.

This went on for a while, until I found out that the deal was that I was supposed to marry the daughter—that's what all the hospitality was about. Well, the gods were looking down on me, because one night we were talking after dinner, and her mother slipped and said, "Well, you're sixteen, you can get married."

I was like, "Thanks, Ma, you got me out of that one." I told them, "Thank you, ladies. Good night, and goodbye."

I split, and right around that time—this was March 1969—the phone rang. It was my brother, calling me from Jacksonville, telling me to come back to Florida.

FRI. DEC. 8th.
SAT. DEC. 9th.
THE STANDELLS
AND
THE HOUR GLASS
No 1
NAVY ST.
VENICE
CHEETAH

At Rose Hill Cemetery in Macon, Georgia

CHAPTER FIVE

Us Against the World

I GOT THESE TWO DRUMMERS . . ."

That was how Duane started his call, and I'm thinking, "Two drummers? Sounds like a train wreck," but he continued, ". . . and a bass player from Chicago."

I thought, "Hmm, okay, that might be nice."

Then he hit me with, "I got a lead guitar player."

"Wait, what do you do?" I asked. "Last time I checked, you were a guitar player."

"Don't worry about it; I'll show you when you get here. What I need you to do is kinda round this whole thing up and send it somewhere. I need you to write something for it."

"Let me hang up so I can get going."

I got the phone almost on the hook and he said, "Wait! And I need you to play a Hammond organ."

"A Hammond organ? Man, I've only sat behind one of those two or three times." After I wrote "Dreams" and "It's Not My Cross to Bear" at the Heart House, I kinda put them out of my mind, so when he said that, I didn't even think, "Well, man, you just wrote two songs on a Hammond."

The first thing I did was call Richie Furay and tell him, "Man, I'm afraid can't make it to tonight's rehearsal—or any more rehearsals, for that matter."

"Really?" Richie asked. "Are you going somewhere?"

I said, "Yeah, man. Actually, my brother just called me, and he's put together a band back home in Florida, and I'm going to go join it."

By some hook or crook, Michael Alexander, the old bass player from the Allman Joys, had been in L.A. looking for a job, and he'd ended up at the Heart House. I saw his car, a Mach 1 Mustang, parked out in front of the house, and I thought, "No way, it can't be. Oh my God, I've got a ride back home!"

First thing he asked me when I walked inside was "Man, you got a few dollars?"

"I do happen to have a few bucks," I told him. "And I'll make you a deal. If you drive me back to Florida, I'll pay your gas money and a little extra," because I had $200 my brother had sent me.

All the way to Jacksonville, he kept bugging me, "Hey, man, can I get a bass-playing gig?"

"Look, man," I said, trying hard not to get his hopes up, "I don't know if I got a fucking job yet. How can I promise you anything?" My brother had parted with Mike on bad terms, because Duane didn't think he was worth a shit.

In the end it didn't matter. We got in the car and hit the road, heading east. When we pulled up to Butch Trucks's house, my brother opened the door and said, "Baybrah! You made it." Then he turned to Mike. "Hey, Mike, thanks for bringing my little brother home."

Duane took me in the house, and slam—he closed the door on Mike's ass, just left him standing there. That was that, man.

I was absolutely elated when I walked into that room and saw the whole band there—my brother, Berry Oakley, Dickey Betts, Butch Trucks, and Jaimoe. Of course, when you walk into a room and everybody knows everybody else except you, it's tough, especially when you're as shy as I am. It was real tense in that room. You could have cut it with a knife.

Thank God they had a real good sound system set up, so when I started singing, they could hear me, and everything came together at that moment. We played "Trouble No More," and it wasn't much different than it is today.

The first thing I noticed was that my brother and Berry Oakley were locked—kinda like my brother and Shepley had been. Oakley reminded me of Shepley a little bit. A skinny little guy with a twenty-four-inch waist, Berry was the bass player my brother had always been looking for. He and Duane had these certain little sarcasms that they shared. They were so tight— spiritually, musically, brotherly—they really had a thing going. Since one of them was a bassist and one of them was a guitarist, they could have easily had a three-piece band—that is, if one of them could have sung. They could have had a good little trio with Butch, but that's not what they wanted.

I thought that my brother must have taken on Dickey Betts so as to get Berry Oakley, because it meant busting up their band, the Second Coming. I couldn't figure out why he wanted Dickey as a guitarist, because Dickey's playing was nothing like my brother's. Dickey's style was much more abrupt. It was loud, and it came in little spasmodic bursts, whereas Duane's playing would just flow, like an angel flying through the air.

That would all change—Dickey's playing and my perception of it—because after he was with my brother for a while, I knew he would either get better or my brother would fire him. I've come to see that he must have been a good guitar player; he wouldn't have stayed in the band if he hadn't been.

The first thing I do when I meet someone is look at their clothes. You can tell a lot about a person by their clothing, and at first look Dickey's clothing was fine, until I got to his shirt. Them ruffled shirts—I just didn't understand that. They didn't fit the person, they didn't fit the occasion, and they made me wonder a little bit. I looked at Oakley, who had a real look going, and then I would look at Betts, who was wearing that damn white-ruffled tux shirt, without a coat, and with the sleeves rolled up. Despite that, I felt accepted by him, as I did by everyone.

They asked me if I had any songs with me, and I told them I had twenty-two, so they told me to play them. I'd get through with one, and they'd ask me, "What else you got?" I'd play 'em another one and they were like, "That was kinda neat, a little potential; what else you got?"

After twenty of them, I'm going, "Oh fuck, I might be without a job here in a minute." I had two songs left—"Not My Cross to Bear" and "Dreams." I showed them "Dreams" first, and let me tell you, they joined right in. We proceeded to sit down, learn that song the same way you hear it today, and I was in, brother. They loved it. I bet we played that thing eleven times in a row, and the more we played it, the better it got.

I told them that it kind of hopped, and back on the drums, Jaimoe got that right off. I'm thinking, "This Jaimoe guy is the hippest cat in the whole crowd," and he still is. It's like my brother always said, "I started with Jaimoe, and then we put the band together." Jaimoe is all right, man. Nothing has changed with him—he's the same cat who came from Gulfport, Mississippi, and happened to be in Muscle Shoals at the same time my brother was. It was fate.

Jaimoe is the strangest man I've met in my life, but I don't mean strange in a bad sense at all. He certainly didn't belong in any institution, but he was just so different, mostly because I was used to hearing people running off at the mouth all the time. Jaimoe never said anything unless it really needed to be said, and the way he would go about saying it would usually end up being so funny.

Jaimoe is very, very intelligent, and eventually I came to realize that he'd been fooling us the whole time, just taking it all in while we'd been running our mouths. The world could use some more Jaimoes, but there's only one. I came to love Jaimoe real quick, and the fact there was a black guy in the band knocked me out. His musical heart comes from jazz, but to get a gig he had to play R&B, which was his second choice. It was amazing how much he knew about music and the depth of his passion for it.

Now, the two drummers confused the shit out of me—and on top of that, there were two guitar players. I kept thinking, "This is going to be bedlam, just pure torture," but of course, it was quite the contrary. I must say, that arrangement had a nice little kick to it. They had all been playing "Don't Want You No More" before I got there, which Berry and Dickey had brought in from the Second Coming. It was scary the power they played it with, and my brother came up with the riff that tied it into "Not My Cross to Bear." Right then and there, I knew we had something special.

I've asked myself many times why my brother was so insistent that I come back and be part of this band. I'm sure they sat down one day and said, "All right, who are we gonna get to sing?" I always wondered if they got me just because they couldn't find anybody else, because back then everybody was a guitar player.

Singers were few and far between, and maybe the ones that were real good were taken.

Still, I always took it as quite a compliment, because it's not the sentiment, it's who it comes from that really makes a difference. Compliments from Duane weren't necessarily verbal—not saying he was a man of few words, but as far as giving me the okay or singing my praises, he would do it in little subtle ways, like he'd wink at me onstage after I sang a verse or did a solo or something. He watched me go up to different levels, and he was always pulling for me.

I was pretty knocked out that first day. March 26, 1969, was one of the finer days of my life. It was a long day, but a great day. I was starting to feel like I belonged to something again.

We spent the first few days just getting to know one another. There was a bunch of beer and a bunch of food, so we partied there for a bit. A couple of filthy jokes always help dudes to get to know one another, and we told some good ones. I've never seen my brother so relieved. He knew we had something, because all the pieces had come together and fit perfectly.

I remember thinking, "Jesus Christ, do other bands have to search the world over to find the right combination, and how many get as lucky as we did? You can have the right group of guys but the wrong drummer, so everyone in that band is a truck driver today." Our thing was so perfect, and on paper it shouldn't have been—we had two drummers, not to mention that one of them was a black man and we were in the Deep South, 1969. The way I saw it, fate brought a certain group of musicians together who just blended perfectly.

One thing that was painfully obvious to me was that while we had this kick-ass band, it came about because we smashed the shit out of this other band, the Second Coming. For a while, I sat around waiting for the bomb to go off, because it seemed to me that everybody else in the Second Coming was vying to be an Allman Brother. I might have been wrong, but it sure seemed that way.

Right after I got to Jacksonville, the Second Coming had a gig at the Jacksonville Beach Auditorium. Toward the end of the gig, Oakley said, "We got a little surprise for you," and my brother and I joined them onstage. We played a few songs, including "Trouble No More" and "One Way Out," and that place went berserk. I had heard a crowd before, but I ain't never heard nothing like that. Those people were howling—that night changed them. It was clear; this was fucking working.

I felt bad for the rest of the Second Coming guys, because they knew what time it was, but I couldn't wait to play again. On the drive back home, all we did was talk about this or that, and this part right here going over there—it was just lined up, man. We could see our destiny, and we set out to get it.

ONCE I GOT SETTLED IN, MY MAIN ORDER OF BUSINESS WAS TO write songs. After showing them those two songs, I became the writer for the Allman Brothers Band. On some of the early songs that I wrote after I got to Florida—like "Black Hearted Woman," "Every Hungry Woman," and "Whipping Post"—my experience with that girl Stacy was probably in my head, but I can't say I was specifically thinking about her while I was writing them. Honestly, I don't know where they came from. The words just appeared.

My brother was staying with this artist chick named Ellen Hopkins, who lived down the street from Butch, so I had a place to stay too. This was in Arlington, which is a suburb of Jacksonville. Berry Oakley, his wife, Linda, and their little baby daughter, Brittany, were also staying there, so I was staying up in the very top of the house, in this sitting room with a real nice couch in it. I was up there, laying on that couch, and I was just exhausted.

I wrote "Whipping Post" the first night I was at Hop's house. It was a huge place that must have been built around the turn of the century, and the house was real squeaky. Despite that, I was told more than once that after a certain time I was not to make a sound.

"If that baby wakes up," Duane told me, "man, we're outta here. Ya dig?" (That was my brother's saying—"Ya dig?")

So that first night, I laid me down to go to sleep on my attic couch, and I dozed off for a while. All of a sudden I woke up, because a song had me by the ass. The intro had three sets of three, and two little steps that allowed you to jump back up on the next triad. I thought it was different, and I love different things. It hit me like a ton of bricks. I wish the rest of them had come like this—it was all right there in my head, all I had to do was write it down so I wouldn't forget it by the morning.

I started feeling around for a light switch, but I couldn't find one anywhere. I was in my sock feet; I just had on my drawers and a T-shirt. I found my way into the kitchen and it was pitch-dark. I had my hands out and I touched an ironing board—thank goodness, instead of tripping over it, which would've made a terrible noise.

I was feeling all around the counters for a piece of paper. I couldn't find any paper or a pencil anywhere, but I did find a box of kitchen matches. A car happened to go by, and its lights flashed long enough to allow me to see that red, white, and blue box. I knew I could use the matches to write with, because I had diddled around enough with art to know that charcoal would work.

I figured the ironing board cover would work as a pad, so I'd strike a match, blow it out, use the charcoal tip to write with, and then strike another one. I charted out the three triads and the two little steps, and then I went to work on the lyrics:

"I've been run down, and I've been lied to . . ."

I got it all down on that ironing board cover, in the closest thing to shorthand as I could muster up. I was really proud that I didn't wake Brittany up. The next morning, Hop raised so much fucking hell with me about that ironing board cover, but it worked out, and we got "Whipping Post" down that day.

This guy down the road was letting us rehearse in his nightclub, which was called the Comic Book Club. They had black lights and girls in little sailor suits dancing on the tables. They smelled terrible! He let us use it until like four o'clock, time enough for us to get our shit offstage before they opened.

The next day I wrote "Black Hearted Woman," and the day after that I wrote "Every Hungry Woman." I wrote most of that whole first record in that one week. I had total peace of mind. L.A. and all its changes didn't even cross my mind. I felt like I was starting all over, which I was.

One rainy day, the guys came over and got me, and my brother said, "We're going for a ride." They took me over to Dickey's old place, because I remember his motorcycle was parked behind it. They put a blindfold on me and led me into this room. They told me, "You can take it off now," so I took the blindfold off, and there it was—they had got me a brand spanking new 1969 B3 Hammond organ. It cost $1,883, and another $1,295 for the 122RV Leslie. They didn't have the money, but somehow Duane had gotten it.

It was plugged in and turned on, and there were four joints rolled—big, big phatties—a nice big ashtray, a garbage can, plenty of paper, and a lot of pencils. They told me, "We'll see you in a few days, brother," and, man, that's when the writing came on. Getting that Hammond helped to finish those songs like "Black Hearted Woman" and "Every Hungry Woman," because although "Dreams," "It's Not My Cross to Bear," and another song called "Demons" are the only songs I've ever completely written on the Hammond, I got images in my mind of what the band would do with these songs, and the Hammond helped a lot.

Writing those songs was work, but it was so gratifying, because it was a true labor of love. Everybody had their minds so nicely open, and we worked so well together. We'd get to one part of a song, and my brother would say, "Well, what about doing this?" and one thing would lead to another. Duane was really encouraging me with my songwriting. He would compliment me, pat me on the ass, or actually kiss me on the mouth, right in front of the other guys. He let me know how much he loved my singing and how proud he was of me.

We were also learning some other songs, like "Hoochie Coochie Man" and "Sweet Home Chicago," which Berry sang. We'd also jam on all kinds of stuff, like "Crossroads" and "Rock Me Baby"—we played whatever came to mind. We also worked up "Stormy Monday," which me and my brother had done for years, as well as "Outskirts of Town," which I never really liked playing because it's really a horn song.

"Mountain Jam" was my brother's thing. He just started playing it one day. It's not that he had a thing for Donovan—it's just a happy little melody, and it makes for a really nice jam. You hear a song, and you can just tell if you can jam on it or not.

We weren't in Jacksonville very long, because Twiggs Lyndon arrived not long after I did. Twiggs worked for Phil Walden at Capricorn Records in Macon, and Phil had signed on as Duane's manager while he was doing sessions in Muscle Shoals.

Jerry Wexler at Atlantic Records always felt that, in a way, he discovered Duane, but it was really Twiggs. Word had gotten around that there was this redheaded guitar player over at Muscle Shoals who was kicking some butt, so Twiggs went over there, on his own dime, to see my brother. He came back to Phil and said, "Dig it, man, you gotta go check out this player over there."

Phil saw him play, and then Twiggs asked him, "Man, are you ready for that? Is that something else?"

"I don't know. Is he good?" was Phil's response, and Twiggs said, "Yeah!" So Phil used him as kind of his barometer, and he called up Wexler.

That's when Wexler came down and said, "Oh yeah, he's good!"

Phil had put Twiggs in charge of getting us up to Macon. He told us, "We got you all a place," which was an old two-story clapboard house on College Street that had been converted into an apartment building. Twiggs rented it and put a Coke machine in there and filled it with beer. I don't think we stayed in Jacksonville more than ten days before we loaded everything up in two vans and headed for Georgia.

Hauling that Hammond around wasn't easy. We didn't have a road case for it, so we just wrapped it in blankets, and belts would go around it, and there was a ratchet thing that would tighten them down. That thing weighed well over four hundred pounds, and we had a lot of second-floor gigs back then. Getting that thing up the stairs always reminded me of a Laurel and Hardy episode. Sometimes we had to use the whole band. We looked like pallbearers, but we usually preferred to use people whose hands were expendable.

Of course, we had to come up with a name for the band. I didn't care too much about a name; I just knew it was the best fucking band I'd ever been in. Duane said, "All right, look. Here's a hat, here's some pieces of paper. Write down what you think it should be, and put it in the hat." Everybody wrote down a name, and it turned out that four of them were the same and two of them weren't.

My choice was "Beelzebub," the right-hand man of the devil, while my brother went with something from *Lord of the Rings*, which he knew wasn't going to fit the music. The other four all said, "The Allman Brothers Band," and that was it. My brother and I both said, "Oh fuck—you all are kidding, right?" Neither one of us had anything to do with the name, and I think the others chose it mainly because of my brother's leadership. So the Allman Brothers Band we became.

Our first afternoon in Macon, we went over to Phil Walden's office for our first meeting, and he blew a bunch of smoke up our ass. The whole time he was talking, he'd only look at Duane. He was used to dealing with people like Percy Sledge, and then they dealt with their bands—and I can see his point in doing it that way, because he had signed Duane, not the band. That didn't last, though, because Duane went in there and told him, "Hold it. My little brother is in this goddamn organization, and you will treat us all the same, or you won't treat us at all. So what's it going to be?"

My first impression of Phil Walden was that he was okay. I knew he had been very successful, and my brother had gone to Macon to speak with him personally. He came back to Jacksonville and said, "He seems pretty solid to me." That was good enough for me and everybody to agree to go to Macon. To look at Phil, with his haircut and the way he dressed, he seemed to be very hip, and he could hold his liquor. I figured, "What the hell, there ain't nothing going on elsewhere, so as long as we don't sign our firstborn away, and as long as the fucking cards are on the table, we should go with this guy."

Phil Walden was taking 100 percent of the publishing, because he was doing "administration." What the hell does that mean? I asked him one time, and he told me, "Well, we make stacks and stacks of cassettes of all the songs you wrote on all the records, and we send them out to Capitol, we send them out to A&M, we send them out to . . ." And he just kept rambling on about all these record labels. What a pile of bullshit that was. The man was taking half my money, and I don't remember him being there while I was writing the songs he was getting paid for.

But my brother trusted Phil, and when I started asking questions about my publishing, he would just poke me and say, "Hey, man, be fucking thankful that we got enough to eat. Just sign the fucking agreement so we can get going, and they'll give us a bunch of money once you sign it." So that's how I signed all my publishing rights away.

Being the writer of these songs, I really disagreed with him, and it hurt me that Duane didn't stand up for me more. I realize that he was looking out for the whole band and its betterment, but still, I think he could have done more, and it ended up costing all of us a shitload of money down the line.

Walden never offered us any direction at all. He would just show us off after we got famous. He strutted his stuff around like a peacock, saying, "Yeah, I'm the manager of southern rock." He could get a record played on the radio—hell, he could sell refrigerators to Eskimos. He didn't sign Otis Redding by being no dummy. Him and Otis's father had to go down to the courthouse when they signed the contract, or it wouldn't be binding—and he wanted to make damn sure it was binding.

BEFORE I'D LEFT CALIFORNIA, I PROMISED KIM PAYNE, WHO'D been a roadie for Heart and who I'd become friends with at the Heart House, that if this new thing with my brother worked out and we needed a roadie, I'd send for him as soon as I got there.

"Bullshit," he said.

"No, man, I will," I told him.

"It's been nice knowing you, Gregg" was all he replied, and he was upset, because we'd gotten real close out there.

Sure enough though, once things began to take shape in

Macon, I sent for him, and he rode his motorcycle all the way out. It was cold and rainy, and all he had on was a pair of Levi's, a pair of boots, a flannel shirt, a T-shirt, and a Levi's jacket. He got off his bike and came over to me, and he said, "Goddamn—some men keep their word."

So Kim joined up with Mike Callahan, who had been the soundman for the Second Coming. Callahan was our only roadie for our first few gigs, and he had a way about him where whenever we got to a gig, he'd talk people into unloading everything. Michael had the gift of gab for sure. He was a hell of a guy, and I can remember laughing with that man until I thought I was going to expire, because I couldn't get my breath. I sure miss my brother Michael, who passed a couple of years ago.

We then added Joseph Campbell, aka Red Dog, who was a wounded Vietnam vet; he had been in the Marine Corps. He'd gotten that nickname in Vietnam, because he was redheaded and he was such a dog—after a while, he had one in every town. Remember that cartoon dog, Droopy? He was a little black-and-white dog with a big fluff of red hair. He had him tattooed on his arm and they had the hair real red.

Red Dog had been everywhere. My brother met him when he was selling weed in the park, these cheap-ass nickel bags that weren't worth a shit. Friendship meant everything to Red Dog, and I mean everything. If Red Dog liked you, he loved you, but if he didn't, forget it—you had no chance. Duane took a liking to him, and he rounded out our first road crew.

In the early days, Red Dog contributed his disability check from Vietnam to the band, but he was paid back in diamonds. Let it show, carved into stone, that Red Dog, God bless him, came along and insisted on giving us that check, because we weren't going to take his damn check—we barely knew the cat. The fact is, he needed a place to belong. He really wanted to be in our gang, because we had a good thing going.

It was kind of a collective deal between the roadies and the band. We'd throw our backs into it, right along with them. We were used to it, because we had been our own roadies before. Butch and Jaimoe would set up their own drums, and we'd help carry everything in. We found that since we were all getting there together, we could unload the equipment that much quicker, and then we'd let them take over. I'm not saying we did their jobs for them or anything like that. But there were only three of them at first. (Eventually we ended up with twelve roadies and, oh God, that was stupid.)

From the start, Twiggs Lyndon really impressed me, because he had been there from beginning to end with Otis Redding, and he had a lot to do with the success Otis had. Twiggs had also been the road manager for Little Richard when the Allman Joys opened a show for Richard and the Coasters up in Atlanta, and even though I didn't meet Twiggs, I did meet Richard and it broke my heart, man.

The Coasters were really funny and great to be around; we really enjoyed them. I got to one of Richard's people, and I asked him, "I've been an admirer of Richard Penniman for years, do you mind if I go meet him?" The guys said, "Sure, come on," and so I went up there. Richard was in his dressing room, and he said, "My soul! Who in the world are you, boy?"

We had just finished our run at Trude Heller's in New York City. We had bought us a bunch of clothes, and I had on a pair of pants that had a little zipper in the back, and a big belt that went over that, and a real nice shirt. He put his hand on my belt, and I said, "No, don't do that," and I backed up. This guy who must have been with Richard said, "In other words, Richard, you better not do that again or there will be a dead nigger around here!" They all laughed, and I just got out of there. Years later, we became "Hey, how are you?" kind of friends, and still, whenever he sees me, Richard always extends his hand and greets me very warmly.

Twiggs and I got along really well. He loved to show me his record collection, and he was a frustrated guitar player. He was so organized and anal about everything—the world was never perfect enough for Twiggs Lyndon, and that's why he's not here anymore. He could drive you nuts with his organization. Twiggs didn't have a short fuse, but if it burned down, look out. He was a little eccentric, and he was way ahead of his time, but then, shit, it seemed like all of us were.

On one of our long drives, it was raining and raining, so of course the windshield wipers broke, but only on the passenger side. We stopped at a gas station, and Twiggs got down there with all these tools, and he was explaining how this catch assembly lock arm should stay next to the band-driven catch assembly on the A-part of the arm. Of course, we all couldn't care less; we just wanted to get going again. After about an hour and a half, we had to tell him, "Shut the fuck up, man," but that was part of what made Twiggs so efficient; he always tended to business extremely well.

Twiggs was the original dirty old man. In his road case was a chart with the legal age of consent in every state of the union, and he had copies made for everyone in the band. He'd hand them out before the tour started, and he kept extras in case you lost it. Twiggs could be a real freak. One time, this chick came out from California to visit me when we were playing somewhere like St. Louis, and we'd been fucking all night, so we went to sleep with nothing on. I woke up, and barely opened one eye, and there's Twiggs. He's got the covers up, and he's looking at her twat. Kim Payne walked in the room, butt-naked, and he said, "Twiggs, what are you doing?" Twiggs just says, "Oh, that." I couldn't believe he said that! Kim looked at me like, "We got to do something about that boy."

Once we got situated at 309 College Street, Twiggs turned us on to the young ladies at Wesleyan College. We boys had been out to sea for a while, and we needed our business fixed. The girls at Wesleyan were more than happy to take care of it. I met this girl the other day, and she told me, "I remember when you guys used to live down the street. I was just a little kid, and my mother would say, 'Don't go down there messing with them boys. They're not churchgoers!'" Of course, her mother was probably banging one of us.

When we got to Macon it was April, and Macon in the springtime is gorgeous, because all the cherry blossoms and dogwoods are blooming. We'd play all day, then go collect enough bottles to get some chicken necks, which we called "Allman Brothers Fried Dead Birds," and we'd grill them up. Masons that we were, we built this big barbecue in the backyard, and there was a big pond back there, fed by this freshwater spring. One day, all of us got in the pond, and we cleaned that motherfucker out—boy, we got muddy, but it looked so beautiful. The water from the spring was crystal clear, and then it rained that night. Man, there was a frog fuckfest like you ain't never seen.

The first time I showed "Melissa" to the guys, we were sitting on the front porch at the College Street place. I played just a little bit of it, and my brother said, "Oh yeah, man—play that one again," and every night from that point on, he made me play it.

Twiggs took us all around town, and he introduced us to Mama Louise Hudson, who was a real nice lady with a restaurant, the H&H. It's always been hard for me to accept any kind of handout or charity, or anything that even resembles it. A lot of times, I'd go down to her place and I wouldn't even order nothing, I'd just wait for the other guys to finish eating. Eventually, I learned that she really loved us and believed in us, and so when she would offer me some food, I'd eat it, but I swore to myself that I would pay her back, no matter how long it took. I have always cared for her: Louise Hudson is a very special woman.

Later on, when we had that jet plane, we'd bring her on it to cook for us if we were in the area. She always wanted a Cadillac limousine, a black one, to pick her up. We'd send one to her to drive her up to Atlanta, wait for her, and drive her back. That was so fun, man. I remember the look on Louise's face the first time we did it; she was just bawling her eyes out. Eventually we got her a gold-plated skillet. It's still hanging up on the wall in there.

Originally our plan was to rehearse at the place on College Street, but it's in a residential section of town, so we couldn't do that for very long. We moved down to Capricorn Studios and started rehearsing there, even though it wasn't quite built yet. The room was all finished—all the bricks, all the floors, the booth, the board was in. All that was left was the machines, and they came in, one by one, and that became our rehearsal hall.

The great thing about our band was there wasn't any bullshit, no preliminary chatter about this or that like there is in so many other bands. We didn't have none of that crap. The music was so important to us that there wasn't any time for chatter—we wanted to play, and we just played and played all day. The only thing we wanted to do was get our sound tighter and tighter, get it better and better. We played for each other, we played to each other, and we played off each other, which is what the Allman Brothers is all about.

We were like Lewis and Clark, man—we were musical adventurers, explorers. We were one for all and all for one. Back then, that novelty never wore off.

We hadn't been in Macon very long when a guy came passing through town from the University of Florida who had a tabbing machine, which is used to make tabs of acid. If you got caught with one of those, it was your ass. You could get caught with all the dope you wanted, but to get caught with a tabbing machine meant you'd never see sunlight again.

This cat came by with a two-quart jar of these little pink pills, about as a big as an aspirin. They were pure psilocybin mushroom extract. We'd get up in the morning, have a little breakfast, and then we'd each pop half a pill. Our shit would be set up, somebody would name a key, and we'd start jamming, and that really spurred on our creative process.

The mushroom logo for our band came out of this early experience. Let me make this clear: that mushroom logo wasn't screaming, "Hey, people, go take psilocybin." It was screaming, "Listen to the fucking Allman Brothers." It's just like the tongue and lips logo screams, "Listen to the Rolling Stones."

There's no question that taking psilocybin helped create so many spontaneous pieces of music. That music would come oozing out of our band. We hit some jams that were out of this world, and they were so powerful that we wouldn't talk for a long time afterwards—no one would say shit. We kept doing that, learning how each other played, learning where each guy was coming from. Our musical puzzle was coming together, and mushrooms certainly enhanced that whole creative atmosphere.

One time, somebody left four or five psilocybin tablets on the back of the toilet at 309 College, and Jaimoe thought they were speed, so he took them all. I think that was the only time I've ever seen fear in that man's face. He had this little transistor radio that would pick up jazz stations, and he walked around with that radio to his ear for pretty near two days. That was the only thing holding him down to the ground—as long as he had that music, he was going to be all right. I was kinda worried about him, and everybody was stashing their shit in case we had to call the paramedics, but he came out of it okay.

AT THAT TIME, THERE WASN'T A DAMN THING GOING ON IN MACON, so we just tried to ease on in and not upset anyone. We made it a point to meet the mayor, "Machine Gun" Ronnie Thompson, and he was all smiles. As for the nightlife, there were a few clubs, Grant's Lounge being one of them. There weren't too many other bands around, even though this one band, the Boogie Chillun, had a bit of a following around town.

Eventually, we became like the Dukes of Macon. People followed us home, and the women would chase us down. Lookswise, I came through all right, fair or average, I guess—I looked a little better when I was younger. There was this one girl who wasn't anything special, but she would call me constantly and just would not leave me alone. God bless her, and I hope she found what she was looking for.

When we weren't rehearsing, we'd pass the time by playing corkball, which is the lazy musicians' game. You get a pool cue, take the smaller end, and cut off about a foot of it. You wrap black electrical tape around the big end of the pool cue, and there's your bat. Then you go to the hardware store and get one of those corks that go into a thermos. Take a penny, lay it on top of the cork—preferably heads up—and then take adhesive tape and wind it around and around, until it looks like a little mummy.

When you throw the ball, you rest the penny against your finger, and you throw it as hard as you can to the batter. A little past the pitcher, there's a marker with "#1" on it, and a little farther there's "#2," and then "#3," and way back was the home run marker. The odds of you hitting that damn corkball with that cue stick were pretty slim, but if you ever did connect with that fucking penny, you'd send that son of a bitch into the next county. We used to play over by Butchie's place—the little triangle park there was the corkball field. It was a great game, man.

In the summertime, we'd get a bunch of inner tubes and go down to the Ocmulgee River. We'd take a little pot in some Tupperware containers because you knew you were going to tip over at some point, and we'd float down them rapids and smoke them phatties, and just laugh. We'd bring girls with us and snatch their tops off—just some good clean fun. We'd have a good old time, but then either we had to walk back or somebody would meet us down there and drive us back.

Good as the summer was, Macon was a general bummer in the winter. The sky was gray, no leaves on the trees, freezing rain and ice, so that first winter we split and went to this place near Tarpon Springs, on the west coast of Florida, called the Weeki Wachee River. There's a place there called Silver Springs, and that's where they filmed all those *Tarzan* movies with Johnny Weissmuller. They have springs there that are like 130 feet deep, and you can look down through these glass-bottomed boats and see catfish that are like eighty pounds. I mean, huge fucking catfish—you could fit a football in their mouths. There are several little tributaries, which all dump into a main spring. It still keeps belching that good old artesian water, and you can swim along and drink it, and it's so delicious.

We would go down there—usually me, Kim Payne, the Hound (which is what we called Red Dog), and Mike Callahan. We would rent canoes and head down the Weeki Wachee. That water is cold—it will freeze your nuts up into your tummy. We'd go out there, and we wouldn't see another canoe the whole trip. Just like back on the Ocmulgee River, we'd put our reefer in

Tupperware to keep it safe from the rapids, and we had bottles of wine, which were half-empty so they would float.

In one spot was a huge oak tree with a rope on it. You could swing out and then drop into the water—boy, we had so much fun. Next time we went down there, we took everybody in the band, and that was really something. I've always wanted to go back there.

My brother loved to go bass fishing. Duane and Butch went fishing all the time, and Duane and Dickey would go fishing every now and then. Jaimoe wasn't no fisherman, but I remember the one time he got a sunburn. I didn't even know that black people could get a sunburn. We were down at my mother's house, because we had had a gig in Miami, and the next one was in Jacksonville, but we had a few days off in between. We got out two lawn chairs, and that sun was directly overhead and beating down on us. Jaimoe fell asleep, and I went inside and got on the phone. After a while, I remembered him, and I went, "Oh shit—I gotta go over and flip him." Oh man, he was as black as a piece of coal, and he couldn't move his arms at all. I had to help him back into the house. He was cooked.

I'll say it again: I love Jaimoe like I loved my brother. Of all the people who have ever been in the band, I love Jaimoe the most.

I met my dear, dear friend Chank Middleton one day at the barbershop that was next door to the studio. I had a pair of Ray-Ban sunglasses with the round backs, and I couldn't stand them, so I gave them to Chank. They were worth like $40 back then, so they'd be like a $200 pair of shades today. Hell, he kept them things for the longest time—I mean, for like fifteen years.

"You mean you're giving these to me?" he asked.

"Well," I said, "you can give me a shine."

"Okay, fine."

I jumped up into the chair wearing sneakers, and I told him, "You motherfucker—I got ya!" He hit me with that laugh of his, and we've been friends ever since.

Aside from Floyd and Jaimoe, Chank was the first black man I'd ever known real closely. We just hit it off, right from the very beginning, and we hung pretty tight. Every time Chank would see us going into the studio, he'd call us into the barbershop to play craps. We had some incredible craps games in the back of that damn barbershop. I learned all about craps in there, especially how fast your money can disappear, and sometimes Chank would have a little smoke for us. You always knew Chank would be in one of three places—at the barbershop; with Carol, his girlfriend; or hanging with us.

From time to time, we would all go down to Rose Hill Cemetery, and we wrote some songs down there. It was a very reverent place to us, very quiet, but I'd be lying if I said I didn't have my way with a lady or two down there. It's cozy, with all those beautiful willow trees and the beautiful river. I don't want people to think that I'm some kind of exhibitionist, but there's nothing like going out and having sex on God's green earth—as long as there are no friggin' red ants.

We shot some pictures for our first album down at Rose Hill, and I thought that was kind of strange, especially that shot of Oakley with arms outspread above the rest of us. Right after we took that shot, a train went by, and the conductor had no idea what the hell was going on. He must have been thinking, "They don't have no white hoods on, so they ain't none of my buddies."

We were absolutely inseparable. We did everything together. We shot pool together. We jumped off cliffs together. Chank turned us on to this rock quarry down on the outskirts of town, and we'd go down there with a watermelon, roll a few joints, and jump off its hundred-foot cliff. We'd make a day of it. It was our gang—it was that simple.

Our family thing only grew stronger, and that included dealing with the perennial redneck questions: "Who them hippie boys and who's the nigger in the band?" We dealt with that second question quite a bit. Keep in mind, this was the 1960s, and we were in the Deep South, so having a black guy in the group came up a lot. But Jaimoe was one of us and we weren't going to change that for nobody. Whenever some asshole came around, all of us, together, would do something about it. Any kind of problem that came from the outside, we met head-on. It was like we had a force field around us. It was us against the world, man.

For the most part, we were fine as long as nothing started within the confines of our gang. Duane and I would do that brother thing from time to time, but it was nothing serious. I'm sure that my brother had words with other people in the band, but he had a way of nipping problems in the bud. The first whiff of any shit at all and Duane took care of it. Why I didn't learn that from him, I don't know, but I wish I had. Letting stuff build up only makes it worse, so jumping on it early prevents hard feelings and grudges.

Back then there was no lingering tension between any of us, and that included Dickey, who has always been a real hothead— even then. Instead of working things out, he'd work them out with his fists, or screaming, or kicking some ass. The fact is, me and Dickey hardly ever said anything, not while Duane was around, anyway. I can't remember Dickey having any big blowups while Duane was alive.

I wore my thirties out and was approaching forty before I realized that you have to watch how you get into it with people, because they might change over time, or you might change, and the two of you might become just what the other one needs, in business, in friendship, or whatever.

I loved the way my brother would deal with Phil Walden. He would walk into Walden's office, and his heartbeat would not change at all. He would never be ungracious or anything, because we were fixing to cut a record and have a career together. He would just go in there and say, "We need this, this, and this." He wore Walden down so much that Phil eventually stopped asking why and gave us what Duane asked him for.

My brother strived to make sure there was a comfort zone in our gang at all times, and there wasn't going to be any bullshit about Duane Allman and his sidemen. We were all equal, all together. A band means a bunch of guys working together for the same goal—that's what the word "band" means, and we defined that. We weren't famous yet, but there was a time in there when we got to watch ourselves create this thing that really worked. Being in that group was the best thing you could ever imagine.

The Allman Brothers Band at Piedmont Park in Atlanta, Georgia, April 1969

CHAPTER SIX

The People's Band

WE JUST WANTED TO PLAY ALL THE TIME, AND IT DIDN'T matter where or for who. Everywhere we went, we played for free. If we had a gig on a Saturday night, then on Sunday we'd play for free at the nearest park. We would just plug in, start playing, and an hour later there would be two thousand people there. Sometimes it would take about an hour for the word to spread and for people to start showing up, so by the time we had played for two hours, the place was starting to fill up, and we'd start over. We'd just pick all afternoon, because we loved to play.

I remember our first gig at Piedmont Park in Atlanta like it was yesterday. This must have been around May '69, and we had gotten enough songs for a real set. It was only about twelve songs, but it was a set, because of the length of some of the songs.

We also had some alternate songs we could use as backups, like "Sweet Home Chicago" or "Love Light."

From the very beginning, we were too loud. I was always saying, "Guys, it's just too damn loud," but the only one who would pay any attention to me was Jaimoe. My brother got double-stack 50-watt Marshall amps, and Dickey got double-stack 100-watt Marshalls. We were playing small clubs, and we were so loud that there were times I'm sure people couldn't hear us.

That's why I've always stayed way over on stage right—to get out of the line of fire. I've always worn earplugs, and I'm about the only guy in the band who doesn't have hearing problems. Back then, they didn't even make earplugs, so I'd just take a bar napkin, roll it up, and stick it in my ear.

We finally called some kind of moratorium on the volume, because it was getting ridiculous. I couldn't even sing over the shit, and that finally was the deciding factor. My brother went to one 50-watt Marshall, and Dickey just turned his 100-watt way down—he never even tried the 50-watt, because he wasn't going to be a conformist.

Duane and Dickey spent a lot of time together, working out all those harmony lines. I'd give them a basic line of what I wanted on some songs, or they would take a basic line out of the melody and try to complement that. My brother was way into that, because he was way into Curtis Mayfield—you talk about king of the guitar fills, that was Curtis Mayfield, and that's what Duane and Dickey tried to do.

I have this ridiculous picture of the first time we went back to Daytona and played the Peabody Auditorium near Seabreeze High, my old school. I had on a pair of white pants and white shoes, with no socks—I look like something out of *Miami Vice*—but I had no tan. You're supposed to have a good tan if you wear white pants and white shoes. Duane had striped pants on, Dickey was wearing that damn ruffled shirt with black cotton pants and his wingtip shoes, and Butch was wearing his *Billy Jack* hat.

Our first trip up to the Northeast was to Boston, to play Memorial Day weekend at a place called the Tea Party. A guy named Don Law owned the Tea Party, and he was a straight shooter. He paid us what he owed us; there was no bullshit with him. The Tea Party itself was a brick building with white trim, and it was next door to a pizza parlor. It had a flight of stairs outside, and then you got inside, where there was another flight of stairs. I remember hauling that Hammond up them damn steps. I don't know which was worse—the ones inside, where it was cool but the steps were velvet, or the shorter ones outside, where it was 104 degrees. They all sucked, every single step. With every step I took, I thought, "I'm not making any money; I don't even have enough to eat. I have a twenty-eight-inch waistline, and I never have a day off." I was thinking of reasons to go home, and I had one for every step. The last thought I had was, "If I leave, my brother will kill me—I'll never get out of here alive!"

What we got paid wasn't enough to get us home, but it was enough for us to eat on until they could get us back into the Tea Party. That's when we went to this slum area over on Kempton Street, and it was rough. There were tenement houses, like row houses, and we found one that was empty, so we snuck into the first floor. Twiggs eased out on a ledge, and eased the window up next door. Nobody was home, so he ran an extension cord from there, and we had power and music. We lived there for about three weeks until they found us. Early one morning, somebody threw an M-80 through the window, and I thought I was going to have a coronary.

While we were in Boston, I did manage to meet one girl who took me in for a bit. I told her the truth—that we were a struggling band trying to get by—because, like my grandfather told me, you can't lose by telling the truth. I would get depressed sometimes, but I would look at how hard everyone was working, pitching in day and night, and there was no way I could quit.

During our stay, we met the J. Geils Band, and they were nice people. We hung out with J. Geils and Magic Dick, the harmonica player, and played a few gigs with them. Since they were from Boston, they were better known than we were. Between our gigs at the Tea Party, we did a free show at the Boston Common, and, man, we blew everyone's shit away. Magic Dick came up and he just started blowing. It was one of those times when all the biorhythms were on.

The people up there were really nice to us, but because it was our first time up north, and there was the way we talked, and we had a black guy with us, I'm sure it was rather confusing for them. They would hear us talk, and they'd be real amused. They used to say, "Wait, wait—sit here and talk a while."

Playing for free in the parks was really starting to get to me. I hated busting our asses like that and just giving it away. Sure, we would pass the hat, but I thought that was ridiculous anyway. It made me feel weird, because I wasn't some dude pounding on a guitar on a street corner in New Orleans, putting a quarter in the hat first. Of course, it did help us become the "people's band," so to speak, because we would go in there and kick all their asses for free. I can see now that it was the right thing to do, because back then we weren't as polished as we are now, we weren't as good as we are now, we weren't as tight as we are now, and we didn't have the songs that we have now. But, by God, we were there, and we were doing it for free. We were doing it for the people, and we were doing it for us, because we loved to play.

Our second gig at the Tea Party was opening for Dr. John, and let me tell you, I thought he was a dork. The way he talked, I thought he was jive, because I figured he was just putting it on. I mean, "They call me Doctor—Dr. John." Well, I walked into this dressing room, and this one broad had two scarves, and she was behind him, and she had them boys tightened down, and these two other broads were popping him in the arm. I froze, and he said to me, "Well, shit, man, they're just my get-together drops. Don't have no kinda conniption on me." "My get-together drops"—that's when I knew he didn't put on an act.

I had three or four reds on me, so I laid them on him, and later he told me, "That was real nice, man, because I couldn't get to sleep. I took my dose"—his methadone—"and popped them reds afterwards, and I had a nice night's sleep."

Meanwhile I was thinking, "Fuck me running, man—that would kill my ass," so I figured that even though I was doing drugs, I must be okay, because I didn't do things in that quantity.

Dr. John also had a gris-gris situation going on too. Basically they were these bags that he had hanging around each shoulder which were leather or goatskin and smelled kinda funky. Inside the bags was this New Orleans voodoo stuff called gris-gris. He threw that gris-gris shit all in my brand-new Hammond—he was throwing whole handfuls of that shit. Gris-gris, my ass. It was gold glitter, and it went down through the keys, down into the stops, gumming the oil up. They had to take the organ apart and scrape down each piece. They said, "What is this crap?" and they charged me $190, which meant I could eat, but I couldn't drink a cold beer for two weeks.

After the gig, Dr. John came up to us and said, "You all are pretty good. You all from down around Alabama? I'm from N'awlins. You know, you all got off to kind of a slow start tonight, and I was getting a little paranoid there, but after a while you all got it cookin', Jack. Them folks were out there, boogying in the house, and they wasn't leaving." I thought the guy was all right.

Dickey, though, was *not* all right. Not long after, he got real sick with hepatitis, which he got from some nasty girl. We ended up having to take him to Twiggs's aunt's house, in Rye, New York. He was so sick, man. I remember we were driving to Twiggs's aunt's place, and it was raining like hell. I had Dickey by one leg, somebody had the other one, two guys held the doors open, and he just barfed right out the back, with the rain pouring down. The poor dude would drink a pint of water and barf a quart, and I'm thinking he might die.

We got to Twiggs's aunt's place, and it was real warm outside. I said to him, "Listen, Dickey, I ain't no doctor, but it looks to me like you've got hepatitis. The whites of your eyes look like lemons, you're barfing like hell, and when you crap, you tell me it's white. To me, that spells hepatitis."

I stayed there with him for the weekend. Twiggs's aunt, Anne Watkins, was a real sweetheart, and she saved our ass, because Dickey was really shook up and so weak. We finally had to put him in the hospital, and we played a few gigs without him around the Rye area, because we weren't going to go back to Macon without him.

We were playing at a place called Harlowe's, in New York City, when Woodstock was going on. Of course we wanted to play, but the roster was full, and we couldn't even go and watch, since we were booked at Harlowe's. They had about nine customers that night because everybody was at Woodstock. To make it worse, we were opening for maybe the worst band of all time, Noel Redding's Fat Mattress. Noel Redding playing guitar—oh Lord! Big buildup, a lot of hype and shit, and they were the fucking worst. Originally I'd wondered, "Why aren't they at Woodstock?" but then I got my answer.

During this period of time, around the summer of 1969, Duane was still doing a lot of session work. He did his most famous sessions after the Allman Brothers had formed, like with Wilson Pickett and Aretha Franklin. The list goes on forever—

Clarence Carter, Irma Thomas, Boz Scaggs, Percy Sledge. He did a lot of things—some of them were big, and some should have been big. That song "Shake for Me," on John Hammond's *Southern Fried*? Boy, if you don't move part of your body while listening to that song, then there's something seriously wrong with you, way down in your soul.

We had never been to New Orleans before, but we were introduced to that city in the best way possible by playing a place called the Warehouse. During our first gig there, the two owners were on the side of the stage, and we must have done real good, because they just flipped over us. From then on, we pretty much had carte blanche, and we could come in and play just about anytime we wanted. The first few times we opened, but after those we only headlined.

The Warehouse was always a good gig for us, because it wasn't that far, it paid pretty well, and we knew that we would have plenty of fun. There wasn't a whole lot of work to playing New Orleans. Anytime you'd mention New Orleans, everybody's eyes would light up—even the roadies, because they knew that after they were done hauling them amps, they could go pick up some good-looking filly, eat some red beans and rice, and have a good time.

I DON'T WANT ANYONE TO EVER THINK THAT I WAS IN ANY WAY the main draw of the band. I was the youngest guy in the group, I had blond hair down to my elbows, and I weighed a rockin' 160 pounds. I've always kinda hoped that it was a group thing, that no one person carried it. But I guess if you do it long enough, you can front a band.

When you get down to it, I was, and probably still am, the least accomplished musician in the band. By accomplished, I mean as far as theory goes, and scoring and reading music—I do none of those. The other guys in the band know more than I do about that stuff, but most of them don't know shit about singing. They're better on their instruments than I am on the Hammond, but only if you don't count my voice as an instrument.

Although I worshipped Jimmy Smith, God rest him, the way I play organ is much closer to Booker T. His style kind of rubbed off on me, because he pretty much puts the gravy on the meat, like I do in the Brothers. I just try to add texture and tone to the song. I try to put flowing notes behind the staccato notes, which is something I learned when we had the Allman Joys.

My brother was rarely critical of my playing, because he knew I was fragile about that sort of thing, and music is not something that I think needs any harsh words. If you want something from another musician, playing-wise, you sure as hell want to ask for it nicely.

Duane greatly respected the fact that I was a songwriter—he knew I was a songwriter before I knew it. When I would write something, and it would still be in its raw form, he could see all the other parts. That would help when we were rehearsing, because he would say, "You all listen to what my little brother has got here," since he already knew what the song was all about.

My brother always listened closely to me: I'd hit a lick, he'd hit the same one. I'd sing, and he'd back it. I'd hit a good lick, and he'd drive it on home in a very complementary way. Nobody has done that since the day he died. With other people, they believe that there has to be a guitar fill before and after the vocal line. Well, I'm sorry, but if you play a note so fast just to fit it in there, it's just going to be one of a multitude of notes; it's not going to create a lot of emotion or feeling. The longer that note or musical passage has to ring or linger, the more impact it has. Less is more, man.

When it comes to soloing, I've always felt you should get in, say what you have to say, and get out. One thing I love about

Warren Haynes, who plays with us now, is that he's always trying to get me to solo. Even though them two guitar players can solo from now until the fucking cows come home, he still wants me to take one.

Duane was the bandleader onstage, but he really let the band lead itself. When he held up his hand, the band stopped, because he wanted those door-slamming stops. He really believed in everybody stopping at exactly the same time, just like he wanted to start at the same time. We had some great door-slamming stops in the studio, and they need to be that way, more so than when you're playing live, because live you can kind of trickle down to a stop and let the song just kinda die.

We'd gotten everything down to the point where we were ready to go into the studio, but our trip to New York City to record the first Allman Brothers album was a bittersweet situation. After doing three nights at a club called Ungano's to get warmed up, we went into the studio. We were staying at the closest Holiday Inn to 1841 Broadway, which was the Atlantic Records offices. Most of Phil Walden's acts were signed to Atlantic—everything that he had was either on Atlantic or Stax. Ahmet Ertegun, Jerry Wexler, and Phil were real tight.

A man named Adrian Barber, a well-dressed gentleman from England, was going to produce the record in one of the most famous studios ever. Ray Charles had recorded on the house Hammond organ, but I set up mine instead, because I couldn't bring myself to play on the same Hammond he'd used.

They told us, "Make good use of your time, because you have enough money for two weeks." I remember looking at the board, and it was so antiquated and small. A red light would go on when we were recording, and it made me so nervous that I'd fuck up. Mr. Barber couldn't understand what bugged me about that red light, but I finally unscrewed the damn thing.

No sooner do we get in there than Dickey set his guitar down and said, "Man, there ain't no windows in this place—it's like a padded cell." He got his 335 unpacked, took it out, and hit a few licks. Of course it sounded dead, because there were all these baffles around. I'm not sure what song we started with, but I know "Dreams" was up toward the front, because Dickey Betts isn't on the recording of "Dreams." He finally packed up his guitar, didn't say a thing, and walked out.

Butch stood up and said, "What in the hell is he doing?"

"Just leave him alone," Duane said.

I couldn't see what the turn-off was for him, but maybe Dickey was such a country boy that at first the studio technology was too much for him. Duane played all the guitar that you hear on "Dreams," and then he left. Duane got Dickey to come back, and then we did the instrumental piece, "Don't Want You No More." My brother must have really liked Dickey, because there weren't too many people that he would take that kind of time with.

Dickey finished the record, because he wasn't going to be whipped, not in front of the whole group. I mean, it does happen to people—it's like taking a little kid out of Sri Lanka and throwing him into a Publix.

I was very unhappy with the vocal sound on the first record. I've always wanted to recut the vocals. They were recorded with the regular old tape echo "Heartbreak Hotel" setting. That was the one thing where me and Adrian Barber—who was actually an engineer and had never produced a record before—did not see eye to eye, but I didn't want to rock the boat, so it's my own fault.

Overall, I felt that we had been rushed through an artistic piece that was only about halfway done. The songs were all written, but we hadn't road-tested all of them, so I wasn't sure about all the different phrasings. When you're that new at it, two weeks is just not long enough—especially if you've got a couple of guys in the band who have never been in a studio. It really slows things down, because you've got to explain so much and it's confusing at first. I've never seen anybody go into a studio who didn't think it was a weird way to go about recording music.

I knew that record wasn't going to make it. We didn't spend enough time on it, we didn't refine it enough, and we were better than that. Phil Walden gave us a pocketful of change, enough for hot dogs and recording, pinned it to our shirts, and sent us on our way. When it came out at the end of 1969, it just barely grazed the charts—No. 188 with an anchor.

We went back up to the Tea Party four or five more times later in the year, and after the last time, we stopped off for three shows back in New York at Ungano's, and then did a gig at Ludlow Garage in Cincinnati. They had rocking chairs in there and a concrete floor. That first time, the fucking place was empty, but eventually we saved that club from going under two or three times.

It was in the last week in December 1969 that we played the Fillmore East for the first time. Man, that venue was something special, and we always had a special connection to it. The acoustics in there were incredible—the kind of perfect sound you almost never get. There was this large, open main floor area where you could just look out at the crowd, and then up above was this killer balcony—all together the place could fit a couple thousand people. Once upon a time it had been a Yiddish theater, but I can't think of a better place to play music.

Having been to the Village a few times by then, I loved it there, and I loved this guy Bill Graham because he was such a straight shooter with us. There were never any confrontations, and he always came back and shook our hands, telling us that we had put on a hell of a great show. He would ask us if we thought the light show was okay, and if there was anything he could to make the show better.

Sometimes it ain't what somebody does for you, it's just the fact that they remember you. We owe so much to Bill Graham. Here we were, out on the road, working our asses off, and the competition looked so tough. Hendrix and Clapton were doing all this incredible shit, and here we were, with one record that had just come out and was going nowhere. At times, I really had doubts about myself, because I was the only writer and I thought I might be holding everybody back. I felt pressure to write songs that were better than the last ones and good enough to compete with all the great songs that were coming out at that time.

What Bill Graham really gave us—and so many other bands— were places to play where you didn't need to know Top 40 hits or Beatles songs. You could play your own tunes, and that's what we needed. Think of the talent that Bill found just by giving bands a place to set up and play their own music. He wouldn't pay you that much, but if you were good enough he'd invite you back, and he was about that matter-of-fact about it too.

That first run at the Fillmore was three nights with Blood, Sweat & Tears, who had just replaced Al Kooper with David Clayton-Thomas and were just starting to make it. They had that big, powerful horn thing going. I loved horns, and Duane did too, but only in their proper place. Their music was very different from ours, and some of the people there weren't ready for blues like we played, so it was altogether brand-new to their ears, but Bill loved us.

When we arrived in New York for that stretch at the Fillmore, one of the first things we did was head up to 134th Street and Lenox, to the S&G Diner. Jaimoe and Twiggs had been there many times, and they turned us on to it. Good soul food, man— collard greens, smothered steak, black-eyed peas, candied yams, all kinds of good shit. It was the funniest place, because the lady behind the counter was as Chinese as she could be, and the people back there, with the pots and the pans, they was as black as the ace of spades. She would take your order and yell it out in Chinese at the top of her lungs. There was one dude back there—I guess he was the interpreter—and he'd translate for everyone. That was the most mixed-up bunch of shit I've ever seen in my life, but let me tell you, the food was dynamite.

When we were in New York, we'd sometimes hang with other musicians, like John Hammond, but we mostly hung with each other back then. New York was a big old scary place, but we found a few clubs to go to, like the Bottom Line down in the Village. I remember talking to Oakley about New York, and I said, "Man, if we could just get New York City by its gonads like we have Atlanta, we'd really have it made," but playing for free in Central Park—oops, we flat-out hit a brick wall there. We figured we best ask before we did it, seeing how that's the only patch of grass they have to share amongst all them poor folks up there. We didn't think we could just plug in and play like we did in Piedmont Park.

The guy who started booking us was named Jon Podell, and he came to us through Phil. Jon was very tight with Bill Graham, and like Bill, he has always looked out for our best interests, which I appreciated so much. From the very beginning, I can honestly say that Jon has never taken a dime from us that he didn't deserve. He has always been very good to us, and he's like me in that he doesn't like to spend money that he hasn't made yet.

After the Fillmore East, we came back to Macon and had a hell of a New Year's Eve party at Idlewild South, a cabin on a lake with about twenty acres outside of town where we would rehearse and hang out from time to time. The party got real psychedelic, and there was a whole lot of wine and beer. It was a good time, and back then we had so much energy, so much drive, and so much want-to.

In early 1970, we made our way out to California for the first time. It was so cold in our van that we had to duct-tape a long pipe to the heater under the dash and push it back to the guys in the rear of the van, since there was literally ice forming inside the van. We were all stacked in there like firewood, head to foot, and it was really freezing. I remember looking up at the ice on the window and asking myself, "Why? Why? How did I let this happen? What the fuck do I think I'm doing? If this is being a damn rock and roll star, I hope I burn out quick!"

We did have our share of comic relief on the road. We loved to make fun of Red Dog and his "Red Dog–isms," as we called them. We would be talking about Carnegie Hall, and he would say, "Oh, that's where they have all those sympathies." We'd say, "Yeah, Red Dog, that's where they have all those symphonies." He'd go, "Yeah, that's what I said—where they have all the sympathies. Sympathy, right? Ain't that it?" We'd tell him again, "No, man—it's *symphony*," but he would never get it right.

We used to write them things down because they were so funny. Another time, someone was reading *In Cold Blood,* and I guess the Hound had heard of it, because he said, "That's the one that was written by that real funny-talking sissy dude, Thurman Capole." Thurman Capole—God, you talk about laughing, that man cracked us up.

California was a bummer, because we were still strangers in a strange land. We got out there, and we didn't have enough money to pay the damn toll across the Golden Gate Bridge in San Francisco. We ended up having to panhandle to get enough change so we could go play the Fillmore, and Oakley got these pretty girls to give us a whole fistful of quarters.

We played four nights at the Fillmore West, where we opened for B.B. King and Buddy Guy. My brother and I got to meet B.B. when we opened for him, and that was really something.

Between the two of us, we had worn out three of his records—played those LPs until they turned white. I couldn't believe we were going to play with him. Buddy was sitting in his dressing room, wearing them old overalls—even way back then, he was wearing them damn overalls.

We played real well at the Fillmore, and the crowd liked it. The thing about San Francisco back then, and I think it's still pretty much like that, is that if you ain't got them by the end of the intro and the first verse, you ain't never going to get them.

After the Fillmore run, we played a free afternoon show at Cal-Riverside University. I met me a nice little honey, smoked me a couple of doobies, drank a little wine, and had some good eats. Next we headed down to L.A. for four nights at the Whisky A Go Go. All I wanted to do was mow everybody down musically with this bad-ass band, but I caught terrible strep throat. I was really hurting, but I kept singing. I felt like I had let the band down, but my brother came to me and said, "You win some, you lose some, and some get rained out. Tomorrow's another day, and we'll come back and get them."

That was when I got the first review that mentioned me specifically, and it said, "Although he sounded somewhat like a black man, he only had a four-note range." I was so upset that I called back home to my family, because I had never had any bad press before and I didn't know what it felt like. They told me, "Son, bad press is better than no press at all—at least they mentioned your name."

My brother did a recording session with Delaney and Bonnie while we were in L.A. It was the album called *Motel Shot,* because it was recorded on the cheap in a motel room, and it was a real acoustic-sounding thing. I was just kind of a bystander to that whole Delaney and Bonnie thing, but God bless Bonnie Bramlett. I thought that Delaney was just out there trying to make some bucks—he had dollar signs in his eyes. I was never impressed with his songwriting; that scored about a four out of ten with me. I was real good friends with Bonnie, but since the day my brother died, I never set eyes on Delaney Bramlett again.

When we weren't playing shows, we found other ways to entertain ourselves. Back then, "What happens on the road stays on the road" was our attitude. The rule was that what you did on the road, whether you were married or unmarried, was nobody else's business. If you wanted to take seven ladies up to your room, and you had the dough, by God, go for it. Nobody was going to say nothing—that was the rule of the road, and anybody who broke it was really a pussy.

I would usually room with Oakley, and the roadies would all room together, because they stunk so bad. Twiggs tried his best to make us as comfortable as possible, and we really appreciated that. My brother really loved Twiggs, and so did I. One night Duane told Twiggs that he was just like a part of the band, that he might as well be in the band. Boy, that meant so much to Twiggs.

As we were getting out on the road more, we needed something new to travel in. We'd had this damn Econoline van that was busting our ass. We went shopping for a Winnebago and found the one we wanted, and it was $23,000. Duane went to Phil Walden's office, and twenty minutes later he came out with a check. Sometimes we would sleep some people in the Winnebago, or the "Winbag," as I liked to call it, or the "Bag," as it eventually became. Somehow, "Winnebago" just doesn't roll off the tongue. If you're talking to a girl and you say, "Well, we travel in a Winnebago"—that's not cool. We would sleep people in there when we had to, or, to save money, we would get a room with two double beds and sleep four guys in there.

We seemed to have endless energy in those days. One meal at

the H would hold me for the whole day, and you wouldn't get the munchies at night. Of course, we never had trouble sleeping at night either. Except for Jaimoe, all of us smoked back then—me and Dickey smoked Marlboros, and Duane smoked Kools like they was going out of style.

On the way back from California, I was still feeling pretty bad, so I slept almost all the way home, except when we stopped off at the Grand Canyon. It was Twiggs's idea to stop there and take some pictures, and man, they had to prop me up—I was freezing cold, I was shaking, and I had a fever. It was the crack of fucking dawn, but Twiggs said the lighting was just right, so we did it.

By February 1970, we were back at the Fillmore East for three nights, playing with the Grateful Dead and Love, and we were the middle act. Uncle Bill, as we called him, had fallen in love with us after he'd heard us that very first time. Not long after that first trip to the Fillmore East, Bill had come down to Georgia and we'd gotten to know him. Even way back then I was thinking that we needed to drop the whole Capricorn bullshit and all the Phil Walden crap and simply talk Bill Graham into managing us. I knew that Bill had something to do with the Grateful Dead, and I thought that if he was managing the Dead, then we could show him what a real band was like.

Before we played with the Grateful Dead for the first time, I had heard all this hype, but I didn't really have an opinion of them. If somebody had asked what I thought of them, I would have said, "I think that their music ain't got no groove to it at all," and it didn't. But they played the music that they played while the crowd did this thing that we eventually called "the Grateful Dead waltz," which consisted of dancing around, twirling, and jerking a whole lot. I didn't understand it at all, and I was the same age as them. I kept looking for something, but I just didn't get it.

"What do you think of these guys?" I asked my brother. He didn't hesitate.

"This is shit. You see them jugs that they're passing out?" he said, referring to the cases of Gatorade that they would electrify backstage and then pass out to the crowd. And then I knew what he was talking about. One tiny sip of that shit and it would be raining fire, man, so no wonder everybody was grooving on that music—anything would sound good like that.

Not that the Grateful Dead had a trick in passing out a bunch of crazy pills so that people would like their music—that's not what I am saying. I'm just saying that that was part of their whole culture, part of their whole deal. I don't know their story, and I don't know any one of them well enough to ask them, "What's the deal with this?" but I really don't give a fuck that much. I just know that there's the Grateful Dead, and they have their place. They're pretty good people; I liked them all right. Garcia called me a narc at one point, so I never really gave two shits for him, but him and my brother got along because they were guitar players. Mostly I just ignored them.

EARLY IN THE YEAR, OAKLEY HAD BEEN LOOKING FOR A BIG HOUSE to rent, and he found one on Vineville Avenue in Macon. He and Linda and Brittany moved in there, and so did his younger sister, Candy, who I was seeing a little bit. She asked me to move in there with her, and I said okay—but I insisted on paying rent, because I wasn't going to freeload on anybody. I've never done that. Duane, his common-law wife, Donna, and their daughter, Galadrielle, also moved in, but they didn't stay there very long.

It was a big place—I remember thinking that we could put the whole band in there—but we didn't want to be on top of each other all the time, since we traveled like that. The "Big House," as we came to call it, was a place for all of us to hang, but it was really Oakley's place.

The vibe at the Big House was always good. We had a real sense of camaraderie, of family, and we would always have one big meal a day—you could count on it. All the girls would get together and cook for us; they'd make a huge pot of chili, and four or five pans of cornbread, and we would hog down, man. Then we would lay around and talk, and play some music on the stereo. We never watched TV; in fact, we didn't even have a TV in the Big House. We talked about all kinds of things, and my brother, being the most well-read of all of us, would talk about stuff that he had been reading, and by the time he was done talking about it, it was like I had read the book myself.

The girls kept that house spotless. They were always telling us, "Take those motorcycle boots outside and leave them on the porch," because they didn't want mud on the floor. Linda and Candy put so much energy into going out shopping at these junk stores to find things for the house. They'd find some great stuff, like say some old tapestries, and then they'd bring it home to decorate the house with.

I remember rainy days when Candy and I would lay in bed and look out the window, watching the cars go by on Vineville Avenue. We'd sit in bed and string beads for hours, and Candy was wonderful at it. She made me all kinds of beautiful pieces, and I don't know whatever became of those, but I would give anything to have them back, because she made them especially for me.

When Candy and I were in love, we really cared about each other. We were friends too, and that's what it takes. We were buds, man. I remember the first time we ever made love, because I thought it was so hip. It happened on the second or third day after we first met in Jacksonville. It was so incredible, and at the end of it I said, "Baby, I just don't know what to say," and she said, "You ain't got to say nothing; it's done been said."

I can't really remember what happened to me and her, but I think it was me. I went out on the road, and there were all these women; when I came back home, it didn't feel right to go in there like nothing had happened. My conscience was bothering me, but I was too chickenshit to tell her what I did, so I just tried to fade on out of there. Plus, she had eyes for Kim Payne, and when I saw that, I felt relieved. It was like going to confession without actually going.

Take a lesson from my life: if you've cheated, either leave or just shut the fuck up and stay in your happy home and don't do it again. I knew there was no such thing as me not doing it again. I became the biggest pussy hound in the world, and I have had my fun when it comes to women.

At the Big House, we listened to music all the time. Linda and Berry had this little community room outside their bedroom that we called the Casbah, and Linda set up a stereo system in there. Jaimoe turned all of us on to so much neat stuff. He gave us a proper education about jazz and got us into Miles Davis and John Coltrane. *Kind of Blue* was always on the turntable—my brother really got his head around that album—and he also seriously dug Coltrane's *My Favorite Things*. Fuck me, man; my brother could soak up music like no one else I've ever seen, and then turn it into something else. He'd be listening to an album or hear a song on the radio, and the next thing you know we'd be working it into our music onstage.

Butchie had a little bit of schooling, and he was into jazz too, even though he came from a band that did a lot of Byrds stuff and electric folk. Me, I was strictly rhythm and blues. I think that's what my brother wanted, a revitalized, up-to-date rhythm and blues band, with the guitar players being very present and playing

Two happy brothers.

My newly married parents in the mid-1940s.

Easter Sunday with our first bicycles.

The clothes make the man.

Me and Duane at Castle Heights
Military Academy, June 1957.

A couple of "big shots" at
Castle Heights.

My
brother
always
knew how
to raise
some
hell for
his little
brother.
He even
tried to
hang me
once,
though
thankfully
it wasn't
from *this*
tree.

Cadet Gregory L. Allman.

Playing the Seabreeze High School graduation party at Oceanside Country Club, 1965.

The Escorts opening for the Beach Boys in Daytona Beach,

All dressed up for an Allman Joys

The Allman Joys eventually morphed into the Hour Glass, and here we are in the studio.

It was tough for the Hour Glass. We spent a lot of time going through the motions.

Forging the Brotherhood at Rose Hill Cemetery in Macon, 1969.
Bottom row, left to right: Butch, Dickey, Berry, Jaimoe; *top row:*
Duane and me.

The first-ever Allman Brothers Band studio session with Phil Walden looking on, in Macon, 1969.

Early morning blues when Dickey was out of commission in Boston, 1969.

Loading the dreaded
Econoline van with Red
Dog and Kim Payne, 1969.

Our first road manager, Twiggs Lyndon,
was constantly taking photos—especially
in the early days. Here I am staring down
his lens.

Passing the time with a game
of cork ball in Macon, 1969.

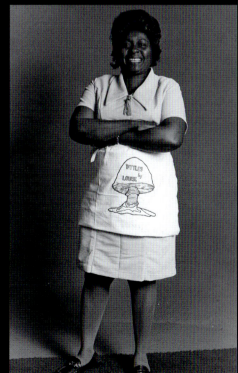

My other mama: Louise Hudson,
proprietor of H&H Restaurant in Macon.

With Duane at Rose Hill.

A "Winbag" pit stop provides another stage for our roadie, the legendary Red Dog.

A quiet moment with my brother in North Florida, October 1970.

My Alabama mug shot.

The one and only Twiggs Miller Lyndon Jr.

The other half of the Brotherhood: our original road crew with photographer Jim Marshall. *From left to right, seated:* Joseph "Red Dog" Campbell, Kim Payne, Joe Dan Petty; *standing:* Mike Callahan, Willie Perkins, and Jim Marshall.

At the top of our game: recording *At Fillmore East*, March 1971.

Hittin' the note at the Fillmore

Brother to brother.

Playing to the masses at Boston Common, summer 1971.

In the backseat with my brother in California, October 1971.

Soldiering on with the five-man band, 1972.

Behind the Hammond B3 at the Warehouse in New Orleans, 1972.

The five-man band outside our first tour bus, 1972.

The Allman Brothers Band with Chuck and Lamar onstage at the Grand Opera House in Macon, September 1973.

Relaxing at the farm in Juliette, Georgia, 1973.

Sitting on the back of "The Blackhearted Woman" equipment truck at the farm in Juliette, 1973.

Headlining in front of six hundred thousand people at Watkins Glen, July 1973. At that time it was the biggest outdoor concert ever.

all this harmony—from the start, you could see that was going to be part of it, those guitars doing the harmonies. And, man, the hours that the rest of us would spend off to the side while those two worked out those parts.

The group Cowboy was on Capricorn, and we played their album *5'll Getcha Ten* quite a bit at the Big House. Scott Boyer had been in the 31st of February with Butch, and Cowboy had a sort of southern-folk sound to them. Then there was Junior Wells and Bobby "Blue" Bland, two of my favorites, plus B.B. King's *Live at the Regal* and John Hammond's *Southern Fried*. King Curtis—my brother thought the world of that man, and he loved Curtis's album *Live at Fillmore West*. Duane wore the grooves right out of that one. The Staple Singers, Taj Mahal—and of course everyone was still listening to the Beatles and Bob Dylan. Dylan's songs are just ageless; they're just like a part of life and they probably always will be.

Dickey and Berry had come more from that psychedelic scene. Dickey was way into Jefferson Airplane—he was a big fan of Jorma Kaukonen, and he loved Clapton's work in Cream too. Eventually the jazz thing rubbed off on Dickey—you can hear it on "In Memory of Elizabeth Reed." Shit, what he and Duane did on that one came straight from Miles Davis. Duane, Dickey, and Berry also picked up on the Butterfield Blues Band sound—that album *East-West* was a killer. Berry and Dickey also were way into the Dead's *American Beauty* album, so you start mixing all that together and you come out with a pretty wicked musical brew, and we used bits and pieces of all of it.

Duane, Berry, Butchie, and Jaimoe all appeared on an album by Johnny Jenkins called *Ton-Ton Macoute!* My brother played his ass off. His Dobro work on "Walk on Gilded Splinters" was just flat-out evil, man, and that's why we still do that song to this very day.

As we were getting ready to record our second album, *Idlewild South,* which we named after that cabin in the woods where we'd spent New Year's Eve 1969, my songwriting was getting better—everything was getting better. We had enough to eat, for one thing. I would just wait, and these songs began to take shape in my head. Sometimes you hear somebody say something and you can get an idea for a song from that. I heard a story about Stephen Stills and Billy Preston. They were at a party, and Billy's date was with him; Stephen's lady was supposed to meet him there, but she didn't show. So Stephen was talking with Billy, and Billy says, "Man, if you can't be with the one you love, love the one you're with." Stephen says, "Fuck, man, do you mind if I use that?" Billy told him, "No, I don't mind," and "Love the One You're With" is a very good song.

That's one way a song can happen. Another way is you can see something happening or going on with someone you know, and it's really fucked up. Maybe you know somebody who really cares for another person, but that person has no idea of it and you can't say anything about it. All these things can inspire a song.

I don't think you can put a time limit on songwriting, but a lot of people do that. They start it, they got a verse, and they want to finish it that night. I let it ooze out, man. It's like some people squeeze too hard on the toothpaste tube. If I squeeze too hard on a song, it will sound contrived.

I've had a few songs that I'm proud of that haven't gotten a lot of recognition, like "Oceans Awash the Gunwales," which was on the album *Just Before the Bullets Fly* from '88. If you've ever seen a picture of a battleship in rough seas, where the whole front end of the ship is underwater, and you wonder how it can possibly stay afloat, but it does—that song is about staying afloat in life.

Actually, it's about overdosing in a New York hotel, which happened to me in 1987. I'd done too much coke and I was under an assumed name. Paramedics got me out of there and were bringing me to Roosevelt Hospital. As they were taking me out on a stretcher, we went by our tour bus, which had the USS *Alabama* painted on the side. I remember thinking to myself, "Battleships don't sink, and by God, I'm not gonna sink either—I'm not going to die." It took a few days, but I got it back together and I started writing a tune about it. When something that serious happens, it will definitely inspire a song.

Another one, also on the *Just Before the Bullets Fly* album, is "Fear of Falling." I'm also proud of "Oncoming Traffic." I worked real hard on that one, and it's a special tune to me. Most of the songs that haven't gotten a lot of recognition would be on my solo records, because it seems that the Brothers' songs are all pretty much accepted and well liked.

If you've got something on your mind that kind of takes over everything else, then you're pretty well fucked as far as writing goes. It helps if you're at total peace, and I guess being out at Idlewild South made me feel like I didn't have a care in the world. Since there were no cops, I could smoke a doob out there, and that was nice. I really liked it out there; it put me in the right state of mind to write, and that's where I came up with "Don't Keep Me Wonderin'" and "Midnight Rider."

On "Midnight Rider," which is the song I'm most proud of in my career, I had all but the last part—so, as I like to say, I had the song by the nuts, I just had to reel it in. The third verse is really important, because it's kind of the epilogue to the whole thing. Basically, you state the problem in the first verse, you embellish on the problem in the second verse—like "let me tell you what a bitch she *really* is"—and then you usually have some music, to let you think about them words for a while and also get lifted up by that music.

The bridge from the music to the third verse is when you want to be different, but you don't want to go all the way from A to Z. You want something that contrasts things a little bit—kind of like matching a shirt with a pair of pants. You want it to be a little different, but not clashing. The bridge is where you say what you want to do about the problem, or what you're damn sure going to do about it. Then the third verse is, like I said, the epilogue to the whole thing.

It might sound like I'm giving you a formula to write a song, but I'm not, because it's never that simple. On "Midnight Rider," I needed something to start the third verse, and Kim Payne came up with "I've gone by the point of caring," which was exactly what I needed. "I've gone by the point of caring"—fuck it—and then, "Some old bed I'll soon be sharing." I've got another buck, and I ain't gonna let 'em catch my ass, and then it's just kinda off into the sunset.

In April 1970, we played a series of gigs around the Northeast—Boston, upstate New York, and SUNY Stony Brook on Long Island. We played a really good show at Stony Brook, and, man, they loved us there. I remember being in the Winnebago heading down to Long Island, and we had this girl with us who sometimes came along for the ride. She was nice and clean, and none of us had anything, and we knew we weren't going to pass anything on, so she would tighten us up every now and then. Nothing will take the blues off of ya like a good head job. Red Dog had to drive the whole way to Long Island though, so he didn't get none.

When we arrived at Stony Brook, we went in for sound check, leaving the Winnebago parked right in the lot. After we finished, we came back out, and right away I heard all this laughter along with a huge line of people. I looked over to the Winnebago, and Red Dog had it rocking back and forth—fucking that girl's brains out. She was moaning like crazy, and everybody standing in line could hear her. That Winnebago was cookin', man—it was just like *Up in Smoke*. I just did a little U-turn and headed right back on in. I wasn't going out there. That poor old girl. She was a pretty little thing from New York, and she liked us, man, and she really did take care of all of us.

And we needed it, because 1970 was a crazy year. We were on the road three hundred days that year, and it wore on all of us. Our next stop was Buffalo—just another gig on the road. Everything had been running pretty smooth up until then, and we got there with no problem, but we were all tired. The place we were playing at was called Aliotta's Lounge, and when we got there I counted seating for forty-seven people, man—forty-seven. We were jammed onto this little tiny stage, and there was absolutely no room in there.

Still, we played, and it ended up being a nice show. I met this beautiful girl with hair down to her ass, but short on top. It was a mullet haircut, but it looked good. It was a Friday night, and we were all tired, but we had to get to Cincinnati to play a free show at Ludlow Garage. The plan was to play that free show, help them keep the place open, and then we were supposed to go home.

On Saturday morning, we were going back to Aliotta's to get our equipment, and me and Oakley were sleeping at the hotel. Twiggs came in our room to use the phone, and he woke us up screaming, "You motherfucker, you're gonna pay us that goddamn money, and we're not going to play another night. We have a contract, and you're gonna pay us, or I'll come down there and cut your motherfucking Yankee guts out."

I didn't think too much of it, but he did have a knife strapped on to his belt. The last time we had been in New York, my brother, being the avid fisherman that he was, had bought this Finnish gutting knife. He'd given it to Twiggs, and Twiggs began to carry it everywhere he went in a leather scabbard.

A little bit later, I overheard my brother talking to Twiggs and telling him, "Twiggs, maybe you shouldn't take that knife with you."

"What's going on?" I asked.

"Don't worry," Duane told me. "The guy is just giving us some shit about paying us." Duane was trying to calm Twiggs down, so I got up, took a shower, and went to get something to eat.

I came back to the room, and just as I put the key in the door, my brother opened it from the inside. He was white as a ghost.

"What is it, man?" I asked.

"Gregory, Twiggs went on down there and killed that man. He stabbed him five times, maybe more." I couldn't believe it, and I got that feeling where the skin on the top of your head starts to crawl.

We were supposed to wait for an attorney to call, Mr. John Condon, who was kin to Twiggs's aunt Anne in Rye, the one who had taken care of Dickey. Mr. Condon called us pretty quick, telling us, "I want you to get in that bus, or whatever it is, and lay down on the floor. Whichever one of you looks the least like a long-haired hippie, get in and drive, and get the hell out of here as quick as you can. I mean, move it—now!"

We were out of there in a flash, because with a name like Aliotta in Buffalo, we didn't want to take a chance.

Now, people have long speculated on Twiggs's mental health, but he was really just overworked. He was so fucking thorough that he didn't realize he was making the job twice as hard. He could have done just fine with only half the energy. Like I said, he didn't snap very often, but when he did, watch out.

There was one night when he was changing some speakers in an amp, and somebody pulled the chair out from under him. He caught himself before his ass hit the floor, and, boy, he stood up and snatched that son of a bitch, bit down on his ear, and spit a little piece of that ear right into the air. There was blood everywhere, and that guy was screaming like you've never heard, but Twiggs went right back to changing out that speaker like nothing had happened.

That was the only other time I ever heard of him losing control like that, but what happened in Buffalo really stunned me. He completely lost it, and it took everything Payne and Callahan had to get his ass restrained after he stabbed Aliotta. This guy was trying to fuck with us, because he had the money we needed to get to Cincinnati and then make it home. Twiggs was gonna make sure we got our money.

What happened really fucked with all of us, especially my brother. He was catatonic the rest of that day and night. He didn't say a single thing, and that worried me. We didn't know if they were going to charge all of us, or if we were going to get sued for everything we had—which wasn't much. Still, if they took it, we were done. All we could do was stay in close contact with John Condon, who kept us informed. John eventually told us that we as a group were out of harm's way, and he advised us to go ahead and finish up our run.

Twiggs ended up doing about eighteen months in jail. In the end, he was found not guilty for reasons of insanity. He spent six months in a mental hospital and was back on the road with us by the spring of 1972.

It was kind of weird that Twiggs had introduced us to Willie Perkins right before that all happened—almost like he knew what was coming. Twiggs had connected us to Willie in Atlanta because a little money was starting to come in and Twiggs didn't want to feel responsible for it. Twiggs was more about keeping the roadies in order, and Willie had a background in banking. But with Twiggs in jail, we hired Willie on as our new road manager, and he stepped right into the job.

At the Grand Canyon, 1970

CHAPTER SEVEN

Come and Go Blues

WHEN I THINK BACK ACROSS MY LIFE, I USUALLY COME UP with positive stuff—like the fun times with my brother, the great times I had with Allen Woody, and all that. My memories aren't about being in jail or my ex-wives. I imagine that most people have enough negative shit in their life that if they dwelled on it long enough, they'd probably blow their brains out, and I'm no different. I just naturally don't dwell on the negatives, just like I naturally don't eat the white part of the turnip—because I can't stand it. Thinking about drugs at this point is another negative, but there's no denying that drugs were a big part of my life.

If you check the records, the most consistent thing about my drug use was that I kept on trying to get straight. I kept coming back, and coming back, and coming back, trying to quit. I must have gone into treatment eighteen times, and the time between each visit got to be a little longer, which I saw as a good thing. That little voice telling me to clean up was always in my head, even though there were times when I could barely hear it.

I started using pills in Daytona, because I had to go to school after playing gigs at night. They were red-and-blacks—they had a little phenobarbital, so they'd take the edge off a little bit. In New York, there was a bit of speed, and I believed in my speed. As long as I had my speed, I was okay, but I never took too much. You know when you're young like that, before you're thirty, you're fucking bulletproof.

When we weren't playing music, we'd do speed and drink or do downers and fuck. We had Nembutals, and we'd grind them bad boys up, sit and wait a bit, and then just fuck for hours. One time, I was visiting Daytona, and we had to go all the way down to Deland to pick up a prescription that somebody had for Nembutals. It was me and these two real pretty girls. We got those pills and chopped them up, put just a bit of water in them, set them up on the dash, and I'm thinking, "Boy, I'm fixing to have me a hell of a time!"

We pulled off on an old country road, did them Nembutals, and then we fucked until the sun went down. I did both of them, one at a time—my dick was like a damn oak tree all day. There weren't no mosquitoes, neither! We didn't have any AIDS back then; there was none of that. Fucking didn't kill you, but it might just make you a little sick or itchy.

I was turned on to cocaine by King Curtis, during the Brothers' first trip out in Los Angeles. I had done a fair amount of speed before I tried cocaine, and to tell you the truth, coke didn't really work on me. It seems that people who had taken speed, when they tried coke, it wouldn't work, and the people who took cocaine, when they tried speed, it wouldn't work. When I first tried coke, it just gave me cottonmouth, and not much else.

I didn't get into coke real serious until I moved up to Macon. This guy who had robbed a drugstore gave me a full sealed ounce of pharmaceutical cocaine, and between me and the band, we about blew our brains out on that shit. You'd do a little bit of coke, you'd pour a real stiff drink so you could level out, and you'd go play some music. Then, when you came back down, you wanted another hit of that damn cocaine, even though you realized that you felt like shit from it and needed that drink to cool out. Doing the same thing twice and expecting a different outcome is the definition of insanity.

Whoever came up with that slogan, "Cocaine is a lie"—well, it is a lie. I don't know how many times I got high on coke, and then sometime between eleven and one o'clock, I felt so fucking bad. I'd be paranoid and jittery, and thinking, "Man, I paid $125 to get like this?" The thing is, then I'd do it again the next night.

After we had gotten into cocaine, we were playing one gig, and we went to count off "Statesboro Blues," and my brother went, "One, two—the band needs some coke!" At intermission, there must have been nine cats come back there with shit to sell. I thought for sure we were all gonna get popped, but we got lucky.

I never did like cocaine by itself, because it made me too nervous. But a little coke and two Percodan and I was ready to fight three lions at once. Then it would stop working, and that was the problem.

Bad as all those were, they were no heroin, man—and it was smack in the middle of that crazy year of 1970 that heroin made its first appearance. We'd been playing so many fucking gigs we couldn't count them all, and by summer we'd found ourselves back in Macon. Back then in Macon, it was really hard to find a nickel bag of reefer, let alone an ounce, but you could buy heroin in a snap—seven dollars a bag.

The first time we scored heroin, we were having a little party over at Duane's house on Bond Street. We had just come in off the road, and we had done pretty good—we each had a couple hundred dollars to show for it. A black dude who was a friend of Chank's came over to me and said, "Hey, bro, try a whack of this." He had a pocketknife that he dipped down into a little plastic bag of off-white powder, and the tip of the knife just barely touched it. He put the point of the blade right under my nose, and I snorted the powder off of it.

It hit me with a big rush, because back then they would cut heroin with quinine, so that it would surge through your blood real fast. I started drifting, and I didn't give a shit about nothing. I felt relaxed, so I sat down in this big leather chair, which was so cool. I remember seeing big purple hippos kinda floating through my head, and that's about all that was going on up there. I thought, "Man, this is neat," because it shut up all the noise in my head.

This cat let me keep enough for about two more little tastes, and then we hit the road for about a month, so I didn't see him. When we got back to town, I ran into him, and the same thing happened again—same amount, same result. It was just as much of a groove, because it hit and I went, "There's that feeling again!"

After that, this cat would kinda be around all the time. After about a month or so, all the band and all the roadies were participating. It wasn't long until everybody associated with the Allman Brothers Band, with the exceptions of Twiggs Lyndon and later Joe Dan Petty, from our road crew, was addicted to opiates. The thing is, no one ever used the word "heroin." The only word that was ever said was "doojee." If I'd had any idea of what it really was, I don't think I would have done it. I honestly didn't know that this doojee stuff was heroin. Maybe I should have, but I didn't.

Heroin is a musician's drug, because you work till you drop, and this stuff would just ease you down off the mountain. You don't think people sneak around and put needles in their arms for nothing, do you? You've never been high till you've been high on heroin. A lot of people who try heroin for the first time will barf up a lot of air and have the dry heaves for about four hours, and it's so terrible that it stops them from taking it again. That didn't happen to us, because we must have taken just enough not to get sick.

At first, there were no needles. We were just snorting it, and we didn't have any accidents. Oakley just loved that stuff. He was an Aries, a fire sign, and the doojee brought him down just enough, but he had enough smarts to never do it two days in a row. Duane liked doojee all right, but blow was much more his thing, and he did a *lot* of it. Me, I had to learn the hard way about doojee; that shit brought me nothing but pain and agony, and it almost took me from this world about six times.

In the beginning though, I never thought we were real junkies—we were just trying to keep a buzz going. We never got too high to play, at least while my brother was alive. Even though those drugs are real habit-forming, it does take a while for the shit to really get into the marrow of your bones, to the point where you wake up and that's the first thing you think of. Thank God that didn't happen but to two of us, but the money we laid down for that shit was unbelievable.

SOMETIMES I'LL SEE AN OLD POSTER, AND IT WILL SAY "$3.50 FOR tickets," and I'll think, "How in the hell did we make it?" Because the promoter took about half, the booking agent took off another 10 percent, and then Phil Walden took his cut.

But by the summer of 1970, we did have some money coming

in, and even though that's a good thing, it also separated us some. What I mean is, with money, if you've got a hobby or an interest or whatever, you can go do it or go buy it. If skydiving is what you like to do, well, now you can go do it. If you wanted to fly down to Jamaica, now you could go. Whereas before one of the band members might call and say "Let's go shoot pool" or "Let's get a watermelon and go down to the rock quarry," and you'd go without thinking, now the answer was "I'm fixing to close on this house."

The thing is, we had absolutely no financial direction. Not that we needed Phil Walden to sit us down on his lap one at a time and explain to us how to invest, but he could have done something. When you're someone who never had any money, and then all of a sudden, you do—whew! Plus, it was never-ending money. All we had to was go out and play and make some more. Come back, spend it, it's gone, fuck—go out and make some more.

That July, we played the second Atlanta Pop Festival, which was actually held in Byron, about twelve miles outside of Macon. It was so fucking hot out there, it was good that we could get back home, because we didn't have no freezing-cold tour buses back then. We had the Winbag out there, and that helped some, but not enough.

The backstage area was pretty nice; they went to a lot of trouble to keep it nice. They kept the mud under control by piling hay on it, and there were plenty of lounge chairs for us to spread out on. There was even a naked chick riding around on a motorcycle, which we were all very happy about.

One thing I'll never forget about that day was getting to see Jimi Hendrix. I didn't see that much of him, and I don't have anything to compare it to because that's the only time I ever saw him, but in all honesty, I thought he could have done better. From what I've heard, he wasn't always all that much when he played live.

It must have been about four thirty in the morning, and I was asleep on the cold-ass hard ground, when somebody came by and said, "Showtime! It's time to play." I'm going, "Show what? What? We got to do it now?" But we got up and did the best we could. As it turned out, we were the first band to play, and the last one to play, and the only band that got to play twice. Just the chance to play in front of so many people—three or four hundred thousand—was great exposure for us. I haven't heard the tape of the show lately, but I remember hearing it right after we did it. I thought we sucked, but people tell me it really sounds good.

I was so critical of the band, always. We were too loud, but every now and then it would get just right. Just when I was I about to say, "Fuck this, I don't need it," a perfect show would come along. One perfect one could make up for a whole bunch of loud ones.

There are a lot of our shows that I haven't listened to yet, and the reason is simple: one day, I'm going to be a fucking jaded old man, and if I can listen to some shit from back in the day that I ain't never heard before—well, shit, do you know how happy that will make this old man's heart? If I could hear something my brother played, it will take me right back in time to that moment. That's why I always used to save me a taste—I was the ratholing-est son of a bitch around.

A couple of weeks later, we played the Love Valley Festival up in North Carolina, and I'm not sure we ever got paid. Love Valley was the idea of this old man named Andy Barker, who was always bragging, "I ain't never smoked a cigarette nor tasted no liquor!" After I'd heard that line enough, I started asking him, "Hey, have you ever had any pussy?"

The local sheriff tried to put my brother in jail, because Duane got a ticket for speeding on his way in there. My brother said,

"Fuck you, and your town too. We've come to play—do you want us to play, or do you want to fuck around?" Andy Barker told him, "As soon as you're done playing, boy, you have to go into that jail." Duane told him to get the fuck out of there, and we just started playing. We were playing good too; we were way into this real heavy fucking thing, and somebody threw mud up on my brother's guitar. Big mistake, because that was it. He finished the set, walked off the stage, got in his car, and left.

It was during this time that a guy named Joe Dan Petty joined the road crew. I met Joe Dan the first time we went down to Sarasota. Dickey was from down there, and he introduced us to this skinny little friend of his who he called J. D. Petty. I always thought it was cool to have a name like that—J. D. Souther, F. Lee Bailey, or what have you—though G. L. Allman, I'm sorry, but that just doesn't fly.

Right away, Joe Dan and I got along. For the longest time, I had no idea that he was a musician. (I also have no idea where he learned how to make boots, but I still have the four pairs that he made for me, and they're still like brand-new.) One day we were in rehearsal, and Oakley wasn't there; he was sick or something. So J. D. went over and picked up that Fender Jazz Bass and started laying it down, with perfect timing. He didn't play a lot of notes like Oakley did; Oakley was a very instinctive bass player, because he knew when to just sink into the repetition of a song, so the bottom was there for the rest of the band.

I've played with many bass players, and Berry Oakley was the perfect bassist for the Allman Brothers Band. If you wanted him to get crazy, he could, but only if everybody else did. He didn't go off on tangents in the middle of "Melissa," and Joe Dan was like that too. He could bring down the band when he had to, because if the bass player or the drummer shuts down, the other guys got to.

The right hand of the bass player and the right foot of the drummer are the main beam of the whole damn cabin; without that, the whole thing collapses. The bass player and the drummer have to constantly think about what they're doing, whereas a guitar player can have his mind in South Georgia somewhere, thinking about being home.

After a while, I asked, "Joe Dan, why are you here?"

He told me, "Well, I'm one of the roadies."

"No, seriously, bro," I said. "You're not really here for that, are you?"

"No, I'm not."

"You're here to watch Oakley, aren't you?"

"Yeah, you got it."

"Then there's going to be a day that you're going to leave and form your own band, right?" But Joe Dan was an excellent roadie, and he was there for us when we needed him. He really was great to have around, because when the shit got too heavy, he knew how to make everybody laugh, and the more you would laugh, the more he would laugh. When Joe Dan laughed, his whole body would shake; that man loved to laugh. And he was truthful. You couldn't beat a lie out of that guy with a ball bat— he would have died first. You couldn't have gotten him to fuck over somebody if his life depended upon it. He was a good man, and it was such a tragedy when he died in a plane crash in January 2000.

Another cat that came along about this time was the Buffalo, Gerald Evans. I spent many a night sitting with him and a bottle of Remy Martin, just sipping away. He was a real sweetheart, and he was the only guy who could ever look at me after I had done something wrong and say, "Do you really want to know what I think about it?"

"Yes, I would," I'd say.

And he'd tell me, "You did wrong, and it ain't right to do that to people."

He had no problem pointing out when I had hurt somebody and didn't realize it. Buffalo wasn't afraid to do that because he was older than everybody else, and he'd been around the block way more than we had. He was as street smart as anyone I knew. He'd look you right in the eye when he spoke to you, and I'll never forget that stare as long as I live. I learned so much from that old man, and he had a big influence on me.

Eventually, Buffalo got a case of the come and go blues. He would go up to Martha's Vineyard a lot and be by himself, because he loved it up there. Buffalo was very wise, too wise to be humping amps. Later on, he became more of an advisor, more of an advance man, for the band. He was like a jack-of-all-trades, and very intelligent, especially when it came to geography. He knew where every place was—not that he'd been to all of them, but he was on his way. Unlike Red Dog, who had been in the Marines but was the most lost son of a bitch in the band. Yet he was the one at the helm of the Winnebago, and he'd get lost in the parking lot.

ON AUGUST 26, 1970, WE WERE DOWN IN MIAMI BEACH, PLAYING a free gig on a stage that the city set up on a big median on Collins Avenue. We were playing "Don't Keep Me Wonderin'," which was the next-to-last song of the night. It would segue with a little jam into "Whipping Post," and I looked out over the crowd, and the people were all standing on the grass, listening. Nobody was doing the damn Grateful Dead waltz, and there weren't no spinners.

I looked over, and I saw this set of beautiful burnt sienna suede boots on this cat who was sitting on the grass with one leg out in front of him. I followed that boot up the pants, up the body to the head, and there was Mr. Eric Clapton. Next to him was Tommy Dowd, grinning like a fucking mule eating in the briars. Jim Gordon, Carl Radle, and Bobby Whitlock were there too—all of the Dominos, but I didn't recognize them.

After I shit myself, I looked over to Duane, thinking, "I hope to Christ he doesn't see him, because this will either be the finest 'Whipping Post' we'll ever play, or this fucker's going to fall apart." But Duane didn't notice anything, so we finished the show with a real good "Whipping Post," and then Duane eases over to me and said, "Baybrah, dig who the fuck is sitting over there."

"Man, I saw him two songs ago," I said.

"Do you see them fucking boots, man?" Duane had a real thing for clothes back then—we both did.

Tommy Dowd, who was Atlantic's house producer, introduced all of us to each other, and then we headed over to Criteria Studios, where Derek and the Dominos were working on *Layla*. We were all hanging out in the lounge, with drinks and food all set up for us. The English people do that, which is something that I admire.

Duane asked Tommy if he could come and just watch some of the sessions, but it turns out that Eric was just as much in awe of my brother as Duane was of him. Eric didn't play no slide at the time, and he loved my brother's slide work. The way I heard it, when Tommy asked if Duane could come watch the sessions, Eric said, "Watch? Hell no. If he shows up, he has to play."

That first night, we all went into the studio together and did that jam thing. The next day, all the other guys left, but I stayed. I watched about three days of the session, and one of the first things they did was "Layla." They played what they already had, and it didn't sound like much. It didn't have that intro on it yet, but once they added that, the song took off. Duane just fit right in, man—from the very first note, it just blended. His guitar and Eric's sounded so good together; it was the perfect blend of a Gibson and a Fender. You could tell that history was being made.

Everybody in the band was so proud of Duane for playing on *Layla,* even though I'm sure that Dickey was green with envy. If I was a guitar player, I'm sure that I would have been too. It goes without saying that everybody in the Allman Brothers has always greatly admired Clapton. Aside from being a fantastic guitar player, he's the same boy his grandmother raised, a true gentleman, very levelheaded, and he really devotes a lot of time to trying to get other people straightened out. Because, like all the rest of us, he was into it pretty heavy.

Many years later, we had a nice moment when he came out during our fortieth anniversary shows at the Beacon. We'd only had a very short rehearsal the afternoon of the show. Up on the top floor, we had a couple of small amps and an electric piano set up and we went over all the stops and starts to "Layla," which are the important parts. Then that night he came out and tore the place up. Backstage, my manager, Michael Lehman, introduced Eric to Duane's daughter, Galadrielle, and everyone got tears in their eyes.

We played the Fillmore East again in September 1970, on a bill with Van Morrison, Sha Na Na, Albert King, and the Byrds. Each act did four or five songs, because this was a made-for-TV event. At the end of the whole thing, they told us that they were sorry, but Oakley's amp was at such a low frequency that it shook the filaments in the cameras and distorted the picture.

They were lying through their teeth, because what really happened is they fucked up my vocal input into the camera, so it's totally missing during "Don't Keep Me Wonderin'" and two-thirds of "Dreams," and that's why it was never televised. Boy, we were mad, and my brother was fucking flaming, because this was going to be our first time on TV. He knew we were getting better, and all people needed to do was hear us.

We were evolving, we were growing, we were maturing in our music and in our lives. Things were getting more refined, tighter, and the set was starting to click. It was exciting, it was fresh, and it was always new. No matter what you felt like during the day, you knew that night we were going to be great.

We rarely talked onstage. We talked to each other, but as far as saying something to the crowd, my brother might say something like "You all sure are quiet," but we really didn't say much. Just like me, my brother could play for a crowd, but talking to them just wasn't part of it. He talked to them through his guitar.

We went to Nashville to play Vanderbilt University in October 1970, and we were staying right across the street from the hospital where Duane and I were born. We had a day off, and my brother was out looking to score some doojee. He didn't find any, but he did find a guy who had some Tuinals and he took one. Then here comes a dude, and he's got a ball of opium with him that's about the size of a baseball. Tuinals and a narcotic do not mix; that's what killed Allen Woody and many, many others. It almost got me a couple of times, until I got wise to it.

As soon as the opium got there, my brother bought a piece about the size of a golf ball and took a big chunk of it off and ate it. A while later, the rest of us were down in the Winnebago getting ready to go, and no one had seen Duane. Red Dog went up to the room to check on things, and he came back down and said, "Man, he won't wake up, and half of his body is turning blue," because his blood was settling—he was almost dead.

"Oh my God, he's going to die, right here where he was born." I was freaking.

I'm getting ready to spring like a damn black panther, and

Dickey goes right over the top of me. When that guy needed to run, he could really move. He was over me, through me, and past me, up to the third floor. He loved Duane—I've got to say that about Dickey Betts. I also have to say that he probably saved Duane's life that night. You've got to give the devil his due, but the thing is, Dickey ain't no devil. He's just a mixed-up guy.

Dickey got to Duane first, with Payne and Callahan right behind him. I was just standing there, frozen in prayer. I got down on my knees in prayer, probably for the first time in my life. They got him downstairs, and he was not moving. The lights were on, but no one was home—hell, the lights weren't even on. Thank God we were parked right across the street from the hospital, because they got him over to the emergency room, and he was in there for the longest fucking time, but they were able to revive him.

God was looking down on us, man, and so were his Angels of Mercy. They say you got two guardian angels; well, I think Duane borrowed both of mine, and a few more from everybody else. My brother must've stayed high for three days, but he actually played the gig the next night in Atlanta. It's too bad we don't have those tapes, because *that* was a rather slow night.

The whole thing really scared my brother, man. He had the fear of God in his eyes after that, and he didn't do drugs again for a long time. He might have drunk a beer now and then, beer or cheap wine, but that was it.

The first time I got dosed with acid was in January 1971 at the Fillmore West, where we were playing four nights with Hot Tuna. I set my drink down, and some Prankster dosed it. I didn't know where I was—it was like *Alice in Wonderland*. There were these big fuzzy things floating around, and everything looked like something out of an R. Crumb comic, I guess because I had gotten turned on to *Zap Comix* right around that time. These

R. Crumb images were coming out of my brother's amp, right along with the notes, and I was like, "What the fuck is going on here?" But it didn't take me long to realize what had happened.

Acid is a brain douche, if you ask me; I've got no use for it, because it just scrambles your brain. It would take me three days before I could even think straight, so I haven't tripped in over thirty years.

WE WERE AWARE OF WHAT WAS GOING ON IN SOCIETY AT THAT time, and we cared about what was happening with the war in Vietnam and what happened at Kent State. The original title of *Eat a Peach* was *Eat a Peach for Peace,* but it got shortened. In truth, though, we were sheltered by the music and the traveling, and, especially for myself, by the songwriting. Writing throws your whole and complete attention into the process, and you get into it so deep, nothing distracts you. Someone would have to inform you that your house was ablaze.

Still, sometimes things would happen that you couldn't ignore. We didn't have any run-ins with the law in Macon, but it seemed like every time we went to Alabama, we got in trouble. One time, when Twiggs was still with us, we were in the Winnebago heading through the hills of northern Alabama, and I had just got done smoking a joint. We heard the sirens and saw the blue and red lights, and this guy pulled us over.

He opened the door and said, "All right, who do we have here?"

"Sir," Red Dog said, "we've got the Allman Brothers Band, a rock and roll band on Atlantic Records, thank you."

The cop said, "Then let me see Mr. Allman, in the back of my car—now."

So my ass got up, and I got my wallet, and I go and get in the back of the car. He asked me a bunch of questions—where we had been and where we had played, where we were going, where we were planning on staying—and this was back when I was up on everything, so I spit it right out to him. He looked over at me, moved his clipboard, and pulled out a big old syringe and started flipping it up and down, catching it.

Then he said, "You know what, Mr. Allman? The judge would absolutely go crazy out of his mind if he knew what you fuckers was out here doing."

"How much, man?" was all I asked.

"Don't rush me—I'm not through with my story." So he finished his lecture. Then he said, "As for the price, I think $300 would be fine. Just drop it over the seat, and I'll give you back your license. And please, be discreet."

I went back to the Winbag, and Twiggs was waiting. He just asked, "How much?" I told him it was $300, and he said, "Man, that's almost going to clean us out." That's when I should have written that song: "That's just the way it is, some things will never change."

Then there was the time we were on our way from Macon to the Warehouse in New Orleans, and we were in a real hurry. We were driving in two rental cars, and Jaimoe was sitting in the back of one of them—keep in mind, this was 1971. We passed through Grove Hill, Alabama, and we were all hungry, so we pulled off the road and went to a restaurant. All of us—that is, except for Dickey, who'd had too much to drink, so he stayed in one of the cars. We sat down, and we were looking pretty rough. Right away, you could tell that people were checking us out.

While we were inside, I looked out the window, and there's Dickey—he's gotten out of the car, and he's barfing like crazy, and the whole place can see him. I thought, "Oh shit," but said, "Okay, guys, I'll have pancakes, and cook the bacon well."

I went to the bathroom and flushed the four or five reds I had on me. I had one bag of doojee, and I wasn't going to throw that away, so I put it in my wallet and walked back out and sat down. When I got back out, I noticed that one of the waitresses was talking on the damn phone and glancing over in our direction. By this point, Dickey was back in the car, horizontal in the back-seat, but the door was still open. I told everyone, "Guys, let's eat up, pay the check, and get out of here." So that we did.

We were riding along, and I was in the back with Jaimoe, while Willie Perkins was driving and my brother was up front with him. Suddenly Duane said, "Goddamn it, they're coming after us. Everybody eat what you got, or throw it out, but do something."

Jaimoe pulled out this bag of reefer that would have choked a mule, and he starts to eat it. It was this big bag of green that looked like a beer you get on St. Patrick's Day—there was no way he could finish it, and the more he ate, the bigger it got in his mouth. Then he couldn't spit it out, so it was like, "Hey, here I am!" Here he is with a bunch of long-haired white guys, and one of them is throwing up.

When I saw they were behind us, I took out that bag of doojee and, instead of snorting it and cooling my jets and making everything easy, I threw it out the back window, and them sons of bitches found it. They saw it in the sunlight when I threw it, and we could hear them going, "Well, it looks like hair-o-win to me, boy. Hey, look out now—don't spill it. You asshole, you're about to spill it." This one guy must have touched the bag, and half of it went out.

They arrested us all and threw us in jail, and I'm in the same cell as Red Dog, so he gets over in the corner and quietly takes off all his clothes. He's got a nut sack that hangs way far down, and legs that are no bigger than a pair of pool cues—I don't know how the hell they hold his body up. He's up on the bars and he looks like the damn Wild Man from Borneo with all that red hair, and that big old dick and them balls. A bunch of old ladies had gathered around the jail, and they just knew he was a heathen!

I knew there was safety in numbers, so I wasn't sweating shit while we were in there. I was hoping that it wouldn't hit the news, but sure enough, that town was so small that word spread right away. We got out of there after one night, charged with disturbing the peace, and we were only fined twenty-five dollars, because Mr. John Condon, the lawyer who'd helped us out when Twiggs stabbed that guy, came to the rescue again. At one point, we stopped playing in Alabama—except for Birmingham, and even that was pretty rare.

Another time we were playing New Orleans. We were staying at the Pontchartrain Hotel, and I had the bottom suite. I had an eight ball in my Levi's, and I had on a blue velvet coat, a white silk shirt with black roses on it, and a pair of blue velvet boots. I had taken my boots and socks off and was having a glass of wine. All of a sudden, here come six guys, banging on the door. "Let us the fuck in, this is the law."

I opened the door and jumped back as they came pushing in. All of them start going through the suite, and one of them got in my face and said, "We're going to sit here and bust you, and then we're going to let you watch us go upstairs and bust all your little Allman friends."

One of them came over and said, "All right, where's the shit?"

I started to say, "If you bust your head open, man, we can dip it out," but I just went, "Where's what? We're not smoking anything in here but cigarettes."

"You just stay here," he ordered, and they never even looked in my pocket—they never shook me down.

Then they went up to Jaimoe's room, and Jaimoe has on a

dress! His friend Juicy Carter was there with him, but I don't know why he had on a dress. The cop opened the door, took one look at him in that dress, and turned around. He just walked away and didn't bother to fuck with him.

Butch had half an ounce of blow, and he put it under the mattress. Boy, how original can you get? This cop picked up the mattress, and if he had picked it up half an inch more, he would have seen it, so Butch got really lucky. Dickey was in bed with his wife, Sandy Bluesky, and as soon as they busted the door open, he jumped up and popped the first guy who came in the room. Another one pulled out his billy club and bapped Dickey across the head and knocked him out cold.

This whole thing happened because the promoters had changed. One promoter had fucked us, so we found a new one, and the first promoter made a call to the police. You should have seen what this fucking warrant said: "Possible possession of barbiturates, amphetamines, hallucinogens, hallucinogenic mushrooms, peyote, heroin, cocaine and marijuana." They also listed some shit I've never heard of, but all they ended up getting us for was Dickey taking that swing at them. It was a dirty, dirty trick, man—somebody really tried to set us up.

Outtake from the At Fillmore East *cover shoot, 1971*

CHAPTER EIGHT

Uppers and Downers

IN MARCH 1971, WE WENT TO THE FILLMORE EAST TO RECORD A live album. We had the recording trucks set up outside, and we knew we had more than one night to do it, so we weren't uptight about it. That was good, because I would have been the first one to make the first mistake, to be the uptight one. Our attitude was to go in there and play our shows, let Tom Dowd figure out the rest, and then we'll have us a record. We played two shows each day, we played for a long time, and the audience was just whupped by the time we were done.

The funny thing is, Tom Dowd almost missed the recording of the album. He was supposed to be on vacation in Europe, but the weather was shitty, so he decided to head back to New York on a red-eye flight. He checked into a hotel and slept until the afternoon of the show. He didn't even know we were recording that night, and we didn't know he was back in town. Tom barely made it into the truck before the music started, but he got it all down on tape. If he hadn't made it in time, the rest of our career might have been very different.

On the first night, we had Randolph "Juicy" Carter sit in with us. Juicy was a baritone sax player, a good old friend of Jaimoe's who had been with him during that New Orleans bust. I think he had been one of the horn players in Percy Sledge's road band, and every now and then he would sit in with us. We enjoyed having him because it broke up the musical routine. We had a lot of guitar solos, so to have a solo on sax, which is the most romantic instrument ever made, was a nice breath of fresh air. But we didn't use any of the songs with him on the album.

Thom "Ace" Doucette used to play harp with us a lot at the Fillmore, and he shows up on part of the album. Thom was from Sarasota originally, and he had the come and go blues more than anybody I've ever seen. My brother really liked him, and gave him the nickname Ace. We would have hired him to be a full-fledged member of the band, but I don't think he wanted the responsibility. I don't think he wanted to have to be anywhere at any time—Thom just kind of drifts, still to this day. Wherever the wind takes him, that's where he goes.

That record shows very well what we could do. Those concerts were so special. It was almost like somebody knew what was gonna happen; it was kind of eerie.

But I have to say that I was still the big doubting Thomas of the whole thing. It goes back to high school—I made the other guys wait to tour until I got my diploma, because, as I told my brother, "Man, we will never make enough money to pay rent doing this." My brother would say, "Gregory, you need to get a little more faith." Anytime I would get in a crisis, he would say something funny and bring me right out of it.

It was the same thing with the live album. The first two records had fallen on their ass. Just barely cracked the charts, if that. Our kind of music was so new that eventually they started calling it a whole different genre of music. I always thought we were just playing some blues with some jazz mixed in, and with Dickey we had a country boy in the band, so that accounted for stuff like "Lord, I was born a ramblin' man"—that's very good as a country song, by the way.

So I thought, live album or not, how many times are you wanting to fail before we finally give this thing up? Not to mention we were working our butts off. In 1970, we played 306 nights, and that was just the gigs; the rest of it was traveling. So we were gone the whole year.

The album cover of *At Fillmore East* was shot by Jim Marshall, who shot all those famous black-and-white pictures of Jim Morrison, Janis Joplin, Hendrix—just everybody, man. For a while, they were pushing us for a cover, and we couldn't think of what to do. Somebody, I think one of the roadies, said, "Why don't we just stencil up a bunch of these cases, go across the street from the studio, stack them up against that brick building, and take a picture?" It was a great idea, because nobody could tell what fucking town we were in, and it looked cold, so you would think we were in New York, but we were really in Macon, Georgia.

I didn't want to be out there, because we weren't really dressed for cold weather. I was wearing a buckskin coat and a pair of thin Levi's, and the wind was blowing, so my ass was cold. The roadies began to unload the road cases and got them stenciled up. They had to do it quick—if you look real close at the photo, you can see where they got some paint on the wall, and when they tried to wipe it off, they smudged it and made it worse.

We were across the street, inside the studio, while they were doing all that, and they finally said, "Okay, we're ready." Jim

Marshall had all his cameras and film, and he shot and he shot and he shot, and he shot some more. How many shots can you take of a bunch of dudes in front of a fucking brick wall? We were getting edgy and ready to walk. Marshall was like, "Look, you sons of bitches, hold still." He was a very successful photographer, and quite bossy.

We were fucking around, grab-assing and everything, because that was back when we were all real brothers. He said, "All right, I'm going to turn around and reload this Hasselblad, and this is the last fucking roll. If you motherfuckers move, I'll never do this again." Meanwhile we're all going, "Boy, I hope not!"

Suddenly here comes the candy man walking down the street, and he ain't never seen nothing like this. My brother goes, "Hey, bro," runs across the street, buys a couple of bags, makes change, runs back across the street, and sits back down just before Marshall turns back around to shoot the picture. That struck us all real funny, and we just cracked up.

Marshall started clicking away, going, "What's so fucking funny?" because he hadn't seen Duane run across the street, so we just laughed harder and harder. He thought we were laughing at him, and the more he thought that, the more we did laugh. We were really laughing at the whole stupid situation, because it was pneumonia city out there, man.

It was Duane's idea to put the picture of the roadies on the back cover. The rest of us weren't too sure about that, but he said, "Hey, man, they work just as fucking hard as we do," so Marshall went ahead and took it.

AFTER THE FILLMORE SHOWS, WE TOOK SOME TIME OFF. I WAS IN such a good mood, because back then, time off was so very precious. We headed up to Gatlinburg, Tennessee, to do some songwriting and rehearsing. We rented out a ski chalet, which cost quite a bit of money.

Once we got there, I started to realize that we had some problems, because as soon as we arrived, Oakley and my brother got into Duane's Volvo 1800E, and they took off for Atlanta and copped. Did they cop for me? Nope, but it didn't matter, because I went up there to write. Besides, I had my own stash anyway.

By the time they got back, we had some new tunes worked up, but we only had two or three days left. On top of that, they were barfing their guts out, so that whole trip ended up being kind of a washout. We did get a couple of my songs learned, and Dickey's song "Blue Sky," and then when we got to Miami to start working on *Eat a Peach,* things moved pretty fast.

In June, Bill Graham asked us to be the last band to play at the closing of the Fillmore East, and that was a big thing to us. That weekend there was lots of confusion, because there were so many bands playing. In those last three days, there must have been ten or twelve bands playing, including Albert King, J. Geils Band, Mountain, and the Beach Boys. The lineup was the perfect example of Uncle Bill's eclectic taste—he liked a little bit of everything, all the way up until the last show. There was actually a bit of tension that night because the Beach Boys were annoyed about having to go on before us. They put up a fight until Bill told them what's what, but they took out their revenge by playing long, so we didn't take the stage until much later than we were supposed to.

When we were finally about to go on, Bill introduced us by saying, "We're going to round it off with the best of them all, the Allman Brothers Band," and that was special. I'd heard a rumor before that Bill had said of all the bands he'd ever worked with, we were his favorite, but I hadn't believed it. So when I heard him say that with my own two ears, I was elated.

I respected, loved, and appreciated Bill Graham probably as much as anybody I've ever known. One day Chank and I were on I-16, heading from Macon to Savannah, and we saw these three Quonset huts right together on the side of the road. A sign said "Antiques," and that's all it took. We pulled in there, and this guy running the place had three crates of 1926 Coca-Cola that still had the cocaine in it. He also had arrowhead collections, rocking chairs, and all kinds of old cans and bottles, just neat, neat shit. He had a wooden box with a glass top and purple velvet underneath it, and when you opened it up there was a .44 cap and ball. The powder horn was there, and the little thing to make the musket ball with, and it said, "Commemorative Model—Robert E. Lee, 1865." I bought it on the spot for Bill.

I wasn't sucking up to him or anything like that; I gave it to him out of respect. He tried three times to give that damn thing back to me. He brought it to a gig once, and he had it in this sack he always carried. He asked, "Are you sure about this pistol?"

"Bill," I said, "if you ask me one more time about that damn gun, I'm going to take it back!"

He said, "Okay," and from what I hear, he went out and bought a black marble pedestal and put the gun on it, right in the foyer of his house. He had a plaque made that said, "Given to me by Gregg Allman." That's what I heard—I don't know if it's true, and there's no telling where it is now.

The Allman Brothers had a special relationship with Bill Graham. Bill was always there when we played the Fillmore, and he'd come in and shoot the shit with us in the dressing room. He'd come down in the afternoon when we were setting up and sit there talking to us. He came down to Macon several times for the annual Capricorn barbecue. He got along real well with my brother and always went out of his way to talk to Jaimoe. I don't know why he connected the way he did with Jaimoe, but maybe it was because Bill was a German Jew. He got out of Europe right before the Holocaust, but his whole family died in the camps, and I think he related best to people who'd had a rough go of it.

Bill Graham certainly had a passion for music, and the live performance of music, right up until the day he died in 1991. He was probably the most assertive person I ever met, but he was real fair with everybody. He didn't give a shit about how famous you were. The opening act got the same treatment as the headliner, and they were made to feel welcome. That was smart on his part, because in three months to a year, who knows? That opening act might be wiping out the whole world.

I remember one night when Jeff Beck wasn't going to play because there was no shower for him. Bill picked him up off the floor, pushed him up against the door, and told him, "You get your little Limey ass out there and play. Quit whining, or I'll give you a fucking shower."

ONE NIGHT WHEN WE WERE IN NEW YORK, OUR FRIENDS PETER Harron and Collette Mimram, who we had met through Ace Doucette, took us to dinner at the apartment of a guy named Deering Howe. Deering either owned or leased the penthouse at 1 Fifth Avenue, and that night Alan Douglas, who had worked closely with Jimi Hendrix, was also there with his girlfriend, Stella.

Deering had one of Jimi's old guitars, strung right-handed so he could play it. When we got there, we all took off our coats, and my brother made a beeline for that damn guitar, plugged it in, turned this little Champ amp on, and started blowing this scathing, molten lava line that went on for about twenty-five minutes. It was like nothing I ever heard him play onstage, and everybody was just in awe. There was a long silence afterwards, and Duane just said, "Nice guitar," and put it down.

Then Collette said, "I'd like you guys to meet some people here," because we hadn't even met Deering yet.

It was funny, man. Duane was just like a kid in the candy store when he saw that guitar, and he burnt that son of a bitch up. It was like his "How do you do?" and it was just perfect. Stella just fell in love with him, and so did Collette. We hit it off with Deering right away.

His penthouse was a pretty cool spot. There weren't any chairs in there, it was all cushions. It was decorated in an East Indian type of thing, and you could almost hear a sitar playing when you walked in there, even though there wasn't any music on. I liked these people from the start; I had never seen anything like them before. They were educated, sophisticated, and just filthy rich, but I had never seen people this hip who didn't play music, and they were just a good bunch of folks. That night was my introduction to Deering Howe, a man who to this day remains one of my dearest, dearest friends.

Later on, when we started to make more serious money, Deering taught me about things and gave me advice, because he had been around money all of his life. He taught me about wine, and certain things you do and you don't do in social situations. He taught me what it was like to have money, and how you should act about money—in other words, that you shouldn't act any different. I'd already heard that people who really understood money wore it like an old pair of shoes, and I guess I've sort of done that. I have nice things, but I don't flash them around. I have my Corvette, but it's just a car, you know?

Having money really was something I had to learn. And it was tough. I blew a million before I saved a nickel. I came close to bankruptcy once, and over the years I think there might have been a couple of bankruptcies in the band. A year or two later, when the money really started coming in, the first thing I did was to get all my teeth crowned, with a little gold inlay in the back, because I was born with soft enamel on them. Then I bought a pair of snakeskin boots, and I paid off my mother's house.

I also used to be a real clothes hound. Every time I'd go to New York, I'd drop a couple of grand on clothes, and back then, that was a lot of clothes. I had quite the wardrobe, man. I would wear Levi's and silk shirts, and velvet jackets and suede boots.

The band and I got involved with the purchase of a 520-acre farm out in Juliette, Georgia. The original idea was to buy a big piece of land and just leave it until we got to be old fucks when we would sell it and make a fortune. Then somebody came up with this notion of AllBroVille or ABBville, or some bullshit. We were going to turn it into a town and we were all going to live there, or some crazy thing. At fifteen dollars an acre, it actually was a pretty good deal, because it was out in the middle of nowhere. That whole thing kind of stunk to me, so I sold my share back to the band and said, "Fuck this." I think I broke even on that.

I loved to buy antiques—real old, old things. I bought a nice car, the Excalibur, and some motorcycles, of course. I bought a bunch of instruments too. I also got turned on to Jamaica, so I went down there a lot. Deering turned me on to deep-sea fishing, and so far to date, I have caught forty-three sailfish and one blue marlin. The last big fish I caught was a 208-pound hammerhead, and it was beautiful, man—gray, and just as white as snow underneath.

For a while there, if it moved, I bought it. That didn't last too long, because as soon as the money moved up to a certain bracket, everybody around us started easing a little bit off the top. They made sure we had all the good highs we needed, but they were stealing from us. I didn't suspect anything, because I always had a wad of money and a checkbook with a full bank account. But keeping a close eye on things was something I had to learn the hard way.

DURING JULY 1971, WE DID A WEEK'S WORTH OF GIGS AT THE STEEL Pier in Atlantic City, and as far as gigs went, that was the lowest of the low. That's where we realized that we were all hooked on that white powder that made us feel so good. We weren't shooting it, but we were hooked.

Everybody knew that something wasn't right, and I can remember waking up in the morning and every fiber of my existence screamed at me that something was missing, that I needed something. I didn't want it, but I damn sure needed it. I had one hit left, and my brother had some kind of detector, because he said, "I know you've got some left," probably because he knew that I'd always hold on to that last one—just it being there made me feel okay.

He knew I had it, but I told him I didn't have any. He said, "You're a fucking liar." I told him again that I didn't have anything, but he kept coming after me. He said, "You know you have a fucking bag," and I finally gave in.

"Yeah, I got one."

"You lied to me, you little motherfucker."

"You're pressuring me about something that belongs to me, motherfucker?"

"Are you telling me you won't even give half to your own fucking brother?" Duane asked.

"Don't you give me any of that horseshit," I told him. "You had just as many bags as I did, you glutton motherfucker. You just did too many. I held one back, because I knew I'd need one today, instead of nodding my ass off last night."

"You little cocksucker, you don't belong in this fucking band if you won't share. I should fire your ass."

"Share it with you, you mean, right?"

"Yeah, I do," and then he walked out, mumbling under his breath about me.

He came back in the room a little later, and I had two lines poured out. Duane says, "Oh, I knew you were my bro," and he hugged me and kissed me, and wolfed a line right up his nose. He immediately felt better, and then we went out and played.

A couple of days later, he came to me and apologized.

"I really feel bad about what happened, and you know I love you. First of all, I couldn't fire you anyway, because this is the Allman Brothers *Band,* and I'd have to call a meeting, and the other guys would tell me that I was full of shit, so I'm sorry."

Just like when we were kids, no matter how hard it would be, he would come back and apologize to me. Same thing happened that time he hung me—a few days later, he apologized.

We headed out to California in October 1971, and that's when *Rolling Stone* sent Grover Lewis out to do a story on us, with Annie Leibovitz taking photos. Annie is okay, but that damn Grover Lewis was an asshole. As little as my brother was, he threatened to punch Lewis out. Those shows went really well, though. We stomped them, but for some reason we never really developed a huge following out there, and we never have, to this day.

After the shit went down with me and my brother at the Steel Pier, we knew something had to be done, and so did a lot of other people. We were at a party in New York City, and Ahmet Ertegun, the founder of Atlantic Records, came up to me and my brother and said, "Could I see you both back here for just a second? I just want to talk to you."

Jerry Wexler, his partner at Atlantic, joined him. I thought they were taking us back there to personally congratulate us, so we went into this room, and Ahmet shut the door and locked it. He turned around, and the face he had on—I knew something was about to come down, and it could only be one thing. I thought, "Here it comes."

They must not have given a shit about me, because they kept looking straight at Duane. Every now and then, they'd gaze over at me as they tore into us about our addiction. Duane just sat there and listened to them, because what could he say? They were trying to help us, and they were doing it in such a way to try and really get through to us. It was delivered in a very stern, fatherly manner.

"Do you have any fucking idea what you are messing with?" they asked. "It killed Charlie Parker, it killed Billie Holiday, and it will kill you too."

They hit us with horror story after horror story, and they said, "And now it's you all—barely twenty years old. That doesn't give you a very long time left, because no one survives the fucking shit."

They went round and round, and they didn't miss a fucking base. Duane tried to be cool about it, saying that he wasn't worried about anything, but we were all worried. It was just like a kid getting his ass chewed out about something and trying to get a few words in edgewise. They kept saying, "Just listen to us," so Duane didn't get to say too much.

I felt like a fucking dog by the time they were done, because I was the one who turned the rest of the guys on to heroin. I had that guilt to deal with, and I had this image of Jaimoe—sweet, nice, pure, clean, wonderful, collard green–eating Jaimoe—lying in bed, a heroin addict, thanks to me. "Thanks to G.A., he's fucked up"—we all were, and I had that responsibility resting on my shoulders.

None of them knew I felt that way, and they told me later, "Man, what do you mean you're responsible? We love it, and we went and bought it ourselves. It would have got to us eventually, you just happened to be the first one in line."

Later on, Tom Dowd got on our asses too. His eyes could bitch you out by themselves, because he wore them big thick glasses. We deserved it, and Tom wasn't trying to do nothing but help. I thought to myself for a minute, "Shit, we really had a great producer, and we fucking blew it," because I was sure that Tom was fixing to say, "I've had it with you." He brought up the party, because he was there when we got bitched out, but he didn't go back there, because he figured that two was enough. But now he had the floor, and there was no getting away from him.

Tom shamed us, man, he did. "You're throwing your fucking life out the window, because you're rolling the dice every time that you do it. Worst of all, you're fucking up your music, and you're wasting my goddamn time."

When Tom used that kind of language, I almost started crying. All of a sudden, I felt like a little kid, and I was really embarrassed. He told us, "If you don't fucking listen and stop now, you're not going to be able to." Little did he know, it was already too late.

Well, maybe it wasn't too late, because we had a band meeting and discussed going to treatment. Everybody was there, crew included. No one had ever gone into treatment, so nobody knew what it was. I thought you went in there for two or three days and they gave you some pills or something, and then you walked out, completely cured. No one tried to deny that they had a problem; everybody copped to it. So it was decided that Duane, Oakley, Red Dog, and Payne would go into treatment up in Buffalo, while I headed home to quit cold turkey.

I got into bed, and rolled round and kicked, man. I went and saw my doctor and got some 'ludes, but they only helped when they knocked me completely out. By the time the guys got home from Buffalo, I was all right. They were there for a week, and they were given methadone, so I don't know if you can say they were really clean or not. That shit is nasty, because it just totally shuts down your endorphins, and it takes more than just quitting to get them to open up again. You gotta wait until they want to come out and play again, and that can be a long wait.

When everybody got back into town, they came over to my house and let me know that they were feeling better. But even though we'd all stopped with heroin, it didn't mean we were clean. Before they'd gone into treatment, I'd given Duane a hundred-dollar bill and asked him to pick me up a gram of blow when they were done because he was going to spend a day or two in New York after treatment. When they got back, I asked him about it, and he told me, "I'm sorry, bro. We saw Buddy Miles last night, and he did all of your blow." That really pissed me off, and I stayed up drinking most of the night.

The next morning, I drove over to Duane's house and I walked in, because he never locked his door. I was going to get some blow or my money back, one or the other. He was asleep in bed, and I mean gone, with his clothes still on. On the nightstand was a little vial, almost completely full with blow. I took me a dollar bill, poured out about half a gram, and snorted it up. He had plenty left, and I put it back on the nightstand.

I got home, and the phone rang. It was my brother, and he was fighting mad. He said, "You little cocksucker, did you come over here and steal some of my blow?"

The last thing I ever said to my brother was a fucking lie, man.

"No, I did not," I told him.

"Okay, man, I'm sorry. I shouldn't have called you up, accusing you of some shit like that. I sure do love ya, baybrah," and he hung up.

That was the last time I ever spoke to my brother.

I have thought about that every single day of my life since

then. I told him that lie, and he told me that he was sorry and that he loved me. I was so dumbfounded, I couldn't say nothing back to him. You never know, man, and right then is when I learned about the power of words.

Let's say that something worse than Hitler happens, and somebody comes over, takes over this country, and places us all in camps. They take all our possessions away—our houses, our cars, our clothing, everything. All you have is the skin on your body, and you only have one thing that's worth something. You know what that is? It's your word.

I had never lied to Duane like that, because there was no reason to. Even when we were kids, and I knew there was an ass-whipping coming, I couldn't lie to him. I could try, but he would see right through me.

I have thought of that lie every day of my life, and I just keep recrucifying myself for it. I know that's not what he would want—well, not for long, anyway. I know he lied to me about the blow in the first place, but the thing is, I never got the chance to tell him the truth.

My brother

CHAPTER NINE

October 29, 1971

I REMEMBER WHEN IT HAPPENED.

I was home and I got a phone call. A woman's voice said, "Your brother had a slight"—she used that word, "slight"— "motorcycle accident." And the way she said it, I just knew. I threw on some clothes and I ran down the hill to where the hospital was. When I got there, Oakley, Dickey, and Jaimoe were already there, and Butch came in soon after.

They didn't take us to the waiting room, they took us in the chapel—that's when I really knew. And there wasn't nothing "slight" about it. Another guy, a surgeon, came out, and he said, "We brought him back up for just a minute or two, but he's gone." He said Duane was just too busted up. I'm so glad that I didn't see him like that, because I don't have to live with that memory.

We set the funeral for the next day. Somebody came up with the notion of putting the casket in front of the band and having us play a gig, and I thought that was the most ridiculous thing I ever heard. I really thought that was ridiculous, the idea of having an audience in a chapel, with a casket covered in roses, and us playing rock and roll behind it. But all the other guys wanted to do it, so I went along with it.

The next morning, I got the news that my mother had arrived, and I was upstairs opening the closet door, getting ready to put on my black suit. There was a tap on my shoulder, and it was Deering Howe. He had been in St. Barts or St. Martin, and he hopped a Learjet and came right to Macon. Deering had a big beaker of the most kick-ass Peruvian flake, and you cannot cry when you do coke. That was the only way we were able to play at the funeral home.

We buried Duane with a silver dollar in one pocket, a throwing knife in the other, and his favorite ring on his hand—a snake that coiled around his finger, with two eyes made of turquoise. Chank told me that someone stuck a couple of joints in his shirt pocket along with a mushroom lighter, and Chank would know, because he went down there and saw him. I just couldn't do it.

There were a whole lot of people at the funeral; people came in from everywhere. And even though it didn't sit right with me, I got up there with one of his old guitars and played "Melissa."

"This was my brother's favorite song that I ever wrote," I said, and it was hard, but I got through it.

After we played at the chapel, we all went out back to smoke a joint. We were standing together, and I think we were all wondering what we were going to do.

"Look, boys," I said. "If you're thinking about stopping, don't. We need to get back to Miami, because we've got some unfinished business down there. If we don't keep playing, like my brother would've wanted us to, we're all gonna become dope dealers and just fall by the wayside. I think this is our only option."

Some of them answered me, some of them didn't, but they all got what I said planted in their heads. Of course, they all felt the same way. When you're in a situation like that, it's great if somebody speaks up and says what everybody is thinking. It's not like I came up with some big profound statement, because I didn't.

After we got home from the service, though, I just fell apart. One of the worst things I saw was, after giving the eulogy at Duane's funeral, Jerry Wexler came back to the Big House and took the dimes out of the pay phone that Oakley kept in the kitchen. Berry kept eight or ten dimes in the little change thing on the phone, for people making calls. Wexler was making a call, and he opened the change thing and pocketed all those dimes. Callahan and I saw the whole thing, and we just started laughing at him—the fucking president of Atlantic Records, pocketing some dimes. Boy oh boy.

Chank hung with me the whole time, and then Deering decided to take me to Jamaica, just to get me away from the madness. Chank saw us off at the airport, and we headed off.

When I got back from Jamaica, it was rough. In my grief, I probably didn't help the band too much at all. I tried to play and I tried to sing, but I didn't do too much writing. In the days and weeks that followed, I began to wonder if I would ever get back that feeling of "Wow, let's go play, man." I wondered if I'd ever find the passion, the energy, the love of making music and making it better—all of that good old stuff.

You get real wicked after somebody dies, and you get pissed off. I was pissed off at Duane for dying, for leaving me behind with all that shit to deal with. Then you get pissed at yourself for being pissed, because you loved them so much. You snap at people for no reason—you just get basically pissed. When that finally gets out of your system, then you're back in the human race. It takes some time, and probably a few glasses of spirits, but somehow the five of us got it together.

We had to take some time off because of our health and everything. We were skinny already, but after Duane died, we got down to nothing. As soon as we were able, though, we got back out there.

I had a lot of other doubts as well after Duane died. I was worried that the Waldens and such were going to take over the band, that it was going to become another McEuen and Dallas Smith situation, because Duane was the assertive one of the band— maybe "assertive" is a little too light of a word. He was the liaison between Capricorn Records and us, between Phil Walden and us. Walden knew better than to bluff my brother, but I'm the kind of guy who doesn't like to have to play those games. The reality, though, is you have to—the world is full of it, and the music business is riddled with it.

Then, on top of all this, the week after Duane died, the *Fillmore* record blew the top off the fucking charts. To be clear, the record took off because of the music, not because Duane had died. In the weeks before his accident, it was already starting to go, but the volcano finally erupted right after he died. It was raining money. There were times when we had been getting by on three dollars a day, which is pretty hard to do, and then suddenly I started getting five-figure checks in the mail, twice a week. That was a real mindfuck, because my brother never got to live to see the big money start rolling in. What we had been trying to do for all those years finally happened, and he was gone.

It's good to sit sometimes and wonder what would have happened if Duane had lived, but that's a hard thing to ponder. Who knows? There might not even still be a band. We could have gone on, but we might not have been what he was looking for. I could say that about anybody else in the band as well, because in this band, nobody is an island.

I'm pretty sure that my addictions would have torn us apart, or his addictions, or both. But I think after we got straight, it's possible we would have gotten back together. I don't believe we would have stayed together continuously for more than forty years, but I know we would have made some great music.

Everybody talks so highly of Duane because he's not with us anymore, and when people talk about him, all they remember is the good parts. Well, there were some shit parts to my brother as well. When he would wake up in the morning, his hair would be all over his head, and God help him if he ever got the damn flu. Nobody in the world had ever experienced a fever and feeling like shit but Howard Duane Allman. Nobody who had ever existed had ever had the shits and the barfs at the same time—nobody. "You don't know what it's like!" So we would just leave him alone. If Duane felt shitty, he wanted to make everybody else feel shitty too.

My brother was a Scorpio, through and through. When we were kids and went to the fair, there wasn't a ride he wouldn't get on. Good God, he was fearless. There was one ride called the Bullet, this thing that just went round and round, real fast. We were just little shavers, man, and I'm hollering, "Let me off this thing!" But my brother was just cackling. I knew I was going to die, but he was having the time of his life. Every time my grandma was around, she'd say, "That boy ain't going to live to see twenty-five."

Duane lived hard, fast, and on the edge, and if you ever heard any of his interviews, you could tell he had a little taste for speed. Somebody listening to my brother today might go, "That's just some fucked-up, crazy hippie." Wrong. He was so intelligent. It would be amazing to see what he would be into today.

When I got over being angry, I prayed to him to forgive me, and I realized that my brother had a blast. His footprints are so deep that he's still being talked about today. In 2003, *Rolling Stone* voted him the number two guitar player of all time, behind Hendrix. That made me feel all warm inside. I wish there was some way I could've shown him, but I know he knows.

Not that I got over it—I still ain't gotten over it. I don't know what getting over it means, really. I don't stand around crying anymore, but I think about him every day of my life.

It was my brother who got me through the first part of my life. Although he was only a year and eighteen days older than me, it seemed like he was much older than that. I looked at him like Merlin the Magician, because he had so much charisma. He had his weaknesses too, but I had the deepest, closest personal relationship with him I've ever had with anyone, because we went through heaven and hell together. Without him, there's no telling how I would have turned out.

I admired my brother so much when I was a kid that it turned into fear—fear of losing him, more than anything else. I was afraid that he would get out of school, he'd take off, and I'd never see him again. They ought to have a mandatory class in school to teach kids how to deal with loss, because sooner or later, somebody dear to them leaves this earth. Children just don't understand that, so they could tell them, "Look, your puppy is designed the way he is designed, and they just don't live very long," because kids don't know that. They want to know why their doggie died, and they don't understand that twelve years is a long time for a dog to live.

It took me a very long time to deal with grieving over anything. I didn't learn to grieve until my brother had been dead for ten years, maybe longer. Before I learned to grieve, every day, every single day I would relive his death. Playing seemed to be the only thing that helped, and being on the road. When we went home and I had nothing to do, my mind would start to run away with itself.

That's why I became addicted—to slow my fucking mind down. I can't stand it when shit gets overwhelming, when you've got this and that happening, and the phone is ringing—I can't deal with it. My brother's way of dealing with that was to just say, "Fuck it, fuck all of you," and he'd just cut. Not cut and run, he'd just cut. He figured out in his soul that life was much too precious to waste worrying about bullshit. That's why he walked out of Castle Heights—he wasn't going to take their shit.

Duane just refused to put up with anybody's shit, and he didn't dig any kind of violence. As for confrontations, they were real quick, and if they weren't quick, he'd just cut out of the situation. Now me, I couldn't do it the way he did. I didn't like confrontations. Of course, I knew confrontations were a part of life, but I wanted to keep them down to a dull roar. I could do them when I had to; I could face the fire, and I could fire a motherfucker.

Whether it was worrying about confrontation or something else, there was always too much happening in my mind. I would get into bed, and I'd have about nine different thoughts spinning all through my head. I would have ideas of how to cut costs for the band, ideas to make the routing of the tour easier. Then there were the pending disaster thoughts: the wondering why you're even bothering to plan shit, because you're going to die anyway. Thoughts of what was I going to do without him, what all of us going were to do without him.

The only thing that would stop these thoughts from racing through my head was heroin. Heroin would bring me some peace from my thoughts. Someone might question why I didn't go to see a psychologist, but fuck that—I could take a little shot of this powder up my nose and everything was all right. Better than all right, way better. The problem is, after a while, it stops working, and so you have to take more and more.

Maybe a lot of learning how to grieve was that I had to grow up a little bit and realize that death is part of life. Now I can talk to my brother in the morning, and he answers me at night. I've opened myself to his death and accepted it, and I think that's the grieving process at work. It's a matter of embracing it and not denying it—because there is no denying it. You're doing nothing but fooling yourself if you think you can put it out of your mind like it didn't happen. A lot of people do that, and they're successful at it for a while, but it usually comes crashing down around them.

I fully believe that there's more to it than just this life here on earth, and I've believed it for a very long time. Do I believe in reincarnation? After seeing Derek Trucks, how could I not? People ask me about Derek and my brother all the time, and I usually give them a little generic answer, because it's a pretty heavy question. But I have very good peripheral vision, and sometimes I'll catch him out of the corner of my eye, and the way he stands looks just like my brother.

Anybody who knows Derek Trucks will tell you that he would be the last one in line to be accused of trying to look like somebody else. Derek is Derek, man. He puts on a pair of Levi's and a T-shirt, plugs his guitar into the amp, and plays. That was my brother, man.

Duane used to make faces when he played—he made the damnedest faces sometimes. You could tell when it was getting good for him. Duane wouldn't have been very good at poker. Derek does it too—just a hint of it, but I catch it. I know when he's really trying and when he's on automatic pilot. I know what he's doing, because he does it in such a similar manner to someone else I knew.

AFTER MY BROTHER DIED, I KNEW I WAS GOING TO DO EXACTLY what he would have done had it been the other way around, and that was to say, "Let's go fucking play." I told the other guys that, in those exact words—"Let's go fucking play." And sure enough, we dove in that much harder.

We went back down to Criteria Studios in Miami to work on *Eat a Peach,* which we had started a couple of weeks before Duane's accident. I was so dinged out, and we were so fucked up. But we knew we had to get back in the studio, and we had to get back on the road, because keeping busy was the only way to avoid going crazy. I knew that, but that's about all I knew. We had to keep going, because I didn't want to think about my brother—or anything, for that matter.

I was looking pretty rough, man. I was weighing out at about 150 pounds, had a twenty-eight-inch waist, and I looked like a rail. I was eating but when something like that happens, food doesn't stick with you. We were taking vitamins, we had doctors coming over and sticking us in the ass with B_{12} shots every day. Little by little by little, we crawled back up to the point where we were standing erect.

We knew we had to finish off *Eat a Peach,* and we did a little work on it. We had already made the decision before Duane died to include "Mountain Jam" on the album, so any notion that we just used it to fill out the record is wrong. If you notice, "Mountain Jam" fades out on *At Fillmore East* and fades back in on *Eat a Peach,* which was what we had planned before Duane died.

We played a few gigs to road-test some tunes, then came back to Miami to finish the album. I remember walking into Studio D at Criteria—the one with the 110-year-old Steinway piano. I saw Tom Dowd, and I knew my purpose, and I knew I belonged there.

We all saw that playing music brought us out of the doldrums, and we actually smiled a little bit. The music brought life back to us all, and it was simultaneously realized by every one of us. We found strength, vitality, newness, reason, and belonging as we worked on finishing *Eat a Peach*.

That's when we cut "Melissa," which we had fucked around with quite a bit before; it was always too syrupy, so we'd just forget it. But I finally decided to cut it while I was on the plane heading down to Miami, and the finest guitar work I ever heard from Dickey Betts was on that song. Dickey brought in "Les Brers in A Minor," and while he had the lick, all us other guys filled in the rest of it for him.

I wrote most of "Ain't Wastin' Time No More" on that old Steinway in Criteria. I had had that lick for a while, and I remember Oakley saying, "Man, what is that little thing you keep playing?" Jaimoe said something about it too, because Jaimoe listens to everything I play—whether we're onstage or if I'm playing a piano in the dressing room, he listens to all of it. I had most of the music down before Duane died, and then the words came after he died. Most of it is about Duane, but some of it deals with people coming back from the war in Vietnam.

Those last three songs—"Ain't Wastin' Time," "Melissa," and "Les Brers"—they just kinda floated right on out of us. They proved that the music hadn't died with my brother. All of a sudden, the cat in the band who didn't play slide started playing it. That baffled the shit out of us, but he made it work. It was really amazing, and it gave us all a shot in the ass. The music was still good, it was still rich, and it still had that energy—it was still the Allman Brothers Band.

Fillmore Management

BILL GRAHAM'S INTRODUCTION OF THE ALLMAN BROTHERS BAND

JUNE 27, 1971

"The last few days, we have had the privilege of
working with this particular group. And in the
past year or so, we've had them on both coasts
a number of times. And in all that time, I've
never heard the kind of music that this group
plays. And last night, we had the good fortune
of having them get on stage about two-thirty,
three o'clock and they walked out of here seven
o'clock in the morning. And it's not that they
just played quantity, and for my amateur ears,
in all my life I've never heard the kind of music that this group plays---the finest contem-
porary music. We're going to round it off with
the best of them all, The Allman Brothers Band."

cheers -

Bill Graham

1548 Market Street, San Francisco, California 94102   415 863-2013

Oakley's last show, November 1972

CHAPTER TEN

"Who's Gonna Be Next?"

A<small>T THE TIME</small> D<small>UANE DIED, WE WERE ONE</small>. W<small>E WERE EQUAL IN</small> every aspect, we loved and respected one another, and we laughed all the time. The guys had just come back from rehab, and it was great that they had come back clean—or so we thought. We were over at my house, drinking some wine, and we had a lot to be happy for. We talked about the future, and we planned it out.

We had all been taken by surprise by what happened. It was like we were all swimming across the English Channel, and right when we could see the bank on the other side, we all had to turn around and swim back. For some of us, that was an impossible chore.

The truth is that Berry Oakley's life ended when my brother's life did. Never have I seen a man collapse like that, though I would never use the word "weak" when talking about Berry

Oakley. He just couldn't continue on without my brother. Maybe Duane was the brother he never had, but whatever it was, the loss of Duane was too much for him.

After Duane died, Berry would start each morning with a case of beer, and it went downhill from there. After the beer, he would start on the Jack Daniel's, and about halfway through the Jack, he was on his knees, man. I don't say this to be critical, but the man could not hold his liquor. Looking back on it now, it seems to me that Berry didn't know how to grieve. He didn't know how to get his pain out, so he just got loaded.

None of us knew what to do, because he wasn't playing like he used to—instead he'd hit maybe every fifth note. It's so odd how things happen. One of the main reasons that Joe Dan Petty was working in the band was so he could watch Oakley play, to help him get ready to go form his own band, Grinderswitch, which was a very good band that never really got off the ground, probably because they didn't want to take Walden's bullshit.

It got to the point where Berry would be so drunk that several times we had to have Joe Dan come in and play. One night at Winterland, we got booed pretty bad. B.B. King opened for us, and the people were yelling to bring B.B. back on, which was tough. That period of time was the closest me and Dickey have ever been, because we took turns caring for Oakley. We would take him out in the afternoon—go to the zoo or something to distract him—and Berry would say, "Let's go get a drink," and we'd tell him we'd get one in a bit, just trying to buy some time and space out his drinks.

We all really tried to pull Oakley out of his depression, but you only had so many tools to work with back then. Time and time again, I have sat and wondered, "God, what in the hell could I have done, what could have anybody have done, to help him?" There was just no getting through to him, because he would wake up on something—he'd be fucked up before we could get to him. You could get to Oakley's house at seven o'clock in the morning, and he'd already be fucked up.

This went on for a whole year, and I was just a fucking nervous wreck. My stomach was in knots; I developed a duodenal ulcer, which I beat because I stopped drinking scotch and Coke and started drinking scotch and milk. I got real frustrated with Oakley, and toward the end Dickey got real mad with him too; you could tell that the situation wasn't going to go anyplace but down. There wasn't going to be no miracle, nobody was going to fly in and tap him with some magic wand and make him all better. There wasn't any chance of taking him to rehab, of him going in there and getting serious about it.

Losing Duane really slammed Dickey too, but he didn't show it. We didn't see too much of Dickey after my brother died. He had this huge garden, and when something would piss him off, he would go out there and sling a hoe or a shovel or an ax for about four hours in the hot sun. He'd come back in for dinner, and he'd be okay. The cat really does have a heart, and I think he really cared about my brother—you don't go naming your child after someone that you don't care for.

When my brother died, Dickey really stepped up. He woodshedded like crazy; I remember him learning how to play the slide part for "Ain't Wastin' Time No More" on the airplane, during the flight down to Miami to finish up *Eat a Peach*. After Duane's death, Dickey was capable of handling things, but he would overdo it every time. He'd just want to get into a fistfight.

I can't say if I ever looked at Oakley and could see in his eyes that he was trying to die. I don't think he wanted to die; I just think he didn't want to live. I can tell you this—I've heard that when Oakley had his crash he drove his bike straight, headfirst into that bus, on purpose. Who knows? Either way, he was drunk when it happened. He got up after the crash, but he wouldn't get in the ambulance. He went home to the Big House and had a brain hemorrhage.

When Berry had his accident on November 11, 1972, I was in New York City, and my wife and I were planning to go to Jamaica. The phone rang, and it was Willie Perkins, our road manager. He said, "Gregory, are you all right? Well, listen. I don't want you to change any plans, just stay where you are, but Mr. Oakley has died." Willie told me, "Just take your tickets and keep on going—there ain't no sense in coming down here." Upset as I was, I kind of breathed a sigh of relief, because Berry's pain was finally over.

When I got back from Jamaica, you could feel the sadness all over town, because now it was two in a year. People were wondering, "Man, who's gonna be next?" I was also getting a vibe like "Where the fuck were you?" I would have been back down there in a heartbeat after getting that call from Willie, but he told me to keep on going to Jamaica. Also, after my brother's funeral, I told myself that the only other funeral I was going to attend, aside from my mother's, would be my own.

When *Eat a Peach* was released, it was the biggest thing for us yet. It shipped gold and it was our first album to hit the Top 10. We'd been through hell, but somehow we were rolling bigger than ever.

Apparently our success was also Macon's. Not only were the Allman Brothers getting bigger, but Macon was getting bigger. By 1972, people from all over the world were coming to Macon. Phil Walden was driving a white 1965 Silver Cloud Rolls-Royce; clearly, he was making all kinds of dough. There were clubs opening all over town. We used to go out to Sam's and watch

whoever was playing. I saw Lonnie Mack there one night, playing the dogshit out of his Flying V. I played with Dr. John there
for the first time. He had come to town for Duane's funeral and
then stayed for a few days.

When we wanted to get away from our old ladies, we'd head
on down to Grant's Lounge, which was a great place to hang out.
We saw a lot of bands, including Marshall Tucker, or Mother
Tucker, as we called them. Toy Caldwell was a good friend of
mine, but I wouldn't give you a nickel for the rest of them. Toy
Caldwell *was* Marshall Tucker—he made that band what it was.

They were a country band, and Wet Willie was R&B, but
somebody decided that any music coming out of Macon, Georgia, would be called "southern rock." That term has pretty much
died out, because people now realize that all those bands were
actually so different from one another.

In 1972, we spent more time at home and less time on the
road. The money was coming in, and that meant more time apart
for the band. I'm not saying that was the only reason, but it was
a big one. We didn't get together and jam like we used to. We
didn't have the cookouts that we used to always have. There were
too many women, and the roadies had roadies, and the money
just kept pouring in.

That year we were finally headliners—our days of opening
for somebody else were over. Opening for other people didn't
bother me that much, because just being on the same bill with
Ike and Tina Turner or Buddy Guy meant a lot. In 1972, we had
a lot of the Capricorn bands that Phil had brought to Macon
opening for us—Eric Quincy Tate, Wet Willie, Dr. John, Alex
Taylor, Captain Beyond, and Cowboy—and it was a very good
thing for everybody. There ain't but one Allman Brothers, and
there ain't but one Marshall Tucker. There ain't but one of any
of those bands, so we weren't worried about them stealing our

thunder or whatever. I would imagine that Lynyrd Skynyrd had more hits than anybody else, but they sure ended up appealing to a real redneck bunch of folks.

For some reason, people think that we all grew up together and we all knew each other, and our friends were their friends and their friends were our friends, like there was one big town of southern rock stars or something. Man, it wasn't nothing like that at all. You might know two or three cats in one band here and there, and you'd see each other passing in the night. If you did a tour together, then you'd see each other maybe a couple of hours a day.

Of course, there was some competition between bands—there has to be. But we weren't out there to sell southern rock, we were out there because we had the best goddamn band in the land. The Allman Brothers Band has had its bad nights, but we are some Super Bowl motherfuckers compared to all them other bands.

In the summer of '72, we started rehearsals for what would become *Brothers and Sisters*. Early on in those sessions, I brought in a song I had written the beginnings of called "Queen of Hearts." It took me a year and a half to finish it, and it's one of my favorite songs that I have ever written. I had the basic frame of the song; it was in 11/4, like the intro to "Whipping Post."

I brought the song to the band during a rehearsal, and because I was a drunk—and nobody listens to a drunk—they turned it down without even really listening to it. I felt like I was begging, and, after all, I was the guy who brought them "Whipping Post" and "Midnight Rider."

"Listen," I said, "why don't we at least try it? The worst thing that can happen is it will be so bad we'll all have a real good laugh."

But the guys were firm: "No, man."

When I asked why, they told me, "Because that song just ain't saying nothing."

Boy, those were the best words they could have ever said to me. You might even say my solo career started right there. I waited until that rehearsal was over, and then I headed into Capricorn Studios by myself. I tried to be on both sides of the glass at the same time, and I did two sessions back-to-back. One was forty-two hours, and after I got about six hours of sleep, I went back and did another twenty-eight-hour session.

I was mentally and physically exhausted, and I had the beginnings of two songs that did nothing for me whatsoever. There was this big round metal trash can in there, so I took those big old twenty-four-track tapes and threw them in that damn can and poured lighter fluid all over them.

I heard the door open, and in walked Johnny Sandlin, of all people.

"What are you doing there?" he asked. "You're trying to be on both sides of the glass at the same time, aren't you?"

"Well, yeah, I am," I replied.

"I got an idea. Why don't you let me help you with this, and we'll start all over again, like nothing's happened. We'll get this damn thing cut, and it'll be your first solo record, your baby."

He asked me what I had, and I played him the Jackson Browne song "These Days."

"Man," he said. "I sure can hear a pedal steel guitar in there."

"Yeah, but it'll sound country as shit," I said.

"Well, not if somebody can play it and have it not sound country—and I know just the guy, and you know him too." It was Scott Boyer, and sure enough, Johnny called him, and he came down, and Scott did great. He played this four-pedal Gibson steel guitar, and he did an amazing job.

When I wasn't in the studio, I was going back and forth to New York, seeing Deering. He had already introduced me to Abdul Mati

Klarwein. Mati, as everyone called him, was a soft-spoken Israeli guy who lived in New York, and he looked exactly like Charlton Heston. He'd painted the covers to *Bitches Brew* and *Live-Evil* by Miles Davis. (That thing with the curlers and the frog feet on the back of *Live-Evil?* It's J. Edgar Hoover.)

I called Deering and said, "Man, do you think you can get Mati to paint an album cover for me?"

"Yeah, for the right amount of money you can get anything done," he said.

"Well, the question is, what do you think he'd charge me?"

"I don't know, man," Deering said. "I know he really enjoys your company. Why don't you ask him, because you'll probably get better results."

So I called Mati, and he said, "Do you have time to come sit for it?"

I told him, "No, but I have a photograph you can use." I sent it to him, and he used that. I loved that cover; I thought it turned out perfect. It cost me $1,500 back then, but today it would be like $50,000, maybe even $150,000.

Not long after I'd started work on my album, Deering decided he wanted to get in on it. Early on, before Oakley died, I had done some demos—including "Multi-Colored Lady"—down at Criteria in Miami as kind of a warm-up thing. Oakley had been there with me, and so had Deering. Deering had some experience with Hendrix; not a hands-on-the-board thing, but he was interested in what I was doing. This is a guy who inherited a rather large sum of money, who went to some fine schools, is very well-read, and has been all around the world. He's seen it all, man—he's seen a monkey fuck a football! It might be true that "work" is just a four-letter word to Deering, but he really wanted to be involved. He told me, "Just put me down as the producer, and I'll put up the

Onstage with Dickey, early 1970s.

Backstage in New
Orleans with my
brother's SG.

Another town, another show…

Stringing up my acoustic guitar, 1973.

A preshow chat with Butchie.

After my brother died, I started playing electric guitar onstage.

Talking over an arrangement with Butch, Chuck, and Dickey.

Riding high
with my
dear friend
Chank
Middleton,
mid-1970s.

In the studio with Phil Walden, president of Capricorn Records.

Some *Eat a Peach* artwork on my Leslie, summer 1974.

Preshow ritual, mid-1970s.

The entire band with Governor Jimmy Carter at our Providence,
Rhode Island, benefit show that helped keep his campaign alive,
November 1975.

Dickey showing me his
custom-made guitar.

Working on some chops with
my Strat.

Hangin' around with Cher in Beverly Hills.

My musical brother Jaimoe is a unique drummer and a wonderful human being.

Bill Graham at the annual Capricorn Records picnic in Macon.

With our longtime booking agent, Jonny Podell

Going nowhere fast with Cher.

The reunited Allman Brothers Band, 1980

At the B3 with the re-formed band.

Bill Graham shares my B3
bench at the Crackdown
benefit in New York City,
1986.

The Gregg Allman Band, 1987.

Floyd Miles, who I'm forever indebted to for bringing me and Duane across the tracks and introducing us to the blues.

With Allen Woody, one of the funniest people I've ever known.

At the Rock and Roll Hall of Fame induction ceremony with Dickey; Jaimoe; Butch; my niece, Galadrielle; and Berry Oakley's children, Berry and Brittany.

The three-headed rhythm monster *(from left to right):* Marc Quiñones, Jaimoe, and Butch.

Words of wisdom from my mentor and longtime producer, Tommy Dowd.

Dickey and I harmonize on "Midnight Rider," 1995.

The young'uns: guitarist Derek Trucks and bassist Oteil Burbridge at the Beacon Theatre.

With Derek at our return to Piedmont Park in 2007. Pretty cool that he's wearing a shirt with my brother on it from Piedmont Park in 1969.

This is what eighty thousand people look like from the stage—Bonnaroo Music Festival in Tennessee, 2005.

To honor my brother, Eric Clapton sat in with the Allman Brothers during our fortieth anniversary celebration at the Beacon Theatre.

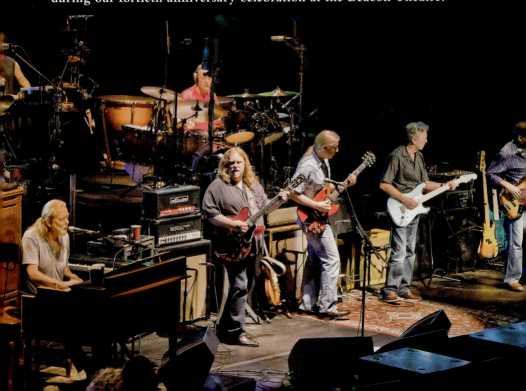

Having a laugh with Warren Haynes, a man I truly enjoy writing songs with.

With my solo band, supporting the *Low Country Blues* album.

Accepting the Lifetime Achievement Grammy for the Allman Brothers Band, February 2012.

With Chank and my manager, Michael Lehman, at the Big House Museum, 2011.

Standing in front of the Big House Museum, a place that I'm truly proud of.

dough for it," so I wouldn't have to fuck with Capricorn. We got a few rough demos down, but then the Brothers started rehearsing again for *Brothers and Sisters,* so I shelved the demos until I had time to get started again in Macon.

I decided that I wanted to call my album *Laid Back.* "Laid back" is a studio term, and to me, it's what you needed when a song is in the right tempo, but it has too much energy to it. What I would always say was "Man, can you make it just a little bit more laid back?" Just a little easier, you know—pull a little of the insanity out of it. I've always pictured it this way: go at it as if you were Mr. Natural, that R. Crumb character. Mr. Natural's feet always got to where he was going before his head did, so "laid back" means don't dive in there headfirst. When I got the guys together who were going to play on my record, I told them to picture a Freak Brother, and they laughed for about half an hour, but they got it.

I got some good players on that record: Bill Stewart on drums, Chuck Leavell on keyboards, Scott Boyer and Tommy Talton on guitar, and Charlie Hayward on bass, who plays with Charlie Daniels, plus Jaimoe, who overdubbed some congas later. I got these guys together and we went to work. Johnny would ask me, "What do you want to hear?" and if I needed something, Johnny would get it for me if I didn't already know where to get it.

He got Scott to play steel on "These Days," and he helped make "Midnight Rider" sound a lot different than the version that was on *Idlewild South.* I told him that I wanted it to sound real swampy, with the image of moss hanging off the trees, alligators and fog, darkness, witches, and shit. That's what I told Johnny, and we took it to the swamp, man.

I did all the harmony work on "All My Friends," the Scott Boyer song we cut. I've always loved the Everly Brothers style of harmony, but I didn't want it to just follow the traditional 1–3–5 pattern. If you listen real close to "All My Friends," that's what made the song what it is, and the same goes for "These Days"—I got those harmonies on that one too.

The Brothers were working on *Brothers and Sisters* at the same time I was cutting *Laid Back,* and it was great flip-flopping back and forth between the two sessions; it was like the guy who has a girlfriend across town so as to keep his marriage together. The wife knows, but then again she don't. She wouldn't admit it, but she knows that if it wasn't for that girl across town, she might lose her man.

With that in mind, *Laid Back* was my mistress; it was my baby across town. It didn't make the other guys happy, because it slowed down the recording process of *Brothers and Sisters,* but making that record was something I needed to do at that moment. And it came out just fine. I wish it could have been longer, because it only had eight songs, but in the end I was really proud of that record, and it took off. As soon as it came out, it got good reviews and went right up the charts. The rest of the band didn't really say anything to me about it, but I could tell that they felt the record interfered with what we were doing as a group. It was one of the first times that I felt a hint of what was to come; to this day, I don't know if Dickey Betts has ever heard it.

Ever since that record was released in 1973, I've had a band on the side. In one band, you're the total leader. You put the band together, and you've got the full run of it. If you're like me, you stay open-minded, and if somebody's got an idea that they want to interject, you encourage it. That's how I am—I never tell the guys in my band to play this or that. If we're doing an Allman Brothers song, it has to be totally rearranged, and I don't think there's going to be much more of that.

After *Laid Back* came out, I decided to go out on the road with that band, plus a full string orchestra. That was a dream I had had for a very long time; I had always had this thing about going out with a big band, like Joe Cocker's Mad Dogs and Englishmen, except with a string section. I knew it was going to be a lot of people and the payroll was going to be atrocious, and I knew we weren't going to make any money, so I decided to record it.

Young whippersnapper that I was, I really wanted to pull it off. We got people from the New York Philharmonic to go out with us; three cellos, six violins, and seven violas. Half of them were men, half were women. At the end of the tour, which lasted about a month, they got a big book, they took one page a piece, and they all wrote something on it and put their picture in there. None of those string players had ever been on a rock and roll tour before, and the girls were crying, because they'd had the time of their lives.

We played only theaters on that tour, real upscale places, because I wanted the best sound quality possible. You can't put that kind of instrumentation in an arena and expect to hear anything. We played Carnegie Hall, and we did the longest sound check I can ever remember, but I wanted the sound to be just right. That place was built for the spoken word, so I told Red Dog to go up to the very top row in the balcony, while I stood in the exact middle of the stage. I whispered my social security number, and he heard every number in it. That's when I knew we had to have the sound absolutely perfect. We made it work, man, and it sounded great. Anybody who was coming to see the Allman Brothers might as well have left, because there wasn't any of that at all.

I was really pleased with how the tour went. Some nights were better than others, but they were all good. I remember we played the Capitol Theatre in Passaic, New Jersey, and we burnt that fucker down. The only thing I was unhappy about was me—I wasn't pleased with my singing. The change from the Allman Brothers to that band was more than I realized. There were times when I would be singing way too loud, and it took me a while to adjust. Everybody had a real good time, they all got paid very well, and after good sales of the *Gregg Allman Tour* album, we made money.

WHILE EVERYTHING HAD BEEN GOING ON WITH *LAID BACK*, OVER with the Allman Brothers we were wondering what we were going to do about getting a new bass player. Unlike after Duane's death, when Oakley died there was no question that we were going to keep going. Jaimoe stepped in and said that he had a guy, his friend Lamar Williams. We didn't really have what you would call an audition. Lamar came and played for us. That was it. Within two weeks we were playing shows again, and we got back in the studio to work on *Brothers and Sisters*. We had already cut "Wasted Words" and "Ramblin' Man" with Oakley, but after Lamar laid it down on "Come and Go Blues," the rest of the album just flowed, man.

I really liked Lamar Williams. He was a nice guy, and we had a very nice relationship. He and Jaimoe were old-time friends because they grew up in the same town, so they hung together all the time. Lamar was a good addition to the band. It was a shame what that Agent Orange shit did to him when he was over in Vietnam—he was only thirty-four when he died from lung cancer a few years later.

Chuck Leavell was another addition who came on board for *Brothers and Sisters*. Chuck had come through town with Dr. John, and after they parted ways, Chuck stayed in Macon. He was hanging around the studio, and he certainly looked the part, but when I heard him play, I knew he was there for a reason. I got him to play keyboards on the whole *Laid Back* record, and he did so well, in addition to being easy to work with. You'd show him something one time and that was it. He'd give you exactly what you wanted, without any questions, and if he embellished on a song, he made it even better. His piano playing was so rich and so good, and it fit perfectly on all the songs.

As we were finishing up the recording on *Laid Back* and the Brothers were getting ready to start laying down *Brothers and Sisters,* I introduced Chuck to the other guys in the band. After *Eat a Peach,* we needed something, and adding keyboards was the right thing to do. He started jamming with us, and everybody liked him right away—especially Oakley, who really took Chuck under his wing for the brief time they played together.

It did take a little while for Dickey to warm up to Chuck. Dickey has that country blood in him, and at first he looked at Chuck kinda funny and would call him "Chopin" or something like that. At the same time, it took some of the load off Dickey as the only guitar player, so he came around pretty fast. Musically, I think Chuck added a lot to the band. He put a little bit of a different sound to things, which was just what we needed.

I wrote fewer songs on *Brothers and Sisters,* and Dickey wrote more, because this is when he started acting like he was the five-star general of the Allman Brothers Band. I was acting like I was a member of the band, which is what I am today. I'm a member of the Allman Brothers Band, and although I'm president of the company, I remain one of the players who tries to make things sound better.

Dickey came to the sessions with songs in hand and just jumped right in, whereas I didn't arrive with much. For some reason, Dickey was upset that more of my songs had been used on the previous records. Well, no shit; that's how it had been since we started the band. I don't know, maybe he had been trying to write since the Second Coming. So he was determined to get his songs on *Brothers and Sisters,* and by that time I was real tired. I was real strung out, and I'd been getting more into alcohol, which was starting to replace narcotics because I was getting tired of chasing that fucking bag.

Meanwhile, Dickey was becoming more serious about his writing; every day, he wrote. At three o'clock every afternoon, he'd sit down and write. I don't write like that, I write when it comes to me. We just had very different approaches that didn't mesh well. He and I did try to write together one time, but it really didn't work.

In songwriting, the first thing that you write down is usually what you want. Dickey would change everything. In our attempt to write songs together, I could have written, "A rose by any other name . . ." and he'd want to change it. "'By any other name, a rose.' No, that doesn't work," and he'd try something else. Then he'd say, "Fuck it. I'm just fucking up your song, man. I'll go away."

About fifteen minutes, a shot of Jack, and a beer later, he'd be knocking on my door again. "Hey, man, how's that song going? Listen, I had an idea. Dig it—if you take this and put it down here, and this over there. Oh, no, that wouldn't match with that."

I'd say, "Why don't you read it like it's written down?" Which should have been the first thing he did.

He'd say, "Well, you know, if you had this line here, and this much of that line up here . . . Oh, I'm fucking up your song again. Fuck this, good night," and he'd leave.

Another half an hour and half a gram later, he'd be back, but I wouldn't even answer the door. So that's why you don't see anything written by Allman/Betts, with the exception of "One More Ride"—we wrote that one during the *Idlewild South* sessions, when we really didn't know each other, and we never really finished it, so there you go.

When something goes wrong or starts to get weird, you try to nip it in the bud. After seeing how he wrote, I thought that maybe Dickey hadn't written before. Then he wrote a couple of instrumentals, and here comes "Ramblin' Man." The son of a bitch goes to No. 2 on the charts, while *Brothers and Sisters* gets to No. 1, our only No. 1 album. Suddenly in his mind he was a seasoned writer, way more experienced than myself. He was then ready to write the rest of the songs for the Allman Brothers for the duration of the band's existence.

There was no power struggle or anything like that. He stood up, whereas I sat down. It's hard to be a frontman when you're sitting behind a 460-pound organ. Up until then, we'd never really had a frontman; Dickey took it upon himself to create that role.

Without Duane and without Berry, there needed to be a leader in the band, and the question that has been asked for years is why didn't I take it? Well, the answer is because the first thing I would have done is fire Dickey and get another guitar player. When I think of the time and money he wasted in the studio and during rehearsal—I mean, there are twenty-nine takes of "Les Brers," and we used the second one. We must have been pretty attached as a band to take that crap from him for so long before we finally said, "Hey, man, you're out of here."

Right before *Brothers and Sisters* came out, we played the festival at Watkins Glen with the Band and the Grateful Dead, in front of six hundred thousand people—the biggest show in history to that point. People always talk about Woodstock. Watkins Glen was like three Woodstocks. I think actually it might've been a little too big. They should have had people all the way around the raceway, and maybe had the stage in the center revolving real slowly, do a revolution in a minute. That's not that complicated.

A show like Watkins Glen was uncomfortable, because you know that you're getting the show across to this many people, but you still got two times that many behind them. You could finish a song, take your guitar off, put it in the case, and latch it up before the last guy heard the last note. Sound ain't all that fast, not compared to light.

When you're playing in that situation, you're kind of thinking about the end. Not that you're wishing it to be over, but you can't even hear yourself—that was back before we had the in-ear monitors. Everything was so loud. You just walk out there and start to wince before you even start playing. It's hard to get any kind of coziness, any kind of feel with the audience.

I guess there's something about that many people seeing you all at once that's real nice, but it's just too much. You're just like a little squeak in the middle of a bomb going off. But it was interesting, and it was a pretty fun day. People were OD'ing all over the place. And of course, Uncle Bill was there, which cured everything. It was exciting to be there and see it—and to be able to make 'em stand up, now that was something else.

THURS., NOV. 1st at 8 P.M.

JERRY WEINTRAUB Presents

THE ALLMAN BROTHERS BAND

CHICAGO STADIUM

1800 West Madison - Chicago, Ill. 60612 - (312) 733-5300

Tickets: $6.50, $5.50, $4.50 | Tickets available only at stadium box office, on sale starting 9 a.m. Saturday, Oct. 28th.

Layin' back, 1973

CHAPTER ELEVEN

Multi-Colored Ladies

Most of my good friends call me Gregory, but my mother still calls me Gregg—and I hate it. To me, the name "Gregg" sounds like a brand name for a product, especially put with "Allman." Gregory, which is my real name, that's all right. To this day, you can tell my good friends, because they always call me Gregory.

I always listen real hard to what people say to me, because if you listen hard enough, you can tell what they're really saying. People will tell on themselves if they're trying to blow some smoke up your ass. Not that I look for that all the time, but I've always picked and chosen my friends wisely. Now, when I was drunk, shit, I'd talk to anybody. But since I became sober, I've been more careful.

Considering all the people I've come in contact with over the years, you would think that I would have developed a lot more good relationships than I have. Some friends genuinely like me for who I am, and if both my hands got cut off tomorrow and I couldn't sing again, they would still like me. Then there are the ones who show me off, and I can tell it just by looking at them. Like if I'm sitting there talking to them and the phone rings, they say, "Hey, I'm sitting here with Gregg Allman." Wait a minute—they didn't have to say that. They did that for themselves.

When you're in a band with someone, being their friend changes things. I have a relationship with most of the people in the Allman Brothers, and I have friendships, and they might not be outstanding, but they're okay. I've never really been tied at the hip with any of my bandmates. In the old days, Oakley was always with Duane. Where Oakley was, Duane was, and where Duane was, Oakley was. I thought it was kind of strange, but they were just like that—and at the same time, they were my cheerleaders. They would come and tell me how great my songs were, and other than Jaimoe, no one else said too much. They made me feel like I belonged, and they made me feel loved.

I think I know how to be a good friend, because I really work at it. Many, many times I've gone out of my way for people, and I still help people on a regular basis. Like my good friend Floyd Miles, who turned me on to rhythm and blues and good soul-moving music. Watching him night after night, I kinda got the idea that that was what I wanted to do. Because of that, he's now one of the members of my band, and when we're not playing, I still pay him. His knees are just about gone, and his wife is on disability, so I try to help them out by picking up their house note. I do think I make a pretty good friend.

I was married and divorced three times by age thirty, and looking back, I think I was trying to find a friend, even if I had to marry one. And that's how I spent a lot of the early '70s: chasing that feeling of friendship into marriage. I had a male friend in Chank, and I had the guys in the Brothers. I had everything I wanted, and that's all well and good, but have you been to Jamaica by yourself? It's not much fun. Even having a tricked-out motorcycle—one you can ride alone and turn a bunch of heads with—isn't enough to make you forget that that's not what life's all about. It's supposed to be you and somebody else, both cruising down the road, enjoying the ride together.

The thing is, I really love women. I always have. I think there's nothing more beautiful than the naked female human body. Nothing else compares to that, and that's the way it should be. The guys from the band back then would all say that I was such a pussy hound, and such a cocksman. My nickname was "Coyotus Maximus," which Kim Payne gave to me. Sometimes after a gig, I would have women in four or five different rooms. Mind you, I wouldn't lie to anybody; I'd just say, "I'll be right back." Lord have mercy, if I had a twenty-dollar bill for every time I told a woman, "I'll be right back!"

I know some people have said that the Allman Brothers got the best-looking women out on the road, but I don't know if that's true. We might have just been a little more picky, you know? It's like that old joke: What's the difference between a pig and a musician? A pig won't fuck a musician.

We did have some lookers, man. I thought we were doing just fine. As far as foxy ladies, there was oodles of them. The hippie days were part of it—that's the way things were back then, free love and all that. And the band had a bit to do with it too: we were different, we had the cute little accents. So for our success level, I think we probably had a little more than our share.

Back then, of course, we didn't have AIDS. I had gonorrhea once, but I never had syphilis, thank goodness. We all had crabs from having sex, but none of us ever had any head lice or body lice—that comes from not taking a bath. I feel bad for the kids today. It was a much easier time back then, in a lot of ways. There wasn't road rage, people weren't carrying guns all the time, and pot dealers wouldn't shoot you.

Women to me weren't something to conquer; it was more of a privilege to be with them. Sometimes, right in the middle of the whole throes, I would think, "My goodness, look at this pretty baby," and I would wonder how I came to get something like her. I would think, "Man, this is too good—what have I done to deserve all this?" To get women, I didn't have to play any role; I just had to play music. That's why I didn't think any of them were serious, because like I said, I didn't get laid until I bought a guitar and played it.

For a time there, I was with at least three different women a week—at least three. They were wonderful, and I thank you, ladies. I liked the variety, and they say it's the spice of life, but after a while that got old. Those crazed first few years with the Brothers gave way to a stretch of time where I felt like I should try to settle down. I went from sowing wild oats to looking for the right one. The thing is, you can't go out there and look for the right one, because all you'll find is the wrong thing, and it will do nothing but hurt you. I learned that the hard way—a few times.

I met my first wife, Shelley, in the summer of 1971 in San Antonio, where she worked for a local promoter. Boy, my brother couldn't stand her—he hated her guts. When I told him that Shelley and I were going to get married, he asked me, "Man, what in the hell do you think you're doing?" I said, "Well, that's really none of your damn business," and he said, "Boy, it sure ain't, and I'm sure glad."

Sure enough, he was right. When I went to Jamaica after Duane's funeral, it was to get away from the madness, but it was also to get away from Shelley. She actually missed the funeral because she was too messed up. That was just one of the problems, though. In the end, the only good thing that came out of it was my son Devon. That marriage turned into a living hell, and it didn't last very long.

Every woman I've ever had a relationship with has loved me for who they thought I was. Maybe they were in love with whatever was onstage, but when the lights are out and the sound goes off, you're left with this dude, and that's me. Obviously, that's the person they didn't get to know, and that certainly was the case with Shelley. She loved me for what she thought I was, and as soon as that knot was tied, she started to try to change me.

I've always wondered why women just don't go down the aisle and pick the model they want. If they want some pussy-whipped whiner who just doles out the money, then go to that aisle. I'm in the "I ain't changing for no one" aisle. Of course, everybody gets older and set in their ways, but I'd really like to think that I have an open mind, because I know I do musically.

In 1972, I met a girl named Jenny Arness when I was in New York. Deering Howe's girlfriend introduced us. She told me, "I have a good friend that I'd like you to meet, and as a matter of fact, she's Marshal Matt Dillon's daughter—you know, the guy from *Gunsmoke*. She's very pretty, very nice, and I'll hook you up on a blind date."

We went out, and she was all right, but the woman really was crazy. I'm sorry to talk about the dead that way, but it's true. She did a lot of blow, and then started giving excuses for why she was doing it. That would drive me nuts, man. I don't know if she was in awe of me or if she thought she had to prove herself.

We weren't together very long—we weren't even really together. She went to Miami with me, when we went down there to finish *Eat a Peach,* and Deering had come down to add some moral support. We were staying at the Thunderbird Motor Lodge in North Miami Beach, and while we were there, one day Aretha Franklin came walking through carrying a five-gallon jug of pickled pigs' feet and wearing a mink coat. She dropped that jug on the tile floor and it busted all over the place. She just kept on truckin', though.

Once I went out to Jenny's father's ranch. As a matter of fact, we did a photo shoot out there, but I have no idea why. We looked like death. It was really horrendous. But I really liked James Arness a lot. One night, I sat in his living room, and he would name off the songs that he loved, and if I knew one I'd pick it for him. He sat there, and I lulled him off to sleep. I played Marshal Matt Dillon to sleep. How about that?

It didn't take long to see that me and Jenny weren't going any- where. I tried my best to let her down easy. I tried to be Henry Kissinger; I tried the most diplomatic way I knew to cut off this thing with her, because we really didn't have a thing. We didn't have any plans for the future, we weren't going to get married, we weren't even in love. The next thing I knew, I was getting information that she had swallowed forty or fifty Tuinals and killed herself.

A friend of hers called me and said, "You son of a bitch," blaming it all on me. Then the phone rang again, and it was James Arness.

He said, "Mr. Allman, don't listen to any of that crap. She committed suicide. I found her, and I found the note that had your name in it. I'm really sorry that these people are calling you and bugging you to come out here for the funeral. I knew how it stood between you and her, and I think I'm right in telling you that you don't have to attend. You will not offend me, sir."

"Thank you, sir. You are such a gentleman," I told him.

"Well, you are too. There ought to be more like you." He went on to tell me that she had tried it before, so I don't think it was all about me. It was nice of him, but I was still really upset about what happened. The last thing I ever wanted was for anyone to hurt themselves.

NONE OF MY MARRIAGES HAVE LASTED VERY LONG—THE LAST ONE was the longest, which was about ten years. Before that, the longest I had ever been married was to Cher, which was for a little over three years. That's about the average—three years—but I don't know why that is. I don't think I make bad choices.

I would say that with four out of six of 'em, everything was cool until we got married. We'd be together for a while and it would be the epitome of being in love—going on picnics and all those sappy, romantic, movie-type things.

But eventually they would start talking about getting married. I would say something like "We both really enjoy each other's presence, and now you—not me—you want to go downtown and have some guy with a big gold badge on say, 'All right, you guys are legally in love now. You've got a contract.' And you want to do that so fast and so quick that I asked you to sign a prenuptial paper and you signed it, just like that? I know you're not after my money, so what's the deal?"

And they didn't seem to have an answer. But sure enough, after we got married, within six months things started going downhill.

I can't tell you the number of nights I wondered where some of my wives were. One time, one of them took off for seven days, and I didn't sleep a single night. Do you know what that does to your brain? You become crazy, man. I cried and cried, and then I stopped crying. Then it was over and the pain was gone. It was a painful lesson, but it was over, and she was out of my life.

While I was working on *Laid Back,* I met a woman named

Janice Blair who had just moved to Macon after a divorce. Her father was there, and he was kind of a jack-of-all-trades—he had some furniture stores, he owned a limousine company. She met one of the apprentices from Capricorn Studios and when I saw her, whew, it just clicked. So I showed off as much as I could.

I had this Triumph motorcycle, and I was out driving it one night after I got out of the studio at about three thirty, four o'clock in the morning. I knew where her house was, and I pulled up to the phone booth outside and called her. I said, "Listen, I was just in the neighborhood and I wondered if you'd like to go for a ride."

She said, "Turn that thing off," because she could hear it out her window.

I said, "Oh, I'm sorry. I get used to the sound." I was hoping like hell it would wake her up.

She said, "Just let me throw on something and I'll be out in a minute." So she came out and, man, she saw that bike and how could she not take a ride? Next thing you know, she's got on her cowboy boots.

Janice was so gorgeous, and I was completely in love. I just worshipped that woman. She's the one on the *Laid Back* sleeve, riding a horse I'd bought her not too long after I met her. We got married in 1973 and started living together in an apartment in Macon. Just like the others, though, it didn't last.

The problems were always the same. They would come to the gig and I would think, "Man, they must be really loving my music," until one night I watched one of 'em. Sometimes in the wings of the stage, there are chairs set up, with a tape line in front that you can't cross. One of them would get a little chair there every night and she would be watching me; when I would lift my head up to sing, well, of course you look at the audience. I'm not gonna lie to you; I'd look at some pretty women. The day you stop looking, there's something wrong with you.

Backstage at halftime, she started reading it off to me: "Yeah, I saw you looking at that bitch!"

A couple of times I had to have that one removed. She was beautiful too, but she got a whiff of that cocaine, and that was the end-all, be-all. I can't say as I turned her on to it. It was just there, around.

I took her out on the road once and she stole a whole ounce from the head roadie. She went and got a key from him by saying, "I'm Mrs. Allman; I have to go in there and get some papers for him." She went in there, and while he was sleeping—I wish to God he'd woken up, but he didn't—she grabbed a whole ounce of blow out from under his bed and took off.

I guess in the hall she did a couple of big whacks, and when she got back to the room she said, "Look, honey, look what I got!"

"Where in the fuck did you get that?" I asked.

"Oh, that don't matter" was all she said back. I'd seen her pal up to this roadie, and she was a coke whore, so I didn't think too much of it. But after the truth got out the shit hit the fan, and I sent her off the tour.

I'm telling you, some crazy shit has happened during my marriages. One day, I came home off the road, put the key in the door, and opened it up. I noticed that my one and only plaque was gone. It wasn't even a gold record, just a piece of press that was so good I'd had it laminated, framed, and hung above the fireplace. I thought "Oh shit, we've been evicted while I was gone and she hadn't gotten to me to tell me, and now I'm breaking into these people's house." I could hear the bedsprings going, and I thought, "Not only am I breaking into somebody else's house, but they're in there fucking." Then I heard this little sound that I recognized, and I went, "Oh no, this only happens in the movies."

This was a strangely set-up apartment; it was an old Victorian manor that had been changed into three or four different apartments, which they did a lot of down south. I heard another little guttural sound that I recognized, and I just walked on into the bedroom. Not only was she fucking somebody else, doggie style, but it was a musician friend of mine.

"What's the deal now?" I said.

He turned around and said, "Listen, Gregory, we've been friends for a long time; don't be walking in on me when I'm taking care of business."

"Man, I got some seriously bad news for you," I said, and I held up the key. "I didn't walk in on you, this is my place." He had no idea; that's why that picture was gone.

He looked back around at her and said, "You fucking bitch." He got up and ran into the kitchen, and she got up and ran into the bathroom. I'm left standing there, and all I can think about is getting the fuck out. He came back, with his naked ass, knelt down in front of me, gave me the biggest butcher knife from our kitchen, and said, "Put it right there."

"Man, get up and cover that shit up," I told him. "I don't wanna look at it. Maybe she does, but I don't."

Then he starts crying, so now I'm trying to console him because he's crying—he put a lot of stock and trust in friendship and stuff like that. I had off my shoes and socks, and my shirt was off, so all I had on was these white Levi's. I hadn't seen my wife since she'd run into the bathroom, but as I came out of the kitchen, I looked under the bathroom door and there was blood just rolling out. She had slashed her wrists, and on the way down she'd locked the door.

I busted down the door and it was a fucking mess. I had blood in my hair, I had blood all over me. I called the hospital and prayed to God she wouldn't die. They came and got her, took her to a hospital that was pretty much right out back behind my house. I went back to console this guy and found Chank. I had called him and he arrived, and of course he made everything a little bit better; he always does.

Bad as that whole scene was, it wasn't even the weirdest thing that's happened with one of my wives. One morning I woke up and my wife at the time said, "Honey, let's go shopping. I think you need to get some new stuff, some new boots, what have you."

I thought, "Aw shit, she ain't been nice like that to me in a while," so I went and got showered, shaved, and all that. She already had my boots shined and everything. We go outside, and it turned out she'd called a limo. I get in the limo and the window goes down by itself, and I thought, "What the hell is this?" This white sleeve comes in the window, and bang, hits me with a needle. And I was out.

When I woke up, I was getting loaded onto a Learjet. Here come that sleeve again with a needle one more time—bam, I'm out again. I wake up and we're in a three-passenger jet. I could see the runway as we were coming into Macon. We landed and I thought, "What the hell's wrong?" My head hurt. Here come that damn sleeve again and I said, "Wait, wait."

Bang. Out.

The next time I woke up, I was in a room that had a cot with a skinny little mattress on it. I didn't know what they'd been shooting in me, but I had to hold on to the damn thing because I was going round and round. This big, huge linebacker-looking black man with big gold teeth was turning the key and locking us in. He looked over at me.

"You might've been free out there to do whatever, but your ass is mine now."

I laid there and there's a big sign that says, "Do not give sharp objects or laces or matches to the patients."

"If you don't mind, my man, what's your name?" I asked.

He told me his name and then said, "You in the big house."

"Wait a minute now, the big house is a prison."

"Well, you in the biggest nuthouse in Macon, Georgia—don't be trying to get out 'cause I'll catch you."

"Hey, why would I wanna leave here?" At least I knew I was in Macon.

Then he said, "If you want your wallet, I've got it." That was good—it meant I had all my phone numbers to all my friends. I called Johnny Sandlin and asked him to help me out. I made an appointment with the house doctor, and his name was Dr. Sykes. Dr. Sykes in the psych ward! I kept thinking, "This is all a fucking practical joke. Okay, you got me, now could you end it?"

I went down to see him, and they patted me all down and I said, "Dr. Sykes, could somebody tell me why I'm in here?"

It turned out that my wife had apparently put out a 643, or something like that, on me. That's when a spouse can lock the other one up for eight days if there's reason to think that spouse is crazy. At the time I had no idea why my wife did this. Later, I heard she had a dude across town and she wanted to roll with it, baby—I guess she just needed me out of the way for a few days at least, and this was the best she could come up with. Or maybe she really thought I was crazy.

"It seems your wife said that you were so out there on the drugs that you might have been dangerous to yourself and other people," the doc told me. "This means you have to be in here eight days. On the ninth day, they take you to court and you have this certain amount of time to tell the judge why you're okay. Then this group of psychologists is going to tell the judge why you're not okay."

"Well, that's a problem," I thought. If this setup meant having to be evaluated by a group of doctors, my odds weren't looking too good. I still had my fucking stage clothes on. Back then, we used to dress up, and I had on a silk shirt, which by that point looked like I slept in it, because I actually had slept in it a bunch of times. I went back to my room and I thought, "Man, this will never do. They're gonna throw me in for a long time."

I thought and I thought, and then I remembered that they had just finished building the new Capricorn Studios. The guys and I were gonna do the first session. Somebody had called and asked to come record there, and it was, of all people, Martin Mull, the comedian who made some albums back then that were kinda hip.

I got another meeting with Dr. Sykes, and it was hard keeping a straight face, but I went in and said, "Dr. Sykes, sir, have you ever heard of Mr. Martin Mull?"

He said, "Why, no, I don't believe so." This guy was totally straight, from way back.

I said, "Well, he's coming to our beautiful new studio."

"Oh, I've heard about that being built—are Mr. Walden and them through with that?"

"They should be totally finished, they're probably testing it out now," I said. "And dig this, Doc—I've been invited to play on a session, and the session is tomorrow night. If you would just give me a pass for one night, as soon as the session is over—and it will probably be kinda late—I'll come straight back here."

I must've put on the most honest face in the world, because he goes, "Well, sure, I'll do that." He was one of these doctors that asks, "What's your name?"

"Gregory Allman."

"Sure . . . sure. Where were you born?"

"Nashville, Tennessee."

"Sure . . . sure . . . sure."

After a while, I'm going, "Where was I born? What is my fucking name?"

So the doc gave me the pass to Capricorn Studios for the Martin Mull recording session. It's all I can do to keep from laughing in that man's face. By now they had issued me a set of jammies, kinda like scrubs, and a robe. It was real cold outside, but I just danced outta that place and went home.

Here's the funny part: that was in late October. More than a month later, it came Christmastime, and they were having the Capricorn office party. I was there, back in Phil's office. We were telling a bunch of lies, cracking jokes, smoking a little reefer, and what have you. There's a knock on the door, and I said, "I'll get it, Phil." I opened the door and guess who it is?

"Hello," I said, and then, seeing who it was, I gave, on the spur of the moment, one of my best performances. "I'm sorry, who are you?"

"Mr. Allman, don't you remember me? I'm Dr. Sykes."

And I said, "Sure . . . sure."

Please Call Home

Take one last look before you
leave,
    Cause somehow it means so much
to me,
    And if you ever need me you
know where I'll be,

[So Please call home, if you
change your mind,
    Baby you know - oh - I don't mind

Oh I saw it coming day by day
But I could not stand a failure
Before you leave there's just one
thing I must say.

I know you are used to runnin
You're lost baby and I ain't funnin
But oh when you call me I come
straight to you side
        runnin
I will confide in you
again

Allman and Woman, 1975

CHAPTER TWELVE

Cher

WHEN *BROTHERS AND SISTERS* CAME OUT, IT WAS LIKE NOTH-
ing that had ever happened before. I mean, none of us
saw it coming—not like that, anyway. Everything that
we'd done before—the touring, the recording—culminated in
that one album, and the thing just fucking exploded, all the way
to No. 1 on the charts.

In July 1973 we hit the road hard to promote the album,
playing shows just about everywhere in the United States straight
through to New Year's. That tour was where we really hit our
stride with Chuck and Lamar. We had great chemistry on- and
offstage—everyone was just having a good time—and our playing was the best it had been since my brother's death. Everything
just came together, and we played some amazing music.

It was during that tour that we were visited by a young, and

I mean young, reporter for *Rolling Stone* named Cameron Crowe. Of course, I had no idea he would go on to make *Almost Famous* nearly thirty years later, and that it would include some of our stories.

When that movie came out in 2000, my only thought was I wished my brother could've been there to watch it, though I'm sure he saw it from his big seat. The way they flipped our story around was very ingenious. They'd have whatever I was doing done by a guy with dark hair and a black mustache, and then they had another guy with blond hair doing something else.

The movie definitely got the spirit right—especially on that *Brothers and Sisters* tour. When I heard about it, and heard what it was supposed to be about, I thought, "Oh God, it could be anything—this could really tear down the Allman Brothers." Now, some of those stories came from Zeppelin and the Eagles. But the jumping off the roof into the pool, that was Duane—from the third floor of a place called the Travelodge in San Francisco. I got up there with him, but I said no, this is too high—I might miss. My brother wanted to do it again, but the cat who owned the place came out shaking his fist, yelling at him. My brother was somewhat of a daredevil, and he and Oakley would do shit like that. We told that story all the time, and I have no doubt that Cameron was around for it.

The funniest thing, though, happened at the end of Cameron's visit. Over the years, in part because of the movie, this story has been spun out in a dozen different ways. Cameron Crowe was so young, he was such a rookie—and of course, we all were once. He was following the tour and taking us one by one, getting a long interview on each of us. So the last thing he did was he came down to my room, and Dickey was there, and we talked for about two hours and it was serious too. We laid it on him.

After he left, we sat and cooked up this idea. We went to

his room and said, "Man, we are so sorry, but there's a couple of clauses in our contract. We were just reading it over, and we can't let you have that interview you just did." And we took it back from him, took his notebooks and everything.

We knew what time his plane was, and just at the last minute, just as he was going out to the cab thinking, "My ass is fired," we handed it all back to him. Cameron was white as a ghost, and he was quite a sport. He's gone quite a ways—he's not "almost" anymore.

As that tour rolled along, the shows only got better. We ended 1973 with a monster New Year's Eve show at the Cow Palace, out in San Francisco. That was a big old smelly place, and it always reeked of cowshit, but we did it for Uncle Bill, who descended from the rafters that night dressed as Baby 1974 and wearing a diaper. By the end of the night, we'd left it all up onstage—just one of those amazing nights. If that tour was as good as we ever played with that group of guys, then that show was our pinnacle.

After a few months off, we then hit the road again from May until August, doing about twenty-five shows, but by the time we stepped off that mini-tour, we were all pissed off at each other and ready for a break, so we did just that. From August 1974 to August 1975, we stayed off the road. We'd worked hard, but we also needed to get the fuck away from each other for a while, man. Dickey was also making noise about wanting to do a solo album of his own, so it just seemed to make sense for us all to get a bit of space. I decided to release another solo album—the live record that had been taped during those performances at Carnegie Hall and the Capitol Theatre in New Jersey on my *Laid Back* tour.

As it turned out, both Dickey and I released solo albums and went on solo tours during that fall of '74, which caused some issues. It seemed like things between us became a sibling rivalry of sorts, which was ironic, because when I'd had a sibling we'd never been rivals over anything. But after I did *Laid Back,* I think Dickey wanted to put his own voice out there.

My album *The Gregg Allman Tour* and Dickey's album *Highway Call* were basically up against each other, as were our tours, and there was a lot of talk about the competition between us. That was made worse by the fact that I had Jaimoe and Chuck in my band. I don't think Dickey was too happy about that; he probably wanted Chuck to play with him on his tour. Butch seemed pissed off too, because he now had no one to play with. The whole thing seemed to frustrate everyone—and it didn't help that we were all taking our turns with whatever drugs happened to be around.

Despite the state of things, I was satisfied with how my tour went—more scaled-down than when I was on the road for *Laid Back* with the string players and all that. It ended out on the West Coast in January 1975, and I sent everybody back home, except for me and Chank. I kept a wad of cash along with some duds, and the two of us stayed at the Riot House—the Hyatt House on Sunset in Los Angeles.

One night Chank and I were out, going to different places and having a drink here and there. I said, "Let's go down to the Troubadour and see Doug Weston." Not that Doug was really a friend of mine, but he's a nice guy, and we'd known each other since the Hour Glass days. We went by and Etta James was playing that night. When I finally saw Doug, though, he wasn't all that happy.

"I'm not doing worth a shit," he told me. "Man, I got problems."

"Shit, you got Etta James playing—you ain't got no problems," I said.

"Yeah, I know," he said, "but I got this other band that's opening up, but they're supposed to be finishing their record tonight in the studio, or the record company is going to take their contract away from them. I got to give them the night off—it's just one of them things that I got to do."

"Well, that's pretty humane," I told him. "Shit, I'll tell you what. I'll do it, I'll play the son of a bitch by myself."

"You're on."

"Now listen, man, I'll have to charge you for this."

"How much?"

"Well, now dig it, bro, I'm a union dude, and if they were to catch me doing any favors for a friend, they'd blackball my ass. It would be at least $2,500." Bam! That money hit the fucking table, with neat little wrappers around it.

But then Doug hesitated. "Now, wait a minute—I need two nights."

I hadn't played by myself since that time in elementary school when those two ratfucks ran out on me, and believe me, mentally, I was right back there. It's one thing playing in a band, but it's a whole other playing by your lonesome ass, because if there are any mistakes whatsoever, it's pretty obvious whose fault it is. However, I'd thought about doing it for years and years, so I said to myself, "Well, shit, I got myself into this." Doug threw in an extra $500 for the second night, and I agreed to do it.

When I finally got up there, I played five or six songs acoustic, then Etta James's band came on. They were one hell of a band, and we jammed on about five more tunes. Then Etta came out, and she looked good. She was in fine spirits, just real happy, and I stayed on for a few tunes before heading offstage. She kicked mucho butt for the rest of the night. That first night was pretty good, because I was able to relax. I was on autopilot for the guitar playing, and I could sing and actually hear myself, and not from the monitors either, but from the rafters of that old place.

It was a good show, but I didn't think too much of it. As it turned out, a woman named Paulette Eghazarian was in the audience that night, and she was the secretary for Cher, who lived out in L.A. After that first show, she told Cher she *had* to come see me play. I think Cher went to the second show just to shut Paulette up. Cher wasn't hip to the Allman Brothers at all—she had heard "Ramblin' Man," but everybody had heard that song.

She showed up with David Geffen as her date, but I had no idea she was in the audience. If I had, I would have had a fear in me. See, a long time ago, I'd had a dream about her. She was by a swimming pool, surrounded by all this beautiful ivy, with weeping willow trees hanging over it, and I'll be damned if that same pool didn't end up in our backyard when I married her.

After the show, Chank ran up to me, going, "Guess who's here? Guess who's here?"

"Who?" I asked.

"I want you to just ease over that railing and look to your right."

Well, I did just that, and there she was, man, looking so good—I couldn't believe how beautiful she was. I wrote Cher a note, asking her to go out with me the next night. I went to Chank and asked him to give her the note.

"Oh noooo. I ain't doing that," he said.

"Come on, Chank, you're my man. Take this note and give it to her," I said. He finally took it down there, and he's gone forever, and a little while past that. When Chank finally came back, he told me, "Man, she gave it back to me and told me she couldn't read it . . ."

"Oh fuck," I thought.

" . . . because there ain't no light over yonder."

"So what did you did do? Come up here to get some light from me? Go back and tell her to take it over by the cigarette machine, read it, and send me back an answer."

"Man, I just got me a raise!" Chank said. (As a matter of fact, I think he got a white Corvette out of the deal.)

I got my guitar and headed down there like I was leaving, and, man, I had tunnel vision. I didn't see no one else in the joint but her. I had met David Geffen on many occasions before, because he used to be Jackson Browne's manager, but I didn't acknowledge him at all—or anyone else, for that matter. I was so rude; I didn't say hello, or kiss my ass, or nothing at all, because I was so blinded by her.

I was walking by, and she was down on the floor looking for something. She looked up and said, "Oh, I lost my earring." Then she said, "Here's my number—call me."

God, she smelled like I would imagine a mermaid would smell—I've never smelled it since, and I'll never forget it. So she split, and as I was leaving I looked around, and I saw David Geffen. I went, "Oh fuck," and thanked God that his eyes weren't locked on mine. I just eased on around to the car and split.

The next day, I called the number, and Paulette, her secretary, answered. I asked to speak to Cher, she asked who was calling, and I told her who I was. She told me to wait just a minute, and then Cher gets on and says, "Well, hello." I asked her if she wanted to go out to dinner, and she said yes.

I went to her house in a limousine, and when she came out she said, "Fuck that funeral car. Let's go in my car," and she handed me the keys to her blue Ferrari.

She really put me on the spot; for one split second, I looked at her like she was a star, instead of just a human being. That was the first and last time I ever did that. This she knows, deep in her heart, and I hope she never forgets it.

We went to Dar Maghreb, a Moroccan restaurant on Sunset. It's a kick-ass place, man, really great. They have all the food in a big tray in the middle of the table, and you eat with your hands, using a piece of bread to grab the food. So we sat there, eating with our hands with the sitars playing. She didn't have shit to say to me, and I didn't have shit to say to her either. What could I say to her? What's the topic of conversation between me and her? It certainly ain't singing, that's for sure.

We finally got through with dinner, and I said to her, "I've got a friend who lives up in the hills, and his wife is Judy Carne." Cher knew Judy, who used to be on *Laugh-In,* from years before, but she didn't realize that Judy was into heroin pretty heavy. We got up to Judy's house, and I had just a little taste of doojee. I nodded out in the bathroom for twenty minutes or so, while Cher was out in the living room with Judy, who's also nodding out.

I came out of there and asked her, "Okay, toots, what else would you like to do?"

"I want to get the fuck out of here as fast as I can," she said.

I walked her out to her Ferrari, and as she got in, all I could think to say was, "Honey, be sure to tell your secretary that I said hello." I really pissed her off when I said that.

I got a case of the braves, and I called her the next day. When Paulette answered the phone, I told her, "I just want to say something to her, and tell her that if she doesn't get on the phone, she's a chickenshit." I knew that would get her, and when Cher got on the phone I said, "Wait, before you say anything—that was possibly the worst fucking date in the history of mankind. We might be ready for the *Guinness Book of World Records.*"

She totally agreed with me, so I said, "Well, listen, seeing how it was so bad, why don't we try it again, because it can only go better this time?"

Cher agreed, and asked, "Where are we going to go this time?"

"Let's go dancing," I said.

"That sounds great!"

That did it, boy. We went dancing, and I don't know how to dance, but I got drunk enough to where I did. I danced my ass off. She's a dancing motherfucker, let me tell you. This is when disco was just taking off, so we did some dirty dancing; a little of this, and a little of that. She had one drink, while I had my twenty-one, of course.

After dancing, we went to a Polynesian place, which had really good food. It really was a glorious night, just a great time. When we got back to her place, she took me out to her rose garden, and all the roses were just starting to bloom with the scent jumping off them. We're standing out there, and all of a sudden, she said, "No, Honky!" This big Rottweiler was sniffing me, but she made him back off.

She had on this gorgeous Bob Mackie shirt made out of beads. Purple going into gold, going into green, back into purple, all beads, and they just covered her tits. That shirt must have cost thousands of dollars. We started kissing, and then she took the shirt off and grabbed my hand to go inside.

"You're not going to leave that out here, are you?" I asked.

"Don't worry about it, it'll be fine," she told me. (The next morning we learned that Honky ate that motherfucker.) "You've got to stay here tonight."

Part of me is thinking, "Gregory, you do not belong here, man," but the other part of me is saying, "Come on, let's go! Get your ass upstairs, boy!" We went up this big huge staircase to the third floor and she started ripping my fucking clothes off. She had this huge canopy bed, and her room had a marble fireplace along with these huge lamps—it was something else, man. All told, the house had thirty-six rooms; you've never seen anything like it. The first time Jaimoe went there, he said, "Shit, man, if this was my place, I'd be renting out them rooms!"

She was hot to trot, man, and we made some serious love. In many of her interviews, she said that I was the best—the best—in the bedroom. I always thought that was nice, because I'm certainly not the most endowed guy there is, but as the old saying goes, "It's not what you got, it's how you use it." So I thank her for that.

AFTER THAT, I ONLY SAW CHER TWO OR THREE MORE TIMES, BEcause I had business to attend to. There was trouble with the band, and I needed to get right back to Georgia. So in February '75, I went back to Macon for a band meeting.

We'd originally been planning to start rehearsing for *Win, Lose or Draw,* our next album, but from the start there was all kinds of bad blood. There had been a rehearsal scheduled and I got back a day late, so that gave them an excuse to get their panties in a wad.

The second I got home, they pummeled me with all kinds of shit, like "You don't love us anymore? You moving to California? What's the deal?" I'd been out there for just over a month, and I didn't see what the big deal was. I said something about being able to move wherever the fuck I wanted, which didn't get the meeting off to a very good start, but they shouldn't have jumped on my ass about where I lived—I wasn't married to the Allman Brothers.

They asked me about Cher, and I told them that I didn't know what was going to happen with her. I didn't understand why they were asking me all these personal questions. I mean, we'd only been on a few dates. I think there was something weird about all the attention that Cher and me had already gotten in the news. I don't think anyone in the band expected to see me in the spotlight like that—I know I didn't. That, combined with the whole

L.A. thing, just rubbed them the wrong way. I finally said, "Fuck it, I thought you wanted to talk about the band," but we didn't get anywhere at all.

Truth is, though, it was clear from the start that this was more about all the shit that had happened the previous fall. This wasn't just about my living in L.A., or about what might happen with Cher—it was also about my and Dickey's solo albums, and of course all the drugs figured into it too. We got to a point where we were all prepared to just move on and play, but there were lingering hard feelings. Unfortunately, this tension didn't end there; in fact, that was just the beginning.

We started to work on the album, but it was rough going—like we were all just going through the motions. I hadn't been back in Macon working on the album for too long before Cher came to visit. She flew into Atlanta, and I drove up to the airport to pick her up. The airline had her stashed in the luggage room while she was waiting for me, and when I got there she was asleep in this big soft chair that they had pushed in there for her.

I took her down to Macon and showed her around. Our first date was at Le Bistro, the finest restaurant in town. We met Phil Walden, and he wouldn't keep his hands off of her. He kept saying things to her like "Why don't you and me go off somewhere and talk?" Really stupid stuff, especially with his wife sitting right there.

Cher kept asking me, "Who is this fucking idiot?"

I said, "Would you believe me if I told you that he was the owner of the record company and the manager of our band?"

"That guy? I thought he was Tony Fucking Joe White!"

Walden loved her because he thought our relationship was a great selling point, and he was trying to convince the band of that, while I'm telling him to stay out of my business. In spite of what the band had been saying, when she would go out with them, everybody liked her, and she made them all laugh. She had the filthiest mouth in show business, and the guys in the band thought she was quite a trip. You get that girl away from Hollywood and she's a whole different person.

Things between me and Cher were working out pretty well, but there was one problem: she didn't realize that I was a hophead. I figured that when I told her it was going to shoot things right in the ass, so I might as well enjoy it while I could. Eventually, though, I had to tell her that I was a junkie, because she started to hint at marriage, which didn't sound so bad because she was a good old gal. I felt that we knew each other well enough and we were on the right track, so I might as well just get it out of the way.

So I woke up one morning and told her, "Look, I've got to tell you something. I'm addicted to narcotics."

"Well, how do you fix that?" she asked.

I didn't have much of a response beyond "Well . . ."

"I know what we'll do," she said. "We'll go back to L.A., and I'll get my doctor friend to write you a big prescription for Quaaludes, and you can just sleep through it. When you wake up, it will all be over."

I tried it—what the hell—but of course it didn't work.

Still, Cher was actually quite elated that I told her the truth about my addiction. She was real positive, saying things like "Don't worry, baby, you can beat that. I'll stand right by you, every minute." She wasn't pissed at all, which made me feel great. I'd been convinced she was going to get up and storm out of the house when I told her, and that would be the end of that. I had prepared myself to say, "Well, it's been a lot of fun, thanks a lot," but she was completely behind me.

Right after that, we went into rehearsals for *Win, Lose or Draw,* but it didn't go worth a shit because the band was convinced that

I was going to split back to California with Cher. And in the end I probably did spend too much time out in California. But at that point it was easy to run; those sessions were the worst experience I ever had in a studio.

It wasn't just me, though; they were bad for all of us. Where the earlier albums had come together pretty quickly, this recording stretched from February to July '75. Very rarely were all of us in the studio at the same time. The only three who regularly showed up were Jaimoe, Chuck, and Lamar. Even so, Jaimoe and Butch still missed playing drums on a couple of tracks—Sandlin and Bill Stewart had to play the drums instead. And then there was Dickey, who seemed like he only cared about playing on songs that he wrote and tried to dictate the entire process.

As dictator, Dickey seemed ready for Chuck to go. I think he was jealous of Chuck; he claimed that Chuck was stepping on the guitar solos, and that the piano runs were too damn long. Dickey accused him of everything that you can think of, but he was doing that shit to everyone. I've always liked Chuck, and we had a good dynamic; he didn't deserve all that.

Things only got worse later that spring, when I fell off my motorcycle and broke my right wrist. Dickey was really pissed, because he thought I did it on purpose so I wouldn't have to go back on the road. He gave me shit about wanting to stay home with Cher because I was so pussy-whipped, but it wasn't like that at all.

For my part, I just wanted to keep my distance—in every possible way. Throughout the spring I was bouncing back and forth between Macon and L.A., which was not a good way to make a record. Things started and stopped, in part because I wasn't always there. I overdubbed a lot of my vocals out in California at the Record Plant with Johnny Sandlin. He would bring out the tapes of the basic tracks, I would cut my vocal parts, and then he would take the tapes back to Macon.

My being in L.A. certainly added to the tension hanging in the air, but it was just the excuse we all needed. It wasn't just me and Dickey who were at odds—me and Butch were going in different directions too. In our own ways, I think we'd all started to question whether it was worth it. Personally, I wasn't sure it was. We'd taken time off, but that had only exaggerated the problems between our personalities. With each day there was more and more space between us; the Brotherhood was fraying, and there wasn't a damn thing any of us could do to stop it.

Meanwhile, Walden kept whispering in my ear that if the band broke up, he'd be there for me. I'm sure the other guys in the band thought that I had a deal with Walden, but they were way off track. Looking back on it now I could have dealt with it all differently. I just didn't even want to bother, man.

In that regard, *Win, Lose or Draw* was a perfect reflection of our situation in 1975. It was basically all over with the Allman Brothers Band. I knew it and everyone else probably knew it too. But none of us could bring ourselves to do what needed to be done.

ONE SUNDAY MORNING, WHEN I WAS BACK L.A. WITH CHER, WE woke up, and she said, "What are you doing today?"

I hadn't thought about it, because I hadn't even gotten out of the bed yet. She said, "Well, listen—Mr. Harrah, who's a good friend of mine, has sent us down his private jet. I was thinking we'd fly over to Vegas and get married." I was awake then, let me tell you!

"Married?" I asked.

"Yeah," she said. "We've been together now for quite some time—what do you think about making an honest woman out of me?"

I thought about it and said, "Well, why not?" I did care about her; I cared about her quite a bit. Well, I cared about one side of her, because there were two sides to that woman. I liked the helpless little girl side she had, but I couldn't stand the General Patton side of her. I already had one five-star general in my life, and I didn't need another one. But I did love that other side of her, so I said, "Okay, let's get married."

On June 30, 1975, we got in the jet and flew over to Vegas. Her good friend Joe DeCarlo was with us, and I really came to like Joe—he was good people to know, and bad people to be on the wrong side of. The three of us headed to Vegas, where we had one of the wedding suites at Caesars Palace.

We were trying to stay as low-profile as possible, which was damn near impossible. First they had to smuggle us downtown to get the license, so they started a rumor that Frank Sinatra was upstairs at Caesars getting married. It worked because then everyone was looking around for Frank. We got back with the marriage license and went upstairs to some meeting room, where they wheeled in two big silver trays with caviar all over them. That was when I got my first taste of black beluga caviar, and, man, I was hooked. The judge came in, but I couldn't get away from the caviar. Finally someone was like, "Can you stop cramming yourself full of caviar so we can start the wedding?" God, I love that shit, and to this day I'm wild about it.

We stand up there, and the judge says, "We are gathered together today to unite these two people in legal matrimony."

I said, "Wait a minute—stop the wedding." Joe looked at me like "What in the fuck are you doing?"

"Pardon me, Your Honor," I said, "but I think I speak for both of us when I say that we've been married before, and I remember that the judge or preacher would say, 'We are gathered together today to unite these two people in *holy* matrimony.'"

He looked me dead in the eye and said, "Mr. Allman, in the state of Nevada, marriage is nothing but a law to protect children."

Boy, that put a damper on the whole thing right there.

"Should I go on?" he asked. I told him to go on, but that's when I should have taken off out of there. I remember standing there during the wedding, thinking, "I wonder what I'd be doing if I was in Macon right now?"

After the ceremony was over, Cher and I got back on the Learjet, and not a fucking word was said between us on the way back to Los Angeles, not a single word. Just silence.

Four days later, she found a set of works in a leather bag that I carried, and naturally that did not go over well. I'd been trying to play the role of a straight man for her, but the whole time I needed a certain amount of this medicine to stay right. I wanted to say, "You shouldn't poke your nose where it don't belong, because you might find something that you don't want to find," but I was in no place to say something like that.

Cher was very much in love, and she was so naive I couldn't believe it. I guess she had thought that one bottle of Quaaludes and it would be all over, I'd be clean as a whistle. I tried to shelter her from the deviousness of a dope fiend, and it was a hell of a place to be in, waking up married and knowing you're still addicted. Sometimes I might do a little too much, and she'd go, "You look mighty sleepy. Are you okay?"

In a way, I was glad it came out, because I'm a lousy liar, and to live with a lie is totally impossible for me. To lie and walk away is one thing, but to lie and then lie there with her—I couldn't do that. When she found my rig, she just got in her Ferrari and took off.

I walked down the stairs, and I saw Paulette and asked, "Paulette, where's Chooch?" Chooch is what I called Cher, because

I used to tell her that she was choochie, which was a word that Deering and I used all the time, meaning "eloquently funky." Like a babe with a pair of old Levi's on, real tight and real faded out, and a brand-new pair of slick-looking boots, and a fox coat— that's choochie, and that's what Cher was.

Paulette looked at me and said, "Gregory, she found something in your bag, and she got mad and took off in her car. I don't know what it was, but she sure was mad."

I said, "Well, I know what it was," and I just waited for her to get home.

When she got back, I sat her down and tried to explain to her what an evil thing it was, but there was no way for her to understand that, because like I said, she was pretty naive when it came to drugs. She gave me the silent treatment for a while, so I sat at the piano and started playing. I was who I was, and I told her who the fuck I was up front. She didn't bother to check into it and see what it's all about. If I'd told her that I had some strange disease, she would have called every doctor, had every book open, trying to find out everything she could about it.

On our second date, we'd gone back over to her house, and I was sitting at the piano, playing her a song. I took out this little bottle of coke, poured some out on the piano, and snorted it. I asked her if she wanted some, and she said, "No, thank you." I asked her if it bothered her, and she told me, "No, not at all." A little bit of blow was okay, but not the heroin, and not my drinking (she really hated that as well). Her father had been a heroin addict, and I guess my addiction took her back to that time. She would get so frazzled about things and wouldn't know what to do.

When she had driven off, she had gone to her lawyer and filed for divorce, but after we talked she decided to let it go. Of course, it was all over the papers that she had filed for divorce after four days, but nothing at all about how she didn't follow through with it.

I called Joe DeCarlo, and I told him what was going on. He said, "Well, shit, man, if I was you, I'd get myself into a rehab," so I did. I went to a place in Connecticut called Silver Hill, which was a pretty exclusive rehab—people used to dress up for dinner. The lady who'd invented methadone opened Silver Hill, and they had me in the Irving Berlin suite—his name was on the door and everything. As soon as I agreed to go into treatment at Silver Hill, Cher withdrew the divorce papers.

On Monday and Thursday nights, we had group sessions. I hated it, because everybody checks everybody else's inventory, and they all wanted mine. I think they went to group for entertainment, to get celebrity dirt or something. I was there for thirty days, I came home for two weeks, and then I was right back in there, but this time it was for alcohol only. Jonesing for a drink, once you've been addicted to alcohol, is just about as bad as jonesing for heroin.

When I got out, things weren't much better with the band than when I'd gone in. Dickey and I still weren't getting along, but what made things worse was that he got introduced to Cher's secretary, Paulette, started dating her, and then got her pregnant. For the life of me, I can't understand why he did that. I would love to think that I didn't have a damn thing to do with that relationship, that it was just a weird twist of fate, but to this day it seems like it was just Dickey Betts trying to fuck with my head.

I think the final turning point for me and Dickey happened after he and Paulette had begun to date. Cher and I were living out in Hollywood, and one morning I came downstairs and who do I see but Dickey Betts. I'll be damned if he didn't walk right by me without saying a word—not a fucking word, man. I didn't say a damn word to him either, because I knew whatever I said would not be said right. It was going to be taken wrong, because I didn't have nothing right to say to him. That did it for me. It didn't sit well with me and it didn't sit well with Cher either, because shortly thereafter she fired Paulette, further pissing Dickey off.

Angry as we both were, the release of *Win, Lose or Draw* did little to make either of us happier or improve things with the band. No one was happy with that release—not the critics, not the fans, not the record company, not us. The six months of frustration in the studio ended with a frustrated album. And maybe the worst part was that the tour hadn't even begun.

The number one band in the country

CHAPTER THIRTEEN

Trials, Tribulations, and the White House

WHEN THE ALLMAN BROTHERS GOT THAT GODDAMN PLANE, it was the beginning of the end.

It was a Boeing 720, and this guy from Daytona, Toby Roberts, who had managed the Escorts for a while back in the day, talked us into getting it. Toby had a whole bunch of irons in the fire, and one of them was leasing aircraft, so we figured for our first tour after *Brothers and Sisters* we'd make a change. This particular jet was burgundy and gold, and had been leased in the past to the Rolling Stones and Led Zeppelin. Finally, Elton John bought it, and he painted little clouds and cartoon things all over and put "Elton" on the tail.

The layout of that plane was in-fucking-credible. It had two bedrooms in the back, with round beds and grizzly bear blankets. Every eight feet in the cabin, there was a TV monitor, and halfway down was a long bar. The first time we walked onto the plane, "Welcome Allman Bros" was spelled out in cocaine on the bar. At the end of the bar was a Hammond, a set of drums, and some amps, so we could jam if we wanted to.

From August '75 through May '76, we did forty-one shows. We opened the Superdome in New Orleans on August 31, 1975, in front of ninety-six thousand people. We played Madison Square Garden, the Spectrum, Boston Garden, the Orange Bowl, Roosevelt Stadium—real big joints. These were some of the biggest solo shows we'd ever played, and the scale of it all was just unbelievable. Everything was over the top, uncalled for, and just flat-out unnecessary. We had thirty roadies on that tour—thirty. Our roadies had roadies. We had a guy whose only job was to open limo doors for us.

Excessive as stuff like the airplane was, it was just a symptom. The truth is, we couldn't fucking stand each other; with each day on the road, the separation grew between us. We didn't talk, we didn't hang, we didn't do nothing together. Everyone had their own limo, everyone stayed in their own suite. Rehearsals slowed down to almost never, and sound checks became a thing of the past. It happened little by little, where you don't even notice that it's happening, until it's wrapped all around you, and then the realization hits you like a ton of bricks.

We all retreated into our own little worlds, and by then we all had our own people, so that made things a lot easier. I had a guy with me named Scooter Herring, who was kind of like my assistant. Scooter was this big, tall, raw-boned son of a bitch who could ride the shit out of a Triumph motorcycle. He used to hang out down at the Sunshine Club, which was this little place down on Hardeman Avenue in Macon. It was a little old biker bar beer joint, with a couple of pool tables and a horseshoe-shaped bar. It wasn't very big at all, maybe two thousand square feet. We'd go in there after we'd been riding, and I'd go a lot with Tuffy Phillips, who drove our equipment truck.

I'd met Scooter there back in '74, and we became real good friends. His relationship with his wife, Karen, probably inspired many of the songs I wrote back then; that man thought the woman made the sun rise and the moon set. I watched them a lot, and I've always been a real quiet observer of people. Like my grandfather always said, "It's the quiet ones that you got to watch, because they're taking it all in."

Around the time I met Scooter, I got a huge royalty check. I was riding high off both *Eat a Peach* and *Brothers and Sisters,* even as much as Phil Walden was taking from me. Scooter's wife wanted to buy a house, and he came to me and said, "Man, Karen is dying for this house."

I had them over for dinner, and I had written a check for $54,000 and put it in an envelope. As they were leaving, I said, "Wait, you forgot something," and I handed them the envelope. I told them not to open it until they got out in the car, and they came running back in, and, man, Karen was just bawling her eyes out. She and Scooter were so happy, and they couldn't thank me enough.

At that point, Scooter wasn't working for me, we were still just running partners, but he was a real friend as well. Soon after that, though, I made him my valet for the *Laid Back* tour, and he did a hell of a good job. He did it like a pupil, but a damn good one. Scooter was a very intelligent man, and he had this amazing ability to do math problems in his head, like no one I've ever seen. He knew about numbers, so I told him to get the book *This Business of Music.* He read the son of a bitch in about three days, and he said to me, "Man, this is a backbiting motherfucking business."

When the Allman Brothers went back on the road in 1975 after *Win, Lose or Draw,* Scooter came out as an assistant tour manager. All the other guys in the band really liked him because they had ridden with him before, drank beers with him, he was always around, and he was just a good Joe. He certainly fit in with us, and he was funny as shit.

But Scooter had another responsibility, one that was for me and for me only: he was my delivery guy, helping me get drugs when I needed them. I didn't ask him where he got the stuff, and he didn't offer it up. But he helped me score whenever I needed it, and back then that was a big job.

I was about as tight with Scooter as I was with anyone on that tour. Scooter and I had some hellacious times out on the road. He had four teeth missing in the front of his mouth, so I got him some new teeth. All of a sudden, he started to look good, and he grew his hair out, and he was quite a sight at six foot six. Whenever he told me, "Here, Gregory, hold my glasses," I knew there was fixing to be an ass-whipping, and it wasn't going to be his. He was one of the most lovable people that I've ever met, and I miss him so bad. There wasn't nothing criminal about that man, nothing.

ONE OF THE FEW POSITIVE THINGS THAT HAPPENED DURING THIS time was that we got involved with Jimmy Carter, which is something that I'm very proud of to this day. I suppose I was the first member of the band to meet him. I was in the studio in Macon, and we got an invitation from him to attend a reception at the Governor's Mansion for Bob Dylan, who was out on his first tour in years and was playing Atlanta. We brought our tuxes and everything to the studio, and we were going to do just a couple of overdubs and then get in the limo and ride on up to Atlanta.

Well, a couple of overdubs became just one more take, and

one more take, and one more take—we one-more-taked our asses until about ten o'clock. I finally said, "Shut it down. We're going right now." We all piled into the limo and hauled ass up there. We got to the Governor's Mansion, which is a huge three-story place with a big horseshoe-shaped driveway and a guard shack at the entry gate.

We got there just as the last guest was pulling out of the drive-way, and I thought, "Oh shit." I got out of the limo and went up to the guard shack and said, "How do you do? My name is Gregg Allman, and here's my invitation. I've been in the studio down in Macon, and we got delayed. Would you please pass this letter of apology to the governor?"

They said that they would, so I turned around to go back to the limo, and just as I got my hand on the door, the guard said, "Mr. Allman, please wait a minute. The governor would like to see you up on the porch of the mansion right away."

I thought, "Oh God—he's either going to be a nice guy or I'm going to get a federal ass-chewing. A state ass-chewing, anyway."

The moon must have been full, because it was real bright outside, and I could see the silhouette of this guy standing on the porch. He didn't have on a shirt, he didn't have any shoes on, and he had on this old pair of Levi's, and they were seasoned down perfect, man—they were almost white. I was thinking, "I wonder who this damn hippie is, hanging out at the Governor's Mansion?" Well, it was him—Jimmy Carter himself.

He had that big old grin on his face, and I thought, "Well, he could be frowning." He said, "What the hell, come on in. You're not too late." We go in there, and there's a bottle of J&B scotch on the table. There was all kinds of food laid out, and they must have had one hell of a bash. So we sat there and told stories, and pretty much polished off that bottle of J&B.

It was getting to be time to leave, and he said, "There's one more thing I want to say to you, Gregory, before you go. I'm thinking about running for president, and I'm going to need a whole lot of money." I had never been approached by any kind of politician; politics and my life were on opposite sides of the world. I'd never voted, though I do vote now. Anybody who doesn't think that it's worth it to go down there and take a few hours out of their day to cast their vote, then they can't have a bitch in the world when we end up with a shitty president.

I told him, "I'll go back to Macon and talk it over with the guys and see what they say—and I really want to thank you for not arresting us for getting here so late." He was a really nice guy, and he was really hip to music. Some of his favorites were Leon Russell and Dylan, and he liked mainstream hippie music. If you ask me, he wasn't nothing but a hippie who had to get a haircut. His mind was young and wide open, and it still is today.

There were two major things that he did right after he took office. I thought one of them was the hippest, greatest thing he could have done; the other one sucked, and the next time I see him, I'll tell him to his face. He gave amnesty to all the people who went to Canada because they didn't want to go to Vietnam and shoot a bunch of folks they didn't know, which was so great. Then he turns around and tells Cuba, "You all come on over!" What the fuck? Fidel Castro empties his jails out and sends them all over here. And with them came the onslaught of a little thing called crack cocaine.

Anyway, after that night at the Governor's Manson, I talked to the guys in the band, and they thought that we should help him out, so we arranged to play a gig to raise money for his campaign. He came down to Macon and met all the guys, and they really liked him. He hung out in the studio and went to eat with us at the

H&H. We talked about music and skeet shooting and fishing—he's an avid fisherman.

The benefit we did for the Carter campaign was in Providence, Rhode Island, on November 25, 1975, right in the middle of the *Win, Lose or Draw* tour. Governor Carter introduced us, and he told the crowd that he was going to be president. I've been told that the money the Allman Brothers raised for him kept his campaign alive, because he was dead broke at that time.

A little over a year later, Cher and I went to the White House for the first dinner President Carter held after taking office. We were back in the private part of the White House, and when they asked Jimmy what he wanted to eat, he just said that he would have what the staff was eating, which I had a lot of respect for. Forget the damn rack of lamb—we ate sweet potatoes, smothered chicken, collard greens, black-eyed peas, cornbread, and sweet tea.

Amy Carter gave us a tour of the White House, and that was something else. She was having a hell of a time showing us around her new home. We saw the Lincoln Bedroom, and his actual bed was in there. I got up there and spread out on it. Nothing magic happened; it didn't make me a better person, but it was cool none-theless. Cher and I had a great time with Jimmy's mom, Miss Lil-lian, who was sitting there watching television. At one point, she whipped out a flask of gin and told us, "This is my medicine—I have to have this." She was just so sweet, man, God bless her.

THE SHOW FOR JIMMY CARTER WAS A HIGH POINT IN WHAT WAS otherwise a rough, rough tour. Sure, that '75–'76 road trip had moments when everything jelled, but those were few and far be-tween. It was nothing like what it had been like on the *Brothers and Sisters* tour. Shows like that New Year's Eve Cow Palace performance were things of the past. A lot of what we were doing was lackluster, and we all knew it. We were just going through the motions, all while doing insane amounts of drugs and spending too much money on it. We were using coke, heroin, pick your poison, not to mention drinking all the time. If you listen to tapes of those shows, you can tell what drug we'd taken that night by how we were playing. Uptempo and edgy? Coke. More jazzy and slow? Codeine. Everybody was doing something, and some of us were doing everything.

When we played the Roanoke Civic Center on May 4, 1976, it would be the last Allman Brothers show for two years. By that point, things had fallen apart. There was no communication going on, and our playing was pretty rough. I had just said, "Fuck it," because I wasn't into it at all. It wasn't the Allman Brothers anymore.

Things continued to go to shit when we got home to Macon and counted our money. At the end of nine months of touring, we had $100,000—and that was the gross amount. To do forty-one gigs at $80,000 apiece, we should have had a little more than a hundred grand. It was ridiculous, and it was all because of stupid expenses. The bills were stacked a mile high. When we'd taken our year off, we'd kept everyone on the payroll. We'd paid people not to work—it was crazy. And then we'd toured some with that plane. You talk about spending money. Good God! The fuel costs alone—you can't imagine.

It wasn't just the plane and the personnel, though. We were out of money because we were buying blow by the ounce, as well as heroin, not to mention our regular clothing dip. Plus we had hot and cold running women, and the best food you could eat. Name it, and we had it.

The thing is, back then we had a real epicurean attitude toward life, just tunnel vision. Eat, drink, get laid, and play some fucking music today, because tomorrow you might just wake up dead. It was kind of the attitude of the day, but the harsh reality of losing two Brothers made it that much more real for us.

We didn't get the bill for all that until we got back to Macon, but when that check arrived, forget about it. That's when the Allman Brothers broke up, right then and there. Technically, it took a couple of months to go through the formalities, but after we all saw the price tag for that tour, it basically was done.

Willie Perkins could have helped us with our money, but he was so afraid of Walden that he wouldn't do it. You would think a friend would help you out, but it wasn't the case. I wasn't paying attention to the money, because I was concentrating on the music; that was the only thing keeping my feet on the ground. Oh, the money we would have today if we had just had some guidance.

We had a meeting about money, and I was afraid that we were actually going to come up with a negative amount. The six of us were there, along with Willie, Twiggs, and Scooter Herring, and once the financial realities became clear, everything that was wrong with the band was laid on my part of the table—and I mean everything. They told me that if I didn't have Laid Back Productions, the Allman Brothers would be doing fine, but that didn't have anything to do with it. Them boys turned against me, man—not Lamar, not Jaimoe, but the rest of them did.

Right in the middle of the meeting, the authorities came in, broke the whole thing up, and took Scooter away in handcuffs. There was a lot of confusion about what was going on and what Scooter had done, but it didn't take long to figure things out. Scooter was being arrested because he'd been helping me buy drugs, but they nabbed him not because he was buying, but because they said he was selling.

That was when I learned where Scooter had been getting the drugs from and what he was mixed up in. He'd been scoring through a guy named Joe Fuchs who was a pharmacist at Harrison's Pharmacy in Macon. Before then, I didn't know about Joe Fuchs, and Fuchs didn't know about me. Fuchs was mixed up with some questionable people, people rumored to be in the Dixie Mafia, and had been selling pharmaceutical-grade cocaine to them as well as to Scooter. It was through his involvement that the authorities had gotten turned on to Scooter, and by extension, me.

The DA in Macon at that time had been in office for about a year and a half, and hadn't had so much as a healthy pot bust. The city fathers and townspeople were getting a little bit ticked, seeing how another load of hippies moved into town every day, so they needed a fall guy. Fuchs was the fall guy, but Scooter was swept up in it too.

On May 28, 1976, Scooter was indicted on charges of conspiracy to possess narcotics with the intent to distribute. By that point, everything pretty much unraveled with the band, and I had left Macon and was back in California with my bride, Cher. The whole thing became a tabloid event overnight. Because of Cher, because of the band, I was front-page news every day. Now, I've never been big on media, but even among people who are, I don't think there's a person alive who likes headlines like that. And it only got worse.

One day the phone rang, and it was Mitchell House, my attorney in Macon. He said, "The federal prosecutor wants you to come to the grand jury hearing on Scooter."

I asked, "Scooter? What?"

He told me, "They indicted him on charges of sales and distribution of cocaine."

I did everything I could to avoid testifying, but it was made clear to me that my back was against the wall; there was no way to dodge a federal prosecutor.

I got that horrible, sinking-type feeling, like a good friend had died or something. Eventually I was granted immunity from prosecution in exchange for my testimony in front of the grand jury and later at the trial. Fuck me, man—I didn't have no choice. I got back to Macon as fast as I could, drove over to Mitchell's home, and Scooter was already there.

I walked in and said, "Scooter, what in the fuck am I going to do when they ask about you?" I was crying, man, and I asked Mitchell, "Tell me what I'm going to do—you're the lawyer."

They got me settled down, and they said, "Just tell them the truth."

I said, "What?"

They told me again, "Just tell them the truth and don't worry about it. One thing we're going to do is save your career."

I told them, "Look, I ain't done nothing to lose my career. All I did was shell out a little dough."

They both told me they knew that, and Mitchell said, "Remember, after everything that you say, make sure you state 'to the best of my memory' or 'to the best of my knowledge.'"

I agreed to appear, and I must have said those phrases three hundred times. I walked into the courtroom—and as a little footnote, there wasn't a single member of the Allman Brothers Band there that day, or any day during the whole thing. None of them had the slightest idea what was going on, and I guess they drew their own conclusions without ever hearing from me. I'm not blaming them, but I guess they just had something more important to do. I don't really give a fuck anymore, but at the time it hurt me real bad.

That was an experience that I hate to relive, because every question was hard, but I know that the judge was totally on my side, or at least he seemed to be. He would ask me if I wanted to take a break, but it was just hell.

It was a rough time, man. People were afraid for my life, because there were some powerful people who thought I knew more than I did. The phone would ring, and a voice would be going, "If you say the name of so-and-so, you'll find a twenty-gauge up your ass." I did get a few death threats. There was all this speculation that Scooter was connected to the Dixie Mafia, but if he was, he never said anything about it to me. He never told me about any chicanery, any theft, any buried treasure, any firearms, anybody getting shot—none of that, and by God, he would have told me something after twelve beers. If there was something, I would have heard about it.

Because of the threats, they hid me out in the barracks at Robins Air Force Base, with four FBI guys assigned to me for protection. Have you ever tried to take a piss with three FBI agents standing right there, and the fourth one guarding the door? I wasn't allowed to read anything or watch TV, but they did give me a bottle of whiskey every night.

The thing lasted for what seemed like an eternity, and it was a complete drag. Every day I was on the front page of the paper, and wherever I went, people would yell shit at me. There was no evidence against me, it was all hearsay. I never understood why John Condon wasn't involved in this trial, because he had been my criminal lawyer since the thing with Twiggs, and Mitchell House had been more of a guy who fixed parking tickets. I'm sorry, but that that's the truth. It didn't seem like he really bent over backwards for me, except when it was time to get his check.

Scooter's lawyers were trying to make me look bad to lighten the load on him, and the prosecuting attorney tried to make me and Scooter look like real, real close friends—I mean, like we were gay. The judge got so upset that he stood up and threw his pencil down and announced, "This man is not on trial here. If you ask him a question that is out of line like that again, I will throw you out of this courtroom."

Scooter Herring never sold me huge quantities of cocaine, but on July 19, 1976, he was sentenced to seventy-five years in prison for the coke he had sold me. The conviction was front-page news when it happened, but what was much less sensational was the fact that Scooter only went to prison for eighteen months, not seventy-five years. Of course, no one pays attention to headlines about getting out of jail—that's why newspapers don't write them.

For his part in all this, Joe Fuchs ended up spending ten years in prison. Later on, I did meet Joe, and now his widow and daughters still come to our concerts. His widow told me one time, "Joe wanted you to know that nothing was your fault at all, and that you didn't do a damn thing wrong, and he doesn't hold you accountable for anything," which I thought was a beautiful thing to say.

I talked to Scooter right after he got out, and he told me, "Gregory, I appreciate everything," because there was a bunch of money in his bank account. I wanted to get together with him and have some dinner, but he said, "It wouldn't look good for you and me to be seen together for at least five years." When he died in 2007, we'd never met up again.

Scooter was my bud, and we certainly had some good times together. In the time that I knew him and that we hung together, on the road or off, we laughed. We were very good friends; he never did anything wrong to me, and I don't think I ever did anything wrong to him. There were situations that arose, and I still don't think anyone knows the full extent of what it was about.

Months later, after the trial was over, I'd be onstage, counting off a slow number, and right in the middle of "one, two, three," you'd hear someone yell out, "Narc!" It wouldn't throw me off; it made me play twice as hard. I'd play right through it, because I knew what the truth was. I knew what I'd done and what I hadn't done, and I just wanted to get on back with my music.

I felt guilty about the whole thing for a while, but as hard as I tried, I couldn't figure out what it was I had to feel guilty about. I wanted some drugs, Scooter got them for me. I paid for them, and that was it—done deal. What was there to feel guilty about? Had I gone out on the street and bought them myself, I probably would have ruined my career. Scooter helped me out as far as that went, but everyone who's buying drugs is getting them from somewhere else. I'm sorry for what happened to Mr. Fuchs, I'm sorry for what happened to Scooter, but they knew what they were doing when they did it. Everybody made their own decisions, man. And that includes me.

THE WHOLE MESS WITH SCOOTER WAS THE LAST STRAW FOR THE band. As if the financial mess we'd gotten ourselves into wasn't enough, most of the guys felt I'd sold Scooter out. They were also scared for their own asses, and worried they were going to get swept into it. And none of this was helped by the fact that we'd all been doing so much coke we were in a permanent state of paranoia.

But when it came down to it, they seemed to feel that my testifying was the worst part of the whole Scooter situation. They felt it was a betrayal of what it meant to be an Allman Brother, even though they didn't have any idea what I'd been through. Because of that it was easy for the other guys to blame me for the breakup.

In August 1976, the band officially broke up when Jaimoe wrote a letter to the Macon newspaper which stated that there was no more Allman Brothers Band. Not long after, Butch and Dickey came out individually and said the same thing, with Dickey doing it in *Rolling Stone*. I remember in that issue, there was a picture of Betts and a quote from him saying, "I'll never play onstage with Gregg Allman again." No problem, brother! I just wish we had held him to that.

Truth is, there ain't one thing or person alone that broke up the Allman Brothers. It was everything and everyone. Scooter, my recording *Laid Back,* my living in L.A., the drugs—they were all just easy excuses, ways of talking around the unavoidable truth: that none of us knew when or how to walk away.

In hindsight, it's amazing we survived as long as we did after my brother died. God knows we tried, but once the money started rolling in, well, it didn't take long for it to take over—there was just too much to walk away from. The second the money well had dried up, we all had to take a good, hard look in the mirror, and we didn't see a whole lot there that we liked.

The feelings, the closeness, the brotherhood that we'd once shared—man, all those things were fucking gone. The Big House was a perfect example. When my brother and Oakley were alive, that place was ours, it was our space. But after Oakley died, Linda moved out, and we had lost our headquarters. The vision of the band that we'd made there, the image of the band that Duane and Oakley had helped create—all that was finished. When we lost the Big House, the band changed. I don't think any of us were the same after that.

It was really strange, but it seemed like we got rich and famous overnight, and when it was over, it was the same way. It was like the whole thing had never happened—like "What the fuck was that?" We had five years at the top, and then, bam, it was over. We had spent so much money, it was unbelievable.

I don't know if my brother is face up or facedown in his grave, he's done so many damn pirouettes over the money we wasted. On the other hand, I'm sure he's very proud and smiling about what we went on to do.

Giving it one more try, 1979

CHAPTER FOURTEEN

It Just Ain't Easy

WHEN THE BAND BROKE UP, CHER GOT BLAMED FOR IT. THE press made her out to be the Yoko Ono of the Allman Brothers. Needless to say, there wasn't much truth to that. When people hear shit, they take it at face value, and then they tell a friend, so a simple rumor can turn into a colossal lie. There's a lot of stories out there that have absolutely no basis in fact. In the end, people believe whatever they want, but the only thing that broke up the Allman Brothers was the Allman Brothers.

Though the breakup really had nothing to do with Cher, its timing did overlap almost exactly with a big moment in my life with her: the birth of our son. Elijah Blue Allman was born on July 10, 1976, and I lived with him until the time he was walking around. I remember this funny little step that he had, and it was so cute. When he would smile, you could see every one of his teeth, and that would make me and Cher just laugh. He could fart like a moose, this tiny little thing in the crib, and it was great. We would crack up, man. I remember when he learned how to swim—he took to the water like a fish, and it took only a day or two for him to learn.

The three of us lived out in L.A. along with Cher's daughter, Chastity. I remember when Chastity had to have one of those Stingray bicycles, with the banana seats and those ape-hanger handlebars. I told her, "You don't want one like everybody got on the street. Go put on some dirty clothes, tie your hair back, and go with me. We're gonna go to a neat place."

I took her to the junkyard, and we found a bike. I had it sandblasted, and then had a kid paint it bronze—real nice paint job. Then I went and bought sprockets and chain and tires, all that stuff, and a leopardskin seat, and together we built that son of a bitch. When we were done, she had the baddest bike in the neighborhood, and I used to be her knight in shining armor. Later on, though, she wouldn't say two words to me, and I don't know why. She probably heard so many ghastly stories about me that were so well embellished that she thinks I'm just a terrible person or something, and that's a shame.

As far as Chastity's sex change, as long as he's happy, he's free to do whatever he wants to do. It's not your everyday thing happening, but I just hope he's happy and I wish him a very long, successful life.

Living with Cher was all right, but there were things about her that drove me crazy. One night we were sitting at home, and it was about eight o'clock, and she said, "I really don't feel like staying in tonight. Why don't we go out and get a bite?"

I said, "Sure, let's go to some quiet, dark place." There was this Cantonese restaurant on the outskirts of Beverly Hills that we liked, so we decided to go there. And wouldn't you know it, there were at least thirty-five fucking photographers waiting for us when we got there. Now, who told them? It sure wasn't me. She loved that, man, but I wasn't from Hollywood, so I never got used to photographers hanging around our front gate all the time, clicking away.

Still, I can't say that being married to Cher was the worst thing in the world, because it wasn't. We had our good times, we had our bad times. We were just different in a whole bunch of ways.

One day I was in the shower, and the next thing I knew, someone was washing my back. It was her, of course, so she turned around and I was washing her. She started singing the Smokey Robinson song, "I don't like you, but I love you," and all of a sudden I came in with the harmony part: "Seems like I'm always thinking of you . . . I need you badly, I love you madly," and it sounded pretty good.

I was really glad that she never asked me what I thought of her singing, because I'm sorry, but she's not a very good singer. When she talks, she has the sexiest-sounding voice, and I tried to tell her that that's the way she ought to let it out when she sings. If she sang like she talked, good God. I guess Sonny must have been on her every move, because he saw the gold mine in her. Without her, he would have been nothing—he certainly never would have become a congressman.

I tried to talk to her about her singing, but she never wanted to hear it, until one day she said to me, "Well, enough other fucking people like it, so if you don't like it, fuck you."

"I didn't say that I don't like it," I told her. "And I'm not saying now that I don't like it. I'm just saying that part of it is contrived."

I tried to show her some inflections, and she showed some interest. Finally she said, "Why don't you produce a record for me?" That led us to start talking about making an album together.

At the time, I'd been putting the finishing touches on my next solo record, *Playin' Up a Storm,* which I'd cut out in Los Angeles. Neil Larsen played keyboards, Willie Weeks played bass, Steve Beckmeier, John Hug, and Ricky Hirsch played guitar, Bill Stewart played drums, and Russ Titelman and Lenny Waronker produced it.

I'll tell you, there were times when Lenny really had to wrangle my ass on that album. Cher and I were having a rough time then, and this one morning I was running late when Lenny came busting into the house. He walked right past Cher, went upstairs, and told me, "Get your ass out in the car. You're not going to be late for this session."

Cher shot me this look and I told her, "Later, baby," and went out and got in the car.

I thought it was a pretty good album, and it was certainly well produced. Because I had moved out to the West Coast, though, Phil Walden thought there was no more Allman Brothers, so he decided to fuck me too. When it released in May 1977, he only printed up about fifty thousand copies, which made it hard for people to buy it.

Cher and I did end up working together on an album, and that album, *Two the Hard Way,* by Allman and Woman, came out later in '77. That record sucked, man. That's the truth, and I know it as well as anyone. It bit the dirt, and it didn't sell worth a shit. There was one, maybe two decent songs on that record, but it was basically terrible, just awful.

In November 1977, I went over to Europe with my band, and we took Cher with us. We did a few Allman Brothers tunes, then we did some of my stuff from *Laid Back* and *Playin' Up a Storm,* and then Cher would come out and we'd do about six or eight songs, including a few off of *Two the Hard Way.* The crowd was pretty interesting, because half the people were in tuxedos—I mean, dressed to the nines. Some of them were even in floor-length tails, because they thought they were going to see Sonny and Cher. The other half of the crowd was all backpacks and Levi's jackets, and they were there to see the Allman Brothers.

It was an interesting mix, and the fights out back were something else. There'd be some dude out there, duking it out in his tux with a guy in denim. It was funny, man. Some old bitch came after me, going, "Why didn't you let your wife sing a little bit more? You would have gotten a lot more claps." I didn't know what to say to her, so I just let it go. "Claps"—good God!

We got to Germany on that tour, and it was snowing like a bitch. We stayed at a hotel that was once a big castle, owned by some squire or somebody. In my room, I had a fireplace that I, at six foot one, could very easily stand up in, and the bed could have slept my whole band very comfortably. The menu was unbelievable; it was truly from the Black Forest. They had quail, venison, elk burgers—all kinds of good, wild stuff that I was just digging the shit out of.

It was right after that—the tuxedos against the backpacks, because I think the Allman Brothers outnumbered the Sonny and Chers—that Cher came to me, and the poor thing was just crying. I asked her what was wrong, and she told me, "We've got to cancel the rest of the tour, because I can't stand the fighting." So we ended it right then, which was about halfway through it. We went home the next day, and that was the last time I ever played with her.

That tour, along with everything else, laid bare the fact that things had changed between us. I had never done anything to hurt her; I'd hurt myself, I'd degraded myself, and I'd hung with some pretty shady people, but I'd never done anything to harm her.

One day, she came to me with this big wad of money, $50,000

maybe, with a big red rubber band around it. She said, "I need time to think about this—I don't know about this anymore."

"You don't know about what?" I asked. She never did quite come out with "what"—she just said she didn't know about "this." Maybe it was all too much for her, or she had lost it for me. I don't know, and I never found out.

She held the money out to me and said, "I want you to take this and get an apartment and stay there for a couple of months, and let me think this whole thing over, and I'll get back in touch with you. We'll see what happens."

I told her, "Honey, you keep your money, because I make a pretty damn good living on my own. You got your reasons, and I sure hope you come to grips with them. You've got my number." So I walked, man, and I went down to Daytona to see my mother.

I STOPPED BY MACON IN EARLY 1978, WHERE I HAD STASHED $12,000 in the bank. I got it out, and I partied my ass off with it. Then I took some of that money and bought myself a new white Trans Am. It made me feel good, plus I needed a way to get around. I got it home, and Mama A loved it.

When I was in Daytona, I would go down and check out the bar scene, and somebody told me about a band called the Nighthawks. They said this band was nothing but straight-on, hard-core blues, and they had a harp player with so many tattoos, that's all you could see when he was playing. I said, "They sound like my kind of guys," so I put on a pair of Levi's, a T-shirt, and a leather jacket and headed down to the Martinique, which had been renamed the Wreck Bar.

I had known the woman who ran the club for years. We called her Ringo, which obviously wasn't her real name, but she looked just like Ringo Starr. She's such a sweetheart, and I love her. She was so glad that I was back home, because I had been gone since 1965.

That night, the Nighthawks were blowing. They took a break and I met them, and then I sat in during the next set. They knew a lot of blues songs, and we sounded really good together. Afterwards, they asked me to come out on the road with them, and I figured, why not? So we went out and did a shitload of gigs, mostly around the Midwest and Northeast.

We had a good turnout from my fans, and I guess I needed that acceptance, because I wanted to know if everybody had turned their backs on us. That really mattered a lot to me, because it took many years to build that fan base. They loved the blues, and they stuck to the blues through it all. I hadn't played any of those clubs in a long time, and they were just dying to see me. I was drinking pretty heavy then, but we played some smoking shows.

On the way back into Daytona after we were done, I stopped at the Pontiac place and got myself another Trans Am, since my mom had taken mine. I'd gotten paid for the gigs in cash, and I had two briefcases full of it with big wads of cash stuffed into every pocket. Back in Daytona, I bought a new Triumph motorcycle too, and I used to ride uptown every night, just to see who was playing at the Martinique or wherever. There were some good shows, but mainly I went into town just to jam, look at the pussy, and drink.

One night I went into the Castaways, and they had a band in there, and a guy had a B3. He loved it when I came in, because I'd play a few songs while he took a break. One night the band was just smokin', and someone asked me if I wanted a drink. Without looking up, I ordered a vodka and tonic. All of a sudden, a bar napkin drops on the table, and the most beautiful hand I've ever seen places my drink down.

I fell in love right there—the hand of fate did it to me. She told me her name was Julie Bindas, and she loved motorcycles, so we rode up and down the beach all the time. Julie was a really nice, together person when I met her, but that changed real fast. It turns out that she was born in the Ukraine, and her father got her out of there just in the nick of time. He was a Soviet diplomat, and when he saw that the whole thing was going to fall over there, he sent her to America.

A year later, in 1979, we got married, and it went downhill from there. Julie was a knockout in her day, but, man, I thought she was crazy. I knew it was over when I came off the road and there was a note from her telling me that she had a Smith and Wesson .45 and she would be glad to use it on me. Welcome home, right? We ended up getting divorced in 1981.

The best thing to come out of that marriage was my daughter Delilah Island Allman, who was born on November 5, 1980. Julie came up with Delilah, and I came up with Island, because we were living on Anna Maria Island, Florida, at the time. Island is the love of my life, she really is. I trust her completely, and that's great, because she was out of my life for a long time.

Not long after I met Julie, in the summer of '78, Dickey tried to call me a couple of times, because he knew that Daytona wasn't too good for me in terms of drugs and alcohol. When we were in Macon together, Dickey had always been afraid of me going back to Daytona. He'd tell me, "Go see your mother, fine; but why don't you just bring her up here?"

One day I was taking a shower at my mother's house, and I was actually planning to call Dickey that night to find out what he wanted. I got the towel wrapped around me and I walked out into the living room, and there sits Dickey Betts. He had actually rented a prop plane from his home in Sarasota to fly over to Daytona, and he asked, "Did you get my messages?"

"Man," I said, "you're not going to believe this, but I was

going to call you back this evening." Of course he didn't believe that, but I really was going to call him. I said, "You don't have a car with you, so what's the deal? Did somebody die or something?"

He told me, "No, nothing like that. I wanted to come down here and talk to you about re-forming the band."

I just said, "Oh," and the words hung there for a minute. I wasn't sure what to say about getting the band back together. I was pretty strung out, because I had been doing Dilaudids and drinking vodka, so I wasn't in no shape to go anywhere at that moment, but I told Dickey I would get back to him.

Thanks to my good friend Bob Merrill, I got into the hospital and went through detox, and within a few weeks I had straightened myself up. The four of us—Butch, Jaimoe, Dickey, and I—got together and agreed to play together again. I'm sure the specific reasons were different for all of us, but my sense was that we all just needed this in our own way. No one was pleased with how things had ended back in '76, and the combination of the passing of time, missing each other musically, and money all made it easier for us to put the past behind us.

In the years since the breakup, all of us had been doing our own thing. Dickey had formed his own band, called Great Southern, which consisted of two guitars, two drummers, bass, and keyboards—go fucking figure. Jaimoe, Chuck, and Lamar had started a pretty hip band called Sea Level, which did this cool jazz-fusion thing; and I had recorded *Playin' Up a Storm*. We had all gone our own ways, but none of us had ventured so far from home that we couldn't find our way back.

As we had been doing all that, Capricorn had been splintering. The year before, we hadn't been getting our royalty checks, and an audit showed that Capricorn was deeply in debt. Phil had borrowed $4 million from PolyGram Records and wasn't even close to paying it back. As we started to work together again, I didn't talk to Phil Walden at all, but we did call Willie Perkins; at that point, none of us were sure if we would work with Phil again.

It was decided that Butch, Jaimoe, and I would join Dickey's band, Great Southern, for a few songs at their concert in Central Park in New York on August 16. As Great Southern was wrapping up that show, Dickey said, "For my last song, I'm going to have to call out some friends to help me." They brought us up one by one, and I was the last one to be called. When we walked out there, the place went apeshit. New York has loved us for so many years, I'm telling you.

We did five songs—"One Way Out," "You Don't Love Me," "Stormy Monday," "Statesboro Blues," and "Blue Sky"—and we just stomped. We ran late and the sky got pretty dark. It seemed like they weren't prepared to have to use lights; maybe they were onstage, but they weren't prepared for the gig to go on into the night. But it did, lights or no lights. That day reminded me how much I enjoyed playing music, and what a fan base we still had, because them people went crazy. Leaving the park, there were people jumping up and down on my damn limo, and they ruined it, man.

The first thing people wanted us to do was get right in the studio, but we said hell no. We had learned to stand up for ourselves, and we knew that heading into the studio right away could put the brakes on this whole thing if we weren't careful. We were going to see how everybody got along, musically and spiritually, and *then* we'd decide if and when we would go into the studio.

About a week later, I drove up to Macon in my Trans Am for the 1978 Capricorn barbecue. Everybody was there, and we jammed a lot, which eased the tension down even more. The other guys had forgotten how I sang, and I had forgotten how it was to play with them. I don't think any of us had realized how much we missed it all until right then. Now we all knew for sure that we were getting back together for the music as much as for the money.

At this point, Chuck and Lamar had decided to stay in Sea Level, so we added Dan Toler on guitar and David Goldflies on bass, who had both played with Dickey in Great Southern. We went into rehearsals in Sarasota, and we all stayed at the Pirates Den, on Anna Maria Island.

I had been living with my friends Chuck and Marcia Boyd. They had a house with an extra room built on, and it had its own private entrance and carport, so that was perfect for me. I had a piano in my room, which was a nice touch, and that's where I wrote "Just Ain't Easy." That song is about Hollywood, and how bad I wanted out of that place. It's about defeat and resignation, being on the bottom, and I think it turned out pretty good. But we decided we'd all stay together at the Pirates Den because we wanted to see if we could get along with each other, and we worked up "Just Ain't Easy" and a few other tunes before we went to Criteria in Miami to record.

The more we played together, the more I kept coming back to something Duane said a long time ago. My brother read all the time. His head was in the books, and his arm was either around a fine girl or around that Les Paul, but that's all he did. I remembered that he had told me about some poet from way back that he'd read. He said, "Gregory, this sounds like you could make a song out of it—it goes, 'The world is made of two great schools, enlightened rogues and religious fools.'"

I told this to the other guys, and I said, "What do you think about calling this record 'Enlightened Rogues'? Because that's basically what we are."

Everyone liked that, so we got in the studio and we cut that damn thing.

It was a pretty interesting little record to cut—and once again there was a house that brought us all together. Criteria had this row of houses along Biscayne Bay that you could stay in. One of them was the title for Mr. Clapton's album *461 Ocean Boulevard.* We stayed about three doors down from there when we were cutting *Rogues,* and we had a huge dinner table in there. We would all sit around that table, and a cook would come in to make breakfast and dinner for us every day. We were all still using and drinking, but everything was more in control that it had been in a long time. That place just calmed us all out—really helped us travel back in time. It was just a groove, man, one big family again. The house was huge, so there was plenty of room for all of us.

It wasn't just the house that was a flashback. I also brought Twiggs back as my manager, advisor, protector, friend, confidant— all good things, but it didn't last too long. Dickey had warned me to not have anything to do with Twiggs. He told me Twiggs was crazy and that I shouldn't bother with him.

One day I was at the studio, and it was getting kind of late. I had to sing something the next day, and I was walking down the hall to my room, and Twiggs was with me. A door opened, and Don Johnson popped out. I said my hellos to him, and he was with Dickey, of course, so we went into the room to talk. We'd met Don in Macon when he was shooting *Macon County Line,* but I hadn't seen him since.

I was having a conversation with Don, and the whole time Twiggs was in my ear, telling me, "Hey, man, it's time you got into bed." I gave him a couple of looks and went on talking. Then Twiggs said, "Hey, man, it's really time for you to get into bed. You've got to be in the studio early."

I told him, "Man, why don't you go to bed? I'll go to bed when I think it's time to go to bed."

That's when he snapped. "Look, motherfucker," he said,

grabbing my arm and pushing me. Then he hit me in the back and told me, "Okay, now I will go to bed, and I'll leave this motherfucking place tomorrow."

"Well, shit, you don't have to go away mad, just go the fuck away," I said.

This whole thing went down in front of Betts and Don Johnson and a few other people, so Twiggs was way out of school. He should have taken me outside if he had something like that to say to me. It really pissed me off, and after he hit me he got that look on his face like, "Oh shit. I better go up and pack."

I hated how that all went down, because I loved Twiggs, but I think he had done gone over the edge. What he had pictured for this whole thing had changed. It had been a long time since he'd been involved. Two of the guys were gone, and everybody else was fucked up. This band had more baggage than Twiggs could manage. It was more than anyone could manage, but the man couldn't handle it when things didn't go exactly the right way—he was just wrapped way too tight.

That was the last time I worked with Twiggs. Later on in 1979, he was killed in a skydiving accident. He was in upstate New York working for the Dixie Dregs, and on November 16, near a small town called Duanesburg of all things, he went for a jump and his chute never opened. A few months later, I got a manila envelope in the mail. In it was a picture of Twiggs walking into the woods with his head down. He's wearing his jumpsuit, with "Allman Brothers" and "Dixie Dregs" running down either side and "Harley-Davidson" across the back.

It freaked me out, man, because it was obviously premeditated. He had somebody mail it for him, because it was postdated after his death. Like I said, the world was just not perfect enough for Twiggs Lyndon.

It was hard letting Twiggs go—almost like it was proof that

things weren't what they once were, or what we wished they would be—but at the same time we were working with Tom Dowd again, and he was a real treat. We hadn't worked with him since he produced *Eat a Peach,* and just like back then, he did his job so well. We had communication, and I mean the utmost communication. Tom was a master at getting everyone's attention focused on one little item, and I picked up so many little ways to go about things from him, and to keep from wasting time.

One thing I learned from Tom was the importance of beats per minute, and it's more important to me than it is to anybody else in the Allman Brothers Band. That might sound pretty strange, and it might sound like I'm insulting three very good percussionists, but I'm not. I'm not a drummer, but I know tempo, and I know that the longer a note rings, and the more of it that you hear, the more of it you get to enjoy. The only thing that's going to keep you from doing that is if another note comes right on top of it and cuts it off.

A note has to have enough time, even if it's in a fast song, to start nasty, get nasty, stay nasty, and end nasty—and do it all in a millisecond. That's easy to do on a guitar, and possible to do with the human voice. You need a certain length of time to allow a note to come up from out of your soul and have it emanate to the microphone, and every now and then you know that you've really touched a nerve.

One night, many years later, I heard Derek Trucks go, "Sing that son of a bitch!" He just couldn't hold it in, and that made me feel good, because it was a note I really tried for, and as you get older it's harder to hit those notes of real emphasis. At the end of "Whipping Post," where I sing, "Like I've been *tied* to the whipping post," that word "tied" gets a little more difficult every year. The ending of "One Way Out" is starting to get pretty hard, but I won't give up on it.

I'm afraid of the day when my throat just isn't going to let me do all the little loop-the-loops that I can do now. I know it's going to happen, because you can't do it forever. I'll do what I can for the rest of my life; I might be able to croon for quite a while. You can always take a different route when it gets to the high note, and sometimes it comes out almost as good.

If your music doesn't have dynamics, you might as well get another job. Just like the rising and falling of a poem, the music also travels, and you have to feel it. It's like traveling on a train, rolling through the hills. It's a journey with your partners, and they're all going with you, and some of them make the same turns, and a couple may go a different route, but they all meet you on the other side. I know that's a strange way of describing how the arrangement to a composition works, but it's like a musical journey.

The main thing a producer does—and Tom Dowd did it better than anyone—is to be the other guy in the band and listen to how the music all meshes together, and hear better than you do because you're busy playing. His job is to make sure it all jibes together properly, and Tom had the incredible ability to make our songs sound exactly the way we wanted them to. Tom was omnipresent, man. He had his headphones and his little beats-per-minute machine, and he kept them right with him. I never saw that man lose anything; he was so organized.

Between Tom producing and all of us playing together, everything went pretty smoothly. The only thing I didn't like about recording that album was David Goldflies, the new bass player. His playing wasn't in the toilet, but it wasn't very good either. The guy must have thought he was getting paid by the note, the way he would play those banjo notes on the bass.

Despite all that, *Enlightened Rogues* was a good record, and I liked it a lot. Looking back, though, I can't believe we did it through Capricorn and Phil Walden, especially since we knew they were in a bad way financially and we'd had issues with them paying us royalties.

In the end, I think we signed a new contract with Capricorn because of Phil himself. Despite the money he owed me, Phil was still one of the most intelligent people in the music business. He knew more about getting a record played than just about anyone, and I guess we thought he had one more miracle in him. Phil was able to worm his way into any situation; he was one of those people, kinda like my brother in a way, only my brother wouldn't lower himself to chicanery. And it was that which finally did in Phil and Capricorn.

In late 1979, after *Enlightened Rogues* was released, the final chapter of Capricorn Records was written when Phil lost Capricorn to PolyGram Records. He'd taken out one loan after another from PolyGram and they finally called all those tabs in. Not even the strong performance of *Enlightened Rogues* or our tour that followed was enough to save that label.

Ultimately, Phil Walden didn't use the right judgment when managing Capricorn, which was so strong and could have been such a good thing. He only thought of himself, and in doing so, he broke the damn company. He borrowed all this money, and I don't know all the whys or what-fors past that, but I know they put a big balloon payment on it, so he took the money out of the till. All the money from all the bands came to one spot—and I'm talking about Charlie Daniels, Marshall Tucker, everybody. He borrowed a big amount of money against all the income all these bands were bringing in, and he couldn't pay it back, so they took Capricorn Records away from Phil Walden.

WPLJ RADIO salutes
THE
Allman Brothers
BAND

JULY 21, 1979
MADISON SQUARE GARDEN

WPLJ 95.5

NEW YORK'S BEST ROCK

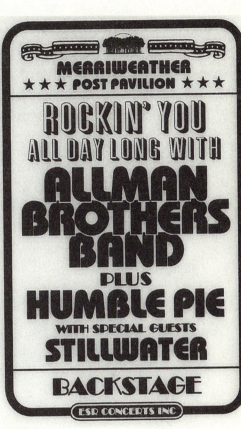

MERRIWEATHER
★ ★ ★ POST PAVILION ★ ★ ★

ROCKIN' YOU
ALL DAY LONG WITH
**ALLMAN
BROTHERS
BAND**
PLUS
HUMBLE PIE
WITH SPECIAL GUESTS
STILLWATER

BACKSTAGE

ESR CONCERTS INC

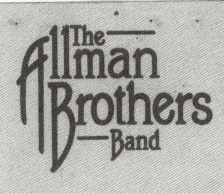

The
**Allman
Brothers**
Band

WORLD TOUR
BACK STAGE

I'm No Angel, *1986*

CHAPTER FIFTEEN

No Angel

THE FAILURE OF CAPRICORN BEGAN THE '80S ON A DOWN NOTE, but in many ways it set the tone for what was my hardest decade in music and the hardest decade for the Allman Brothers. Looking back on it now, there wasn't much that went right for us during these times. The hangover was long and it was bleak. These were some rough years, and the end of Capricorn was just the start.

When the dust settled with Capricorn, we signed a deal with Arista Records, but the honeymoon phase that had enabled us to record and promote *Enlightened Rogues* did not last long. We did two insipid albums on Arista—*Reach for the Sky* and *Brothers of the Road*—and you won't find a copy in this house, and I doubt that any of the other guys have those records either. It was like a whole different band made those records. We had background singers, songwriters, synthesizers—fuck me, man.

In truth, though, I was just too drunk most of the time to care one way or the other. After *Enlightened Rogues,* I just fell off the deep end. Before then, my drinking and drug use had been more or less in check. I'd have my bad days, but most were pretty good. By the early '80s, those good days were hard to come by.

I was drinking a minimum of a fifth of vodka a day, and even though I knew things had gotten out of hand, it didn't feel like there was a damn thing I could do about it. I remember one time around then; I was living on the west coast of Florida, and I was visiting my neighbor. She was watering her flowers. I didn't have a driver's license at this time, so I asked her if she would give me a ride down the street. She said, "Sure," so we got in the car and I told her to turn in at the ABC liquor store. I got a quart of fresh-squeezed orange juice and two pint bottles of Smirnoff Red.

I got back to the car, and I poured about half the orange juice out, and I took one of the pint bottles of vodka, poured it in, and shook it up. She's just looking at me, and by the time we drove the six blocks, I had pulled out the second bottle of vodka and dumped it in.

My neighbor asked me, "My God, Gregory, you like to do this often?"

I told her, "Honey, I don't like to do this at all, but I have to do it. If I don't, my muscles will start cramping up on me, and I'll get the sweats and vomit. It's just terrible."

Of course, she couldn't understand, and looking back on it, I can't say that I blame her. That was my morning regimen for years and years, but it was at one of its worst points in the early 1980s. I was so out of it, man. I wasn't listening to the music or really paying attention to what was going with the band—I was just a total fucking mess. Those two awful albums for Arista were the price I had to pay for that drinking—and unfortunately all our fans had to pay that price too—but the real crime was how I lost sight of the music.

Before we recorded *Brothers of the Road,* Jaimoe and Dickey got into it over where our money was going, and Dickey fired Jaimoe. After Duane died, Dickey's crown had gradually gotten bigger and bigger, and it only got worse when we'd gotten back together. At first, things had been better, but I think he took reuniting as a sign that he was going to be running things. He certainly didn't have much finesse when it came to dealing with people. He's just not a natural leader, and firing Jaimoe was the prime example of that.

Now, the Allman Brothers have had our share of conflict over the years—hell, show me a band that's been around as long as we have that hasn't fought. But one of the real blights on the history of the Allman Brothers Band was that Jaimoe, this gentle man, was fired from this organization. The thought of that makes me want to throw up, but sadly I was too drunk to put a stop to it before it happened. I thought that Dickey Betts had pulled some pretty low shit in his day, but that was the worst. Old Man Time has a way of coming back around, and now Jaimoe is right here with me, and we're having a hell of a good time without Mr. Betts.

When Dickey axed Jaimoe, I should have checked out then. It was 1976 all over again, but I wasn't together enough to see what was happening. Thankfully, this time the end came much more quickly.

We appeared on *Saturday Night Live* on January 23, 1982, and that was it for the Allman Brothers Band. We had a gig scheduled in Sarasota, and I heard that Dickey said he wouldn't play in Sarasota with me because he thought I would get drunk and embarrass him in his own town. Now, mind you, I'd lived there for six and a half years, and he says some shit about "his town." Excuse me, you know?

We were supposed to play at the Playground South, so I accepted the gig and decided to play it with the Gregg Allman Band. I think it was all for the best, so I put a band together and hit the road, and didn't look back. We were released from our contract with Arista, which was a good thing—with all the shit going on in the band, it just wasn't working anymore.

By that point, I didn't like to think about the Allman Brothers, I didn't like to talk about them, and I damn sure didn't like to play with them. You would figure that they would have appreciated all the songs I had given to them, but because of the alcohol, they pretty much lost all respect for me. They just kinda put up with me because of my last name, and I'm pretty sure that's why they kept me in the band. I mean, they couldn't fucking fire me and still call it the Allman Brothers Band, could they?

The breakup of the Allman Brothers in '82 wasn't all about me, though. The '80s saw the onslaught of electronic music—synthesizers, electric drums, disco, all that bullshit—and our kind of music just fell by the wayside. That decade wasn't worth a shit musically. There was hardly anybody playing live music, and those who did were doing it for not much money, in front of some die-hard old hippies in real small clubs.

It was like going back to square one. It wasn't like I was washed up—I never thought about that shit. To this day, I don't ever think about being washed up. I don't waste my time thinking about where we lie in the public's eye. Who gives a shit? The only thing I think about is where we are going to play next. Two hundred people or twenty thousand people, I just want to play.

I actually first started thinking about writing this book in the '80s, when the Brothers broke up. Between '83 and '89, when we got back together again, I started writing stuff down, a little bit every day. I kinda wanted people to know me past what they see onstage. I've watched John Wayne all my life, I've always dug the Duke, but I know nothing about the man.

What got me started was the thought that maybe the band was really over. The first time we broke up, in '76, I thought there was at least a chance that we'd get back together. When we got back together in '78, we figured that'd been enough time. But the second time we broke up, that's when I thought it really might've been over.

It was a relief to be out of the Allman Brothers. It's like having a constant pain, and you get so used to it that when it finally goes away, you realize just how much pain you were in for all that time. It's like what my brother used to say about banging your head against a wall, because it feels so good when you stop. I couldn't deal with all the hypocrisy, and we just let the band fade away. Nobody called anybody, it just kinda ended.

As I was trying to figure out what to do next, I had a whole different thing to think about. One day I get a letter from Mary Lynn Green. Back in 1965, there was a club in Daytona called the Bat Cave A Go Go, of all things. It had a great stage and great sound in it; they built this place perfectly, and it was out of sight playing there, except for the fucking name.

Mary Lynn was one of the waitresses there, and, to be real blunt, I punched her ticket in the car out in the damn parking lot one night. Twelve years later, I get a Christmas card. I open it, and there's a picture of a little kid, sitting behind these drums. The card says, "This is your son, Michael, and he's doing fine."

A few years go by, so it's about 1981, and I was living on Anna Maria Island. I get this letter from Mary Lynn, and it said, "Gregory, some things have come up. I would greatly appreciate it if you would take Michael and keep him for the summer."

So here comes this guy, and he's about six foot four, and he knows shit about shit. We did have a great old time; I bought him a fishing rod, and I took him out one day. We hit a damn redfish hole, and he was catching them right, left, and in between, just having the time of his life. He'd never been to a strip joint, he'd never been on a motorcycle, so we did all that. It came to be the end of the summer, and time for him to go home. He was like, "Oh, Dad, can't I stay here? You can put me in school down here."

Michael stayed for a while, and I tried, man. I really did. It just wasn't a good situation, so after a time he returned home, and that was the end of that.

When I started playing with the Gregg Allman Band, there wasn't as much money, but everybody was in a good mood, and how much is that worth? I got on the phone, put a band together, and started rehearsing, because we weren't going to play Allman Brothers songs, we were going to play my songs, and so we had to learn them real quick. Eventually I put together a solid lineup, with the Toler brothers—Danny on guitar, Frankie on drums—Bruce Waibel on bass, Tim Heding on keys, and Chaz Trippy on percussion. We went out there; we were tight, and we hit it hard.

I used to call Frankie Toler "Franklin Delano Crash Pad" for some reason, even though his real name is David. They called him Frankie because one night some chick mistook him for somebody else and called him that, and it just stuck. Frankie was a lot of fun, and boy could he fight. Me and him were in the French Quarter one night, at a place called Black Beard's, shooting some pool. We were getting ready to leave when these three black guys came in. They started in on us, giving us shit, and we tried to ignore them, but they wouldn't have it. They grabbed Frankie and took him down, and one of them stomped on Frankie's hand. Another one was holding me back, but Frankie got loose and grabbed a pool cue, broke it in half, and stuck one of those dudes right in the gut with it. We got the hell out of there, and I don't know what happened to the guy he stuck, but, man, they might have killed us.

Bruce Waibel went from roadie to guitar player to bass player, and that's when the band really started cooking. Bruce played just what needed to be played, and he caught on so fast. I couldn't believe it when I found out he committed suicide in 2003. I wish he had called me before he did it, because I would have told him that there's nothing worth killing yourself over. Suicide is a permanent solution to a temporary problem. Life isn't a bowl full of cherries, but it's not a bowl full of shit either.

For his part, Tim Heding was a great keyboard player. There isn't a horn on either one of those records; Tim played all those parts on keyboard. The thing about Tim was that he was a cheap drunk—three beers and he was done for the evening!

That was a good band—I really had a lot of fun working with those guys. Frankie and Danny were both good at bouncing ideas off of each other and helping the creative process. That band was really good when it came to arrangements. There was never any arguing about this part or that part. It was one of the most easygoing organizations that I've ever been in, and it's too bad that we were so poisoned, because it took away from the direction we had going. For me, the poison was alcohol; for the other guys, it was Quaaludes. We'd play a gig, and after it was over we would look for whatever we could to get a nod going with. It wound up being anything from cough syrup to pills, but it was more me than them.

During this time, we did some shows with Stevie Ray Vaughan, and good God almighty, what a player that man was. The people just loved him, and they gave me credit for bringing him, since he was opening for me, but I had nothing to do with the talents of Stevie Ray Vaughan. I was real heavy into drinking, and Stevie was just getting sober, so he and I drifted apart, but, man, we had some nights.

I enjoyed the playing, but the pay sucked. My manager at the time was Alex Hodges at Strike Force Management. Alex had been at Capricorn before it all fell apart, and I'd thought he was the only person who came out of there that I could trust, but I was wrong. Strike Force Management, my ass—the only person who got struck was me.

I couldn't believe that Willie Perkins, who was my road manager then, let that go on for so long. Willie wasn't as bad as Hodges was; I think that Willie's an honest man at heart. He didn't tell lies; he just didn't say nothing at all. Here's a man who we picked up on Twiggs's recommendation, and who I thought was a real friend. What those guys made off of me, you could probably retire on. I hope they still have some of their stash left.

When you've got a band, a tour bus pulling a trailer, and you're staying at a Holiday Inn, you've got to get paid $5,000 a night just to break even. Every now and then we'd made $10,000 for a gig, but for most shows we got paid $7,500. I was getting paid a certain amount, but with all the things that were being taken for various expenses, I was bringing in about $150 a week—just enough for smokes, basically.

One thing that really helped was going over to Marcia and Chuck Boyd's house, where I'd been staying during the rehearsals for *Enlightened Rogues*. I finally wound up living with them so I would have somebody to talk to. When I moved back in with Marcia and Chuck I'd been living in this damn one-room apartment with all these yuppies around the communal pool, and I needed to get out. I just didn't fit in with the scene there at all. Before I moved in with Marcia and Chuck, I was never really happy living in Sarasota. When we would come in off the road, I would think, "Well, shit, now the damn tour is over, where do I go now?" That's why it was so great when I moved in with them, because it gave me a place to call home.

Marcia and Chuck made me feel welcome, and I loved Marcia's cooking, especially her chicken and biscuits. I lived with them for the majority of the seven years that I lived in Sarasota, and they were so good to me. They had a bunch of dogs and gave one to me, whose name was Professor Dodsworth.

I have a real thing for animals, and I always have. I've never been without an animal. My first dog was a little black dog, and all four paws were white, so we named him Boots. I have a picture of me and Duane and Boots sitting on my grandmother's steps. I really enjoy having God's creatures in my life. Not too many, though—I don't take in just any animal.

When I wasn't hanging with Marcia and Chuck, the Toler brothers lived just a few blocks over, which made it easy to go down to Telstar Studios for rehearsal. We'd call them up, and they would open up for us. They would turn on the big speakers, and all the instruments were set up, ready to go. We got a lot of shit written in there, including most of the songs for my next two albums. I wrote a lot with Tony Colton, and he also provided the comic relief. Tony is the funniest British cat I have ever met in my life—that guy could make me laugh like no one else.

In between the laughs, though, there was no doubt that I was having a tough time. I might have been playing in a band I liked, with a good group of guys, but we were making peanuts and I just kept on drinking. The cops down in Bradenton/Sarasota didn't like me too much either, and everybody knew it. I played a lot around town, because I'd get drunk and go jam anywhere. I was well-known, of course, and the cops were just gunning for me—they were always looking to pop me for drunk driving, or just to be a general pain in my ass.

I remember the only time I had to go to jail was back in the '80s. I got five days because I had a DUI. It was the middle of the night and I had just gotten this new Pontiac, one of those 6.6 Trans Ams, a real heavy car but a lot of engine. And I was boogying, man.

They made me go down there and sleep it off. The judge gave me five days and fined me a grand. He almost made me serve another five, because when I came to serve I showed up rotten drunk. He didn't appreciate that, but somebody spoke up and saved my ass. Maybe there was a fan in the crowd.

Doing those five days, I got sick as a dog. As I remember it, you didn't have a room and a bed; you had to just sleep on the hard floor. Thank God I had a big heavy coat. I was in there with a bunch of other folks and then they moved me in with three other guys. And I got so sick. I don't know if it was the food or if it was nerves, probably a combination of both, but I about went nuts. Incarceration? I can get through a lot of things, but not that. Just the thought of incarceration makes my tummy kind of flip-flop.

No two ways about it, the '80s were rough. When the Brothers were broken up, from '82 to '89, my drinking got much, much worse. It was seven years of going, "What is it that I do?" Being self-employed your whole life, that becomes a certain rock, a reinforcement. When that's gone, not only are you bored stiff, but you just want to cry—"What do I do? I know I used to serve a purpose." And subconsciously, there's that fear of everybody forgetting about you.

Despite that, I always kept writing, always kept looking for more ways to make music, but with the music of the time being what it was, it was just hard to find an audience. The thing is, no matter what I did with my solo career back then, no matter how much I clicked with my band, it never was the Allman Brothers.

I knew it as well as anyone. And it was that, as well as the money, that kept pushing me back to familiar places.

In the spring of 1986, my band did two runs with Dickey and his band, which allowed us to play bigger venues. Much as I knew the troubles that came with Betts, the money was good, and I was just tired of not making shit. We'd each do a set with our own bands, and then both bands would come out and play some Allman Brothers tunes together. Everybody was really fucked up. Dickey was cussing his guys and bossing them around like they were a bunch of field hands.

It wasn't how I ran my band, but it was typical Dickey. Still, hard as it was to watch all that, that tour led to two Allman Brothers reunion shows later in the year, one in July at the Charlie Daniels Volunteer Jam, and then the "Crack-Down" benefit show at Madison Square Garden on Halloween.

The bottom line was, musically, me and Dickey needed each other, so we would put up with each other as long as we could. It would always ease things out when we had new material—but it had to be good material, not just something thrown together or contrived. Even with decent material, though, everything was always temporary. Something would happen, tempers would flare, and once again we'd go our separate ways.

BEFORE THAT RUN WITH DICKEY, I HAD GOTTEN A CALL FROM Forrest Hamilton, who is not with us anymore. Forrest was the younger brother of Chico Hamilton, the famous jazz player. Chico was a good friend of my brother's, and a good friend of mine for that matter. At that time, I didn't have a recording contract or nothing, so Forrest called me up and said, "Man, I got three songs that I'm going to send to you—tell me what you think."

I'd been in California at the time and I liked what I heard, so

I called him back and Forrest said, "Listen, why don't I fly you out here to Los Angeles, and let's see what happens." I'd taken Danny Toler with me to Rock Steady Studios, and we'd cut those three songs in two days, recording my version of the Beatles' song "Rain" with a huge choir singing background. We also brought "I'm No Angel" out there and did a demo of that one.

In September 1986, with those songs in hand, Epic Records offered me a recording contract, and we headed into Criteria Studios to record *I'm No Angel.* I had a lot of hope for that record, I really did. The sessions went well, and it felt good to be back in Criteria again. Frankie Toler, at one time, was one of the finest drummers around. If you listen to *I'm No Angel* or my follow-up, *Just Before the Bullets Fly,* there's some incredible drum work on those albums.

When we got to Criteria, Don Johnson called me up and said, "Hey, man, it's Don. You need some help with that record over there?"

I told him, "Yeah, I do. I'll tell you what—I'll leave three songs that you can pick up, then give me a call after you listen to them and tell me which one you want to do." He chose "Evidence of Love," and we worked for four hours on it, and we got it. The key was really bothering him, but we worked it out.

Don was really Dickey's friend, from back in the Macon days, so I wondered about that phone call, because we were never really that close. I think he might have done it for the exposure, because he had just finished cutting a record, in the same room at Criteria that we were using for *Angel.* Maybe he did it just to see if he could, I don't know, but whatever his reasons were, he did his very best. The best that was in that man came out on "Evidence of Love."

I'm No Angel was a good album, overall. The title song had a good hook to it and did well on the radio—thanks to Tony

Colton for writing that one for me. The album eventually went gold, and led to the recording of *Just Before the Bullets Fly* in 1988.

Those two albums are really just one long one. We got in such a groove making *Angel* that by the time we were finished we had four or five songs left over. Rodney Mills was the producer, and while I didn't know him that well, we worked very well together. There was no bullshit, and it was a comfortable experience. He caught on real quick to how I work in the studio, and he was very attentive to all the instruments. He treated the other guys very well, and I liked that.

The recording of *Bullets* went real easy too. We were in the same room at Criteria, same producer, same guys in the band, same guy changing the tape, same guy bringing in the food. Same exact experience as *Angel,* except it didn't sell, and that's a shame, because *Bullets* has some of my favorite songs on it. It is a really good album, but I don't think Epic supported it like they did *I'm No Angel.* I don't think they promoted Dickey's record *Pattern Disruptive* either, probably because they wanted us back in the Allman Brothers.

And eventually, their plan worked.

As I kept touring around, I continued to meet women wherever I went, and with my drinking being what it was, I continued to get myself in trouble.

In late 1988, the Gregg Allman Band was playing what would be its last tour of the West Coast. From San Diego to Vancouver, we riddled the place with gigs. During that time, we ran into two girls from Capistrano who started coming to the gigs. One of them was named Shannon Wilsey. She had this white, white hair, and her friend had this real black hair—the two of them looked like they could have done that black-and-white scotch commercial. This was back in the day of the real short one-piece dress, the five-inch spike heels, and no underwear.

One day, both of them came over to my room, and they started a pillowfight. One of them sat on my knee, and oh boy, that did it. She told me, "Nope, not now. It wouldn't look right," but the next day, oh God! Shannon was incredible, and shit, she was just barely of age.

We ended up staying together for about a year, but our relationship just kind of faded away. Let me say this: I never, ever gave Shannon any heroin. Later on, her mother accused me of all sorts of things like that, but I never turned Shannon on to heroin. In fact, the last time I saw her, she opened her makeup kit and I saw a bunch of needles in there, and I told her never to do that stuff, because I knew what it felt like to be strung out. I tried to talk her out of it, but she didn't want to listen to me.

Shortly after I stopped messing with Shannon, she got into porn, using the name Savannah. Somebody told me that she had gotten into porn, but said, "She's only with women." Well, I ain't messing with nobody who's in porn flicks. That stuff isn't like spin the bottle, you know. To each his own, I suppose, but I have never associated with anyone in that business.

When I asked her if she was making porn movies, she kept avoiding the question. Finally, she said, "Look, that's really none of your business."

I told her, "I'll take that as a yes, and with that, I'm gone."

It was too bad, and it was even worse when I got word in 1994 that she shot herself. That upset me, because despite all the accusations, I knew the truth about what had happened. I was not going to have that on my karma—that I somehow turned her on to that shit.

I've always believed in karma, even though I didn't know the word until I moved to Los Angeles. All it boils down to is the golden rule—do unto others as you would have them do unto you. If everyone would live by the golden rule, then the world would be at peace.

All in all, it was a weird time for me when it came to women. My next wife, Danielle, was just from another planet. I don't know why I married her. That was a midlife crisis, I guess, because I was really doing well. I was out in Los Angeles, singing the opening track for the movie *Black Rain*. I was staying at the Riot House, and Steve Winwood was in town. He was playing at the Universal Amphitheatre, and a couple of the guys in his band were some of my old players. Randall Bramblett was playing with him, and so was Mike Lawler, so I had to go.

I went over there and had a good old time. What a gracious gentleman Steve is, and his wife is just a sweetheart. A lot of British guys you meet are real cocky, especially about the blues issue. They try to talk to me about the "British blues," and I don't want to hear that shit. My brother hated that too. There was some Brits playing some blues, but there ain't no such thing as British blues—that sounds like blues that was made in Great Britain. Rock and roll and blues is America at its finest. British blues is like a parrot that lives in Greenland, man.

Danielle was staying at the Riot House with this redheaded bass player I knew from New York, and I was there by myself. I offered to take them to the Winwood show, but he couldn't go, so it was just me and her. We had a good time, and she was dressed up real pretty that night. I was in my mid-forties, and I was thinking, "Man, I'm going to get old and ugly one of these days, and them girls aren't going to look at me no more," so I figured I needed to find me a babe and settle down.

She looked real good, so I flat-out told her, "I've got to go to

Nashville tomorrow"—that's where I was meeting the band for the rest of the tour—"and if you want to go with me, be ready at nine o'clock."

That's how I left it with her, and sure enough, she was in the lobby the next morning. It surprised me, because she didn't seem the type. As I found out later, she was a pretty hard woman.

We got married in Vegas, and right after that I OD'd back at the Riot House, so our marriage started off with a bang.

At first we had a lot of fun, but we didn't have much in common. Even just going down to a funky blues bar like Blake's in Berkeley, where I met John Lee Hooker. I took her there one time, and she said, "Christ, how can you stand the stench of this place?" I knew right then that this thing was on its way out.

To tell you the truth, I was scared of Danielle, especially after one time when she hit me square in the face—God knows what she thought I did to deserve it. She wasn't afraid of much. One night I was at the Silver Dollar Saloon in Nashville, and I drank twelve kamikazes. She came in and told me it was time to go. We walked out on the street, and this guy was there, trying to fix his Triumph motorcycle.

I said, "Shit, man, you ought to get yourself a Harley-Davidson."

He told me, "I wouldn't have one of those pieces of shit."

I don't like anyone talking badly about Harleys, so I said, "Those of us who can afford them love them." That son of a bitch got up, came over, and the next thing I knew—bam! He cold-cocked me. Danielle jumped up on that boy's back and started sticking her fingernails in his eyes and ripping his nose. Man, he was bleeding and screaming like a butchered hog. That guy was scared, because he thought he'd lost both his eyes. That was something, man.

A little later, I was getting ready to leave for Europe for some shows, and Danielle had called all her friends and relatives in Europe, lining up dinners for us to go to. I came in and told her, "I've got some news for you. We're not going to be able to take any of the wives to Europe." She said, "Well, okay," and she was really nice about it.

She helped me get packed just perfectly, and I left. When I got back, that place was cleaned out. There was one bag in the middle of the floor that she had left for me, and it was full of peace of mind. I loved it, man.

After about my fifth wife, I realized that maybe I shouldn't be married. Instead, I tried having three or four different girlfriends, but then they'd bump into each other, and there would be a catfight. I'd split and tell them all to get fucked. I've never understood why some people think that a relationship is somebody owning somebody else. When you love somebody, that includes trust, and if they're going to go with some other dude, they're going to do it. There ain't a damn thing you can do about it—now, tomorrow, yesterday, a week from now. If it's going to happen, it's going to happen. There was always this sense that I was going to change. That just wasn't going to happen.

From what I see in relationships, the tightest ones are between a man and a man, because a man will step in front of a bullet for his friend. It's too bad, because you'd think that a man and a woman should be the tightest, but it just hasn't been that way for me. I've always known which guys have my back; it's why I pick them the way I do.

The Allman Brothers Band, 1992

CHAPTER SIXTEEN

Ain't Wastin' Time No More

IT WAS EARLY SPRING IN 1989 WHEN THE ALLMAN BROTHERS GOT back together. And when that happened, things started to turn around.

About this time, someone had come up with the idea of "classic rock" radio stations, and they started popping up everywhere. Man, they played us over and over. We put out a box set called *Dreams,* and that thing just took off. All of a sudden, I get a call: "Hey, man, this is Dickey. What do you think if we just get together up in Tallahassee and talk?"

It was a real déjà vu, because we'd also gotten back together in '79—there seemed to be a pattern. I remember how cool it was outside when I was driving up to Tallahassee in my brand-new white Trans Am, thinking about the drive to Macon I'd done ten years before.

We met at Butch's studio. Everybody was drinking beer, and before the meeting was even over, we were all doing a line on the table. Way in the back of my head, a little voice was going, "See, same old thing." Part of me was thinking, "The Allman Brothers again?" But what appealed to me the most were the memories of the good times. I wanted to go back and feel that way again.

I've played with some real killers in my career, but there's just something about playing with the Allman Brothers. It's like a special fishing hole that you have—that one over there is good, but this one down here is a motherfucker. When the Brothers were on, and if Dickey was having a good night, no one could touch us.

One positive was Warren Haynes, because he served as kind of an anchor for Dickey. Warren was Dickey's choice as the other guitar player; it was a package deal. That was Dickey's choice to make, because I sure wasn't going to do it, and the drummers weren't going to either. I had met Warren earlier, around '86 or so, and I liked him right away. I liked what he brought to the table, because he could play, write, and sing, so he helped make it desirable to put the band back together.

Johnny Neel was the choice for the other keyboard player, even though I thought he was a little bit squirrelly. His being blind got me, I guess, but I really didn't like having him in the band. Dickey wanted him and I went along with it, because it did save me from playing a lot of stuff I didn't want to play anyway.

Then we had to audition for a bass player. I had never really done a full-blown audition, and I hated it doing it this far down the line. Just through word of mouth, something like eleven bass players showed up. We played the same three songs all day long—"One Way Out," "Dreams," and "Whipping Post."

There were some good players; there wasn't a one of them that was bad. And they were everywhere—we took a break and I went into the bathroom and there's a guy in there with a bass and a Pignose amp hanging around his shoulder. He was standing in the door, grooving. I bumped into him, literally, and I said, "Oh, excuse me." And he goes, "Hey." I didn't know who he was; he was from New York, and he was a very, very good bass player. A cartoonist could do a real number on that whole thing.

There was another dude with real long hair who had four basses lined up, just beautiful machines. He sat over in the corner, waiting to be last. Well, that was Allen Woody. Just the way he grabbed his shit and plugged it in—he had this air about him. He had a very confident look, which is just what we wanted. All through the other auditions, I kept looking at him. Before he even played a note, I thought, "That's him."

When he played, he played somewhat like Oakley, but no one can play like Oakley could. We even told all the bassists before the audition that they weren't there to fill anybody's shoes, that those shoes can never be filled.

So we played and we played, and it was kind of like *The X Factor*. There's a lot of truth to that X thing. Some people had it, but Allen Woody was covered with it. He just had that charisma. It was like having a revolver with a bunch of unmarked bullets and trying to fit them into the cylinder, and then finally one just slid right in there.

It wasn't necessarily his chops. There were some guys that were more technical, and they could lay down the groove and support the band and all that. This one guy played well—he played a lot like Willie Weeks—but he was just a raging geek. I imagined riding on a tour bus with him, and it just didn't fly.

We got through the longest day in history there. We told everybody to go home, that we'd contact them. We're all sitting in the band room, and it was just hands down. Somebody goes, "Man, Allen Woody was a son of a bitch." I hadn't remembered his name—I'm not too good on names, but I'm great on faces. I've heard quite a few names, you know? We come to find out he was from Nashville, where I was born, and had been playing just about as long, played with people that all of us knew. I just thought that this guy was meant to be here. It was unanimous.

Once we had Woody in place, the déjà vu just continued when the people at Epic Records tried to get us straight in the studio, like Capricorn had ten years earlier. And just like last time, we all said in unison, "Fuck that. All we've done is sit down in a room over in Tallahassee. We seem like we're going to get along together, but let's see how we do over a long stretch." We told them that we were going to do a tour, and if everything worked out—spiritually, musically, and personally—then we would go into the studio and do a record.

For the crew, I brought in Bud Snyder and Rich Cramer from the Gregg Allman Band, and Joe Dan and Red Dog came back to work for us. Joe Dan had been making custom boots in Macon, and Red Dog was doing stagehand work in Tampa. It was good to have them back, and we always tried to take care of those guys.

Some years later, me and Red Dog had a falling-out. Red Dog got fired, but not necessarily by me. He probably just left us as much as he was fired, because he was just getting too old to be humping amps. Last year he passed, and it was right as my own health was a problem, so I couldn't go to the funeral. They called me and told me he was real sick, that he had lung problems. He was a heavy smoker. He got COPD and quit smoking, but it was too late for him. Boy, I miss that old coot. I will always hold him in the highest of respect, and I don't think there's a person in this band who didn't just love him.

At first, we really didn't have any management looking after the band, but then Danny Goldberg, who had worked with Led Zeppelin, Bonnie Raitt, and a whole bunch of other people,

stepped into that role. Danny told us to go ahead with the reunion tour, and then, if we were still cool, we would record an
album with a chunk of money at the end of that. So that was our
mind-set as we set out on the *Dreams* tour in the spring of 1989.
In March 1991, we didn't renew Danny's contract as our manager, and Bert Holman, who had been our tour manager, took
over and has been running the show for the last twenty years.

Having Woody in the band reminded us all where we used to
be. It was a real refreshing injection. Suddenly, everybody felt a
few years younger. Like when you learn a new song and it's really
killer, and you sit there and play it six or eight times, it renews the
whole project. You spit out a new one and it's like "Well, I'll be
damned, I can still do this."

Sometimes you feel like you're getting stale. You've gone
around the horn and played all these songs, maybe in a different
order, but over and over still. You go to so many far-flung places
and you get new people and new audiences, some who have never
heard you. But still, after a while, you need to get new life in the
band—new material, a new player. Especially with a new bass
player, which is like the backbone of the band, everybody kind of
plays a little bit different. It's a good revision of the same thing, a
good breath of fresh air, and you have a new outlook.

I really enjoyed that tour, because we had been apart for
almost a decade and people had matured, at least musically. At
first, I think fans showed up out of curiosity—"Let's see what
you old fucks still have left"—but they liked what they heard, and
they started coming back for more. We had to build a fan base
all over again, but as word of mouth spread about how good the
music was, more and more people took notice. It felt great, man,
and that really helped the music.

I was so happy I got picked to travel on the bus with Warren
and Woody, because those two were just so funny, man. They

were like Martin and Lewis, or maybe like Eddie Murphy and Martin Lawrence. We'd get in the back of the bus and have some serious fun. All Woody had to do was say something and we would just crack up—he was a naturally funny man.

Warren and Woody didn't know each other all that well before joining the Brothers, but I sat there and watched a relationship develop that went all the way to them forming a band together, Gov't Mule. Warren knew Johnny Neel from Dickey's band, and Woody knew Johnny a little bit, but Warren and Allen didn't really know each other, and it was great watching them come together.

Warren gave the music a different flavor, there's no question. It was like adding a great spice to a pasta sauce; it just makes it that much better. He also has this intestinal fortitude where he'll just walk right up to whoever it may be and just say, "Hey, hoss. Your name is what? James Taylor? Well, come on, let's go over here and pick some." It's the same exact kind of balls that Duane had.

Good as the new additions were, that's not to say that some of the old personality rubs that had been there before didn't show up again. Dickey and Butchie got into it right away over a couple of things, and it showed once again that Dickey still wasn't into working with people; he was into telling people what to do. Meantime, my drinking was still there, but at least it wasn't interfering with my playing. I was what they call a functional alcoholic—that's what they call it in the big book. It wouldn't be too long, though, until I just gave it all up.

The first time we played at the Beacon Theatre was also in 1989. Our old friend, the legendary promoter Ron Delsener, took a chance on us, and it paid off big time. Ron has always been good to us, and he set the table for us to come back year after year. We got in there and just knocked 'em dead, man. From the first night, it was like, "Wow, guys, did that feel like the Fillmore to you?"

The guys in the band were saying it was like an indoor Schaefer Music Festival, or an indoor Woodstock, on a small scale.

Not knowing their wants and needs, we came to town the first time and just raised the roof on the place. And they must've gone, "Whoa, what do we got here? A satisfying band that plays longer than thirty minutes?" Whatever happened with the chemistry of the Brothers and the people of New York, I'm so glad it did, 'cause they're wonderful people. I'll play there till I can't play anymore. This I swear.

The Beacon started asking us, "Hey, can you come back next year?" Then they started wanting to contract us for two and three years at a time. I don't know how long the damn contract is now—till death do us part.

In the early '70s, Atlanta was our town. When we started playing the Fillmore East and the Fillmore West, we used to just bounce back and forth, and when we started doing that, then New York became our place. New Yorkers are no bullshitters. The Yankees get paid a lot of money, and I can see why. New Yorkers don't want no old, watered-down crap, they want the real deal. They seemed to get satisfied when we get off the stage; they were totally worn out, and that's just what we want.

After playing the Beacon more than two hundred times, you just feel at home, whereas other places that maybe you've played once or twice, it's more like, they live here; we're just visiting. Those feelings don't get in the way of your playing, but it's so much nicer to play in a place that's not stiff. You don't feel like you're being judged and you feel at home. By the second or third time in there, we knew, this is our place—how often can we get in here?

By the time we finished that reunion tour in '89, there was no doubt that having Allen and Warren in the band put a good, fresh wind in our sails. Those two together made the band really click. In fact, things were going so well that we went into Criteria in the spring of 1990 and cut *Seven Turns,* which I think is a very good record.

That album has a lot of songwriting and a lot of singing. There are songs written by me, by Dickey, by Warren, and by Johnny Neel, and we all sang as well. That gave me a vocal break, which left me all kind of throat to really do it right when I sang.

While we were making the record in Miami, Butchie says, "C'mon, guys, I wanna show you something. It's down in South Beach."

"I'm there," I told him. This was when it was just bad women down there, just naked as hell—anybody'd wanna go down and take a look at that.

Me and Woody were hanging pretty tight about then, so he agreed to go too, and Warren also jumped in. I think Warren knew where we were going. We kinda went in the back way and come up a one-way street, and there were these two little guys with ball caps on and gloves, throwing a ball back and forth at the ass end of this club called Tropics International.

Butchie didn't say nothing. I guess he'd already called and said, "We're coming up the back way, just don't say nothing and we'll walk by." We went in and it was one of those clubs, like in New Orleans, where you have the bar and the bottles and the band is back behind that. If you stepped forward, you're right in the bottles.

So we're sitting there and they announced the band back on and they said, "Derek Trucks." Butchie looks over and gives us a shit-eatin' grin and says, "Wait till you see who it is." Suddenly I see the two kids from outside who'd been throwing the ball and they walked onstage. It was the same way with me when I'd started playing. If you're underage, when you left the stage, you had to leave the building where they're serving alcohol—as if somebody wouldn't bring you one.

I said, "That's your nephew—that's your brother's kid."

And he said, "Yep, that's my nephew, but hang on to what you got when he puts that guitar on."

They came in and put on their gear, and Derek was just barely taller than that Gibson. He started with that slide—matter of fact, slide was all he knew how to play at that time, and I thought, "Well, that's a first."

But he blew the roof off that place. After the first song, Butchie leaned over to my ear and said, "And he's not a bully." I laughed—Dickey was such a fucking bully.

I said, "Man, how old is this guy?"

He said, "Well, he's *almost* ten."

I love Derek Trucks, and I always have. Derek has turned out to be a fine musician and a fine person, one of my favorite people in the whole world. Now he's all grown up, has two kids, he's outta sight—and his wife, Susan, is too.

Recording *Seven Turns* went so well that a year later we decided to do another one. We recorded *Shades of Two Worlds* at Ardent Studios in Memphis, and that went pretty well. Percussionist Marc Quiñones came in to play on a few tracks, and we loved him so much, he never left. It's funny—my brother had always wanted a percussion player in the band, and we got one twenty years later.

I was mostly sober for that whole recording session, and that certainly helped. It was much easier for me, because I could concentrate on what I was doing. Tommy Dowd noticed it too, and he would say funny little things to me like "Thanks for not making me wait two weeks for those vocals."

Let me tell you something; that man lived a full life up until he died in 2002. He had done everything I had done twice. He could run any technical stuff there was, and built some of it. People don't realize that Tommy worked on the Manhattan Project in World War II. Good God, from the Manhattan Project to cutting rock and roll records, the man did it all. I had my heart invested in Tommy Dowd—I loved him like he was family.

It was about this time that I also got involved in acting. I'd done my first movie back in 1988, and it was called *Rush Week*. I'd played a guy who had been in college so long that they finally decided to make him a member of the faculty. His name was Cosmo Kincaid, and he was like the president of the student body, kind of a liaison between the students and the faculty. The movie opens with Cosmo sitting across from this girl who was naked and cross-legged. The truth is, I had some pretty fucking lame lines; it was a real B movie. We shot for three days in Los Angeles, and it was freezing the entire time.

Then in 1991, I did the movie *Rush*. We shot it in Houston, and collectively I was there about a month. I had to keep commuting back and forth from Houston to Memphis, where we were recording *Shades of Two Worlds*. The experience was great, because Sam Elliott and Jason Patric showed me the way and held my hand through the entire process. They told me not to sweat anything and really made me feel comfortable.

One night we all had a night off, so I looked in the paper for entertainment, and I saw "Dan Electro's Guitar Bar: Live Band on Tuesday Night." I thought, "Man, it's Tuesday, and that's the place." I got Sam and Jason and told them, "C'mon, man, let's go downtown and I'll show you what I do in my spare time." We go to the bar, I picked up a black Les Paul, and the guys in the house band knew every tune there was. We had a blast, man, let me tell you.

Rush was directed by Lili Zanuck, and she and I look like brother and sister. She is so sweet, and I'm just in love with that lady. From the moment I met her, she made me feel at ease. One day I told her, "If it wasn't for Richard"—her husband—"you'd be in real trouble!"

There was one shot where they washed my fucking hair seventeen times. I finally told them, "Listen, if one more motherfucker washes my hair, I'm done. If you ain't got the take in the can, then you ain't got the fucking take, because this hair ain't getting wet again!"

Despite that, I really enjoyed the whole process. It was a different facet of the entertainment industry, and I wanted to see how those people worked together. I didn't have all that many lines in *Rush*; it was more of an attitude thing. Also, if I did another movie, I wouldn't want it to be so serious. *Rush* was some serious shit.

That same time, I met a woman named Shelby Blackburn and we got together. I told her that I had four kids, and the way the world was going, I couldn't see bringing another child into it. We were together for a couple of years, and everything was fine; she was on birth control and all that. Then, right when it was looking like we were fixing to split up, she got pregnant. It felt like entrapment, man.

Her family came out from Indiana to visit. Her father, mother, and two of her brothers were there. I sat them all down and said, "Now, look, your daughter is pregnant. I've been married five times, and I'm not getting married now. If Shelby wants this baby, it's hers, and I will pay a certain amount to support her. So she can have it, or we can abort it while it's still a little drop of water." They all said, "No, no," so this little drop of water grew into Layla, who is a singer and a songwriter now.

Her full name is Layla Brooklyn Allman. There's no particular reason why her middle name is Brooklyn; Layla Brooklyn just seems to roll off the tongue, and I thought it was a really hip name for a girl.

Then one day in 1994, my daughter Island came to live with me in California. I really hadn't seen Island since her mother, Julie, and I had split in 1981, and all of a sudden there she was. I'd been drinking off and on at the time, still trying to get sober, and the bottom line was Julie wanted Island to live with me.

So I took Island in, and at first it didn't work. I sent her to a school nearby, and she just didn't do shit. It was a Catholic school, because she had been raised as a Catholic by her mother. It's one of the finest Catholic schools in the world, and it just happened to be right down the street. Her grades were terrible, and she would lie about things just for the sake of lying.

One night, after she'd been living with me for about five or six months, she was in her room, and when I went back there I could smell cigarette smoke. I knocked on her door, and she opened it just a crack. I asked what was going on, and I started to walk on in. She put her hand right in the center of my chest, and I asked her what she thought she was doing. I told her to get her hand off of me, but she didn't. Man, I got madder and madder, and within five seconds, I was as mad as I could get.

"Island," I said, "I'll tell you what I'm going to do. I'm going to go into the family room, and I'm going to sit down, and I'm going to cool out for about an hour, and then I expect you to meet me for a talk. Don't be late." If I hadn't walked away, I would have done something violent, and I didn't want to do that. I'm not proud of that reaction, but that's where I was at that point.

Sure enough, she came out, and I told her that while she was living in my house, she would do as I say, and I told her that I loved her. After that, she stopped doing all that shit, because she saw that I really cared about her. She'd really thought that I was going to come in that room and beat her, because she could see how upset I was. When I didn't, I showed her how much I loved her, and that really surprised her.

Eventually we got to liking each other, and somewhere in there, she grew up real quick. I don't know when it happened, but it seems like it happened over a weekend or something. I swear to God, she got better and everything was fine. Thankfully Island overcame all that stuff, and she loves me—good God. She's really proud of the fact that she's the first Allman ever to graduate from college, and even from graduate school, and so am I. Island is the love of my life.

I moved out to Marin County for most of the '90s; that was where Island and I lived during this time. The Allman Brothers never felt like we fit in musically in San Francisco, but I have a lot of real close friends out there, so it seemed like a good spot for a bit. I liked living out there; it's just that there were too damn many people. You got a freeway with six lanes on each side. If I wanted to ride my bike, I had to load it up on a trailer. Everything's either uphill or down. I had to load that heavy piece of iron up on the trailer and back it down a long driveway—which is all downhill. That was scary, but I made it every time.

I'd drive my hog up to the Sonoma area, up in the wine country, which was great. Sometimes we'd check into a bed-and-breakfast up there, and then I'd have Saturday and Sunday to ride. That was more worth it. But when I'd have only Sunday to ride, I had to get up early, load that thing up, take it down that long driveway, haul it all the way up north into Sonoma, unload the bike, ride around Sonoma all day—which was real fun. Then my tired ass had to load that sucker back up, drive it back down to Marin, load it up that hill, and take it out of the trailer. And I wonder why I have arthritis today.

I've loved motorcycles since I was little. I was riding one before it was legal to ride. When I was growing up, you would get a learner's license at the age of fourteen, and you could drive a motorcycle on the street as long as it wasn't above 10 brake horsepower. You didn't get much sauce out of that—it's like a scooter or a moped.

On the front of my *Searching for Simplicity* record, there's a picture of me at the ripe old age of fifteen. When we would go back to Nashville to see my grandmother in the summer, this guy named Tim lived down the hill. He looked just like George Thorogood, same haircut, flopped down in his face. I loved that guy. He had a Harley-Davidson 125 Hummer. That's when I learned to drive, sitting in front of him, way up on the tank. He must've had a lot of faith. But he said, "Once you get the hang of it, man, you got it."

When the family—meaning my mother and me and Duane—moved from Nashville to Daytona Beach in 1959, there was no I-75, no 95, there weren't any interstates. Eisenhower was in office, and he's the one who put in all that infrastructure. On the way, we were coming down 301, and we came through Savannah. It was in the early morning; I loved that time of day. We were going down the street and there were all these oak trees, it was like this tunnel. At the very end was a Harley-Davidson shop and they were all out there, different colors, looking like little pieces of candy. I thought, "I oughta come back to this place someday." Sure enough, I did.

I didn't hesitate to get back on after Duane's accident, or Berry's. Not at all. Think about it—it has nothing to do with me riding a bike. It only has to do with them. My brother had two speeds—ninety and parked. At one time, just about everybody in the band had a motorcycle. Mostly, we all had Triumphs. We'd go riding, and my brother would be like seven blocks ahead of us. We'd say, "We're going to go to this certain beer tavern up here," and when we got there, he'd already be there.

"Is Duane going?"

"Well, he's kinda going, you know?"

He didn't seem to get enjoyment out of riding; he got enjoyment out of speed.

Oakley had just learned to ride after we put the band together, and he was the same way. He had a Datsun 280Z, when they first came out, and he used to fly around in that thing.

You gotta let the motorcycle become a part of you, and of course, you gotta drive defensively. I don't go on the freeway; I stay on the two-lane. I usually just putt. If it's wide-open spaces, with nothing on either side of the road, I might open it up then. You gotta see what the ol' boy can do—once, at least.

Riding a motorcycle will just blow the stress right off of you. It's a total feeling of freedom, and having control of that much power just does something for you. It's not an ego builder or anything like that, but it's a real good feeling. Some people got it, some people don't—some have the fever for it, and some people live their whole life and wouldn't even go near one. That's totally understandable, because not only can you get killed on one, but you can get just about drawn and quartered.

But that's a rarity, and now there's so many of them. Drivers used to ignore bikes on the road, but now there's not a time I go riding I don't see at least ten of 'em. Man, just talking about it has me itching to ride.

BECAUSE I'D JUST ABOUT DONE MYSELF IN BY DRINKING SO MUCH during the '80s, I honestly wanted a change—it just took a while.

When the band got back together in '89, I really did try to quit drinking, but I didn't get any help from Dickey. He was drinking just as hard as me, and he looked at me like, "You poor trash." He would call me a hypocrite, anything to make what he was doing right and what I was doing wrong. Of course, I tried to ignore it. I didn't bear him any malice. I wasn't judging anybody, and I never have. I'm not a judgmental person—I do not have the right to say anything about what other people do, because whatever it is, I've done it.

But we had some great years, despite Dickey. The name of this section could be "And one more time, it worked." We were back in the saddle again. After Allen came in, we just steadily kept getting better and better. I started writing new stuff and everything was fine, except for Dickey. I would catch myself saying, "It's always something"—you fix this end, that end goes wrong.

Still, I think it was the fact that the band was working out so well that allowed me to make the change that I really needed and get sober. Early in the '90s, I was drinking real heavy. I'd given up on drugs, but I just traded one for the other. It's such a sleazy way of living. When you sweat, you smell like vodka. You know, I say I "traded," but if drugs just fell into my hand, if somebody came by and they had some killer blow, we'd do it. I just didn't reach out for it, didn't have to.

Musicians get famous and they're sitting ducks for it. "Here, man, try some of this; it'll get you going onstage." Then, "Here, man, try some of this; it'll settle you down after you get off of the stage." And sure enough, it does for a while, and then it becomes a way of life. It's insidious. And cigarettes are right in there with it.

The more you drink, the more you have to drink. At one point, I was up to one and a half, sometimes two quarts a day. And the whole time I was drinking I had no idea that I had hepatitis C, which affects your liver. I've often wondered, if I'd known back then that I had hepatitis C, would I have drunk as much? I'd like to think not. It was a rough ride.

The Brothers went to Japan in '91, and that was good. I was still one of those twenty-four-hour drinkers, though, with a pint under the bed because the next morning I would have the shakes so bad. In Japan they had vending machines on the damn sidewalk; you got a pint of vodka in there and you just put the dough in, if you can figure out which coin is which.

During the day, I would try not to drink too much, and some days I would get it just perfect. The band tried every way in the world to help me, but it's something a person's got to do on their own. I'd go on these benders and then I'd come down—to come down off alcohol is rough, man. You see spiders and all kinds of stuff. I don't know if it's as bad as heroin; it's just different. I don't think it's any less scary.

It finally got to the point where, right before I quit drinking, the other guys were gonna throw me out of the band. That just crushed me, to think that the only reason I was in the band was because of my last name. But they were like, "Man, you let us down," and I can't say that I blame them. I started having introitis—I would forget intros. I would know the song, I probably wrote it. But they'd call "Black Hearted Woman" and I'd think, "How does that damn thing start?"

Which brings me back to the Rock and Roll Hall of Fame ceremony. I was totally disgusted with myself for letting myself get drunk that day. I knew I shouldn't have gone out of the room. I was so repulsed. But I didn't stay long at that rehab in Pennsylvania either. I caught the plane back to California, and I might have had three drinks on the plane just to make it back. It was a nightmare; it really, really was.

A few days later, somebody came over and showed me the footage of me accepting the award. When I saw that, I was just mortified, to the point where I hired a male nurse to come into the house. Now I was bound and determined to get released from booze, and I thought the best way of doing it was by myself, in my digs, in the familiarity of my house.

At the time, I'd been seeing a woman named Stacey Fountain, who I eventually ended up marrying. She was so proud of me then, saying, "You've got to stop wearing this chain—you look bad, you smell bad." Then she grabbed me and said, "But I love you anyway. I don't want to lose you, not to that fucking bottle."

She was right, and she had a lot to do with saving my life, not only with my drinking, but also during my treatment for hep C several years later. But the one it started with is me; a person has to want to be set free from that shit.

Mind you, I'd been to, like, eleven rehabs, but I always had that little spark back there saying, "All right, go ahead and dance for 'em, get 'em off your back for a while. I'll meet up with you later." Not this time. This time, I didn't go to any rehab. I just called in a nurse—actually two guys, who switched twelve-hour shifts. Now it seems like I just kinda blacked out, but for about the next three or four weeks I was just limp. I didn't have any want though; the more time that passed, the stronger I got.

And then it was all over. I mean, it was over, man. It was flat over. I quit drinking, I quit smoking, I quit snorting anything—I quit all that. I had prayed to God, "Man, get me off of this shit," and he did. I thought, "I have been released."

First, you're just so glad that it's over. For weeks, that's the only thing on your mind. Your mind is free. You want to go out and tell everybody. Then I realized that people started saying, "Man, you're looking good." You know, they never said, "Hey, you look bad."

But then you wonder, how the fuck did all this happen? Did I get any positive anything out of all that? And you've got to admit to yourself, no, I didn't. You can see what happened and that by the grace of God, you finally quit before it killed you.

When you're an alcoholic, you don't ever stop to think, "I wonder how much my body can take?" And you don't really think about death. But as soon as it's over, you start thinking about how close you came to actually killing yourself. You hear of people having esophageal hemorrhages, when that big vein in your esophagus just pops. My blood pressure was always way up there. Now it's like 120/65, which is like someone in the NFL.

It takes over your brain. There's not much left to think with, it's all floating in booze. It's not something you can really imagine—it's like nobody knows what it's like to be locked in a cage with two big grizzlies until they do it. And even then they probably wouldn't know what to tell about it, anyway.

I only went to AA once, and it was years before I quit. I walked in, and these three girls dragged me in the corner and asked me if I'd sign this and that. One of them was hitting on me pretty heavy. I looked at them and said, "Anonymous, my ass." I walked down the street and got drunk. I showed them, didn't I?

Because AA didn't work for me, I thought I was weird until I talked to Waylon Jennings about it. Waylon told me, "Me and Johnny"—meaning Johnny Cash—"we can't go to the AA meetings or NA meetings either. But I'm gonna tell ya, brother, all you need to have an AA meeting is two drunks and a coffee pot, and that big book." And that's basically what I did.

Now I look around at my beautiful house on the water, and part of me says, "I don't deserve this," but I realize that's just an alcoholic's way of thinking. Alcoholics don't believe they deserve anything, which is a reason to have a drink. "I'm not good enough for this house, I'm not good enough for this woman, I'm not good enough for my cars and motorcycles." I've fallen off the wagon after I received a gold record—I don't know if it was because I didn't feel worthy of it or "Hey, let's celebrate, just for one day."

The truth is, I worked hard for all of this and I love having it, but every now and then I'll think of all the hell I caused other people over the years. To some people, I was just a little pain in the ass, but, next to myself, I was roughest on the band and my loved ones. That's the thing about being an addict—people say, "I'm only hurting myself." Well, that's bullshit, because you're hurting all the people around you. They haven't done anything wrong; all they've done is love you.

I always thought my alcoholism was punishment for what I had done in the past, only I couldn't figure out exactly what it was I had done. I guess it was feeling like a failure after my brother died, and he was still kicking my ass from up there. It was like he was saying, "Baybrah, I leave you, and then you go and get fucked up."

I was trying to be as a good a person as my brother, because he set the pattern for my life to follow. The way people try to be like their dads, I tried to be like my brother. The thing is, he was such an outrageously confident man and I'm just the opposite, so there was no way for me to match up to him. It made me feel like I was a failure, so I drank.

I wonder if someday they will find an answer to addiction. If they don't get an answer to this crack stuff, somebody's going to invade us, and ain't nobody going to be ready, especially if they got that pipe in their hand. That shit is like taking a hit of paranoia, man. I only tried it once, and it was awful. Crack is a terrible waste of money and brain cells—at least that's one drug that never got me.

The bottom line is that drugs are a nasty trap. All I can say is don't do it—don't fucking do it. Don't anybody do it, for any reason. If I can get through to one cat who has tried heroin once and knows that groove, and if I can convince him to stay away from that second hit, then cool. I believe in my heart that over the last few years I have saved a few people from making that mistake.

In most every interview I do, they ask me what I would change if I had it to do all over again, and I tell them that the one thing would be the drug use.

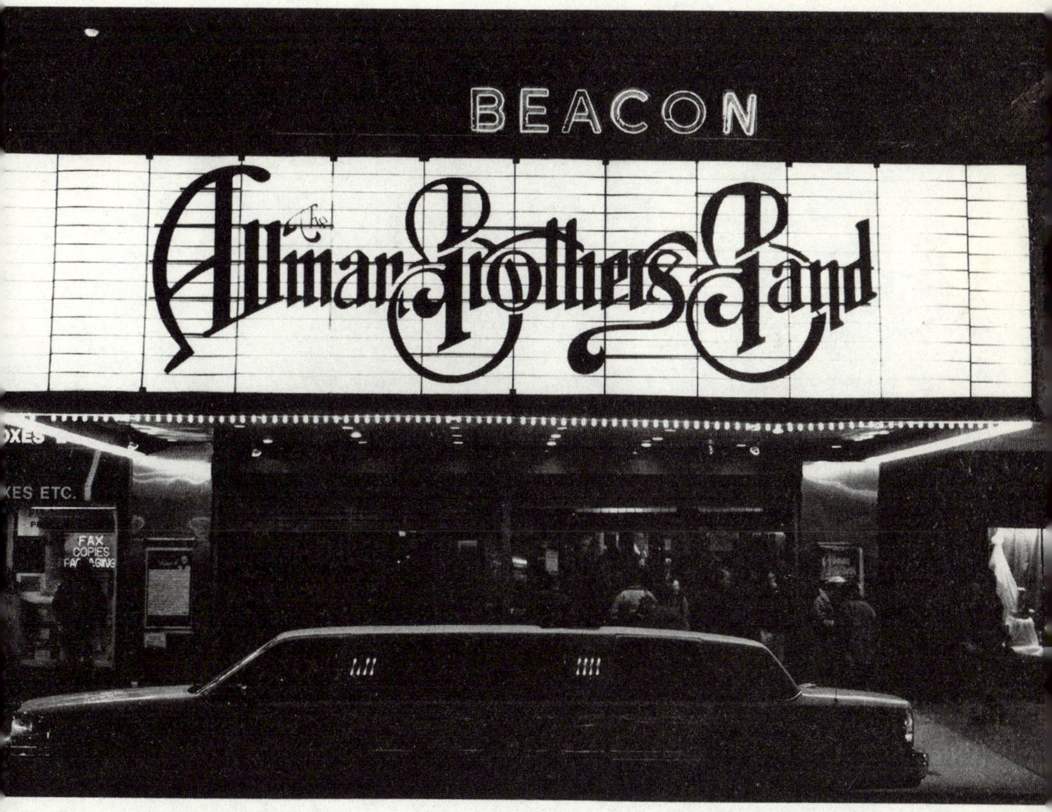
BEACON
The Allman Brothers Band
FAX
COPIES

The Allman Brothers Band in New York City, 2006

CHAPTER SEVENTEEN

One Way Out

THE ALLMAN BROTHERS KEPT ROLLING THROUGH THE '90S. We recorded *Where It All Begins* in 1994, which was a solid album overall and eventually went gold. The best part of it was recording up at Burt Reynolds's ranch in Jupiter, Florida, with cypress trees all around; it's just a gorgeous place.

And once I'd gotten sober, man, for the first time in years I was able to just sit back and enjoy it. Marc Quiñones let me know how proud he was of me for getting sober. So did Butchie, and Jaimoe too, in his own way. When we'd play shows, it was a sweet sight—the fans, the crowds. We were playing huge shows in front of packed houses. The best part was that now I was actually aware enough to appreciate them. Once we got that momentum going, we never looked back.

Still, there were problems—only this time they didn't have a thing to do with me. Now it was Dickey heading off the tracks. *Where It All Begins* was the last studio album we ever did with Dickey because both his behavior and his playing were becoming more erratic, and issues developed between him and Allen Woody.

Basically, Woody was tired of taking Dickey's shit, and it got pretty ugly between them. Warren too had grown weary of Dickey's subpar playing and the fact that Dickey's solution was to just crank it up and play even louder. The volume certainly had something to do with his drinking, which he was doing a lot of. At one point, we outlawed any kind of alcohol onstage, since I was sober. Suddenly, he didn't have anybody to drink and play with, because nobody else in the band drank.

The end result was that Warren and Allen were through. They'd wanted to devote more time to Gov't Mule anyhow, so they decided to split the band after the '97 Beacon run. I was bummed to see them go, but I completely got it.

Even after Warren and Allen left, we still tolerated Dickey, and instead of doing something to try and get him to change, we once again went through the tough process of replacing two premier musicians. Thankfully we got lucky. Jack Pearson was one of the best guitar players in Nashville, and an old friend of Warren's. We knew right away he was the guy. Jack Pearson is tops—he can do it all. There's no question that he's one of the most accomplished cats I've ever played with; Jaimoe said that Jack's playing is the most like Duane's of anyone who has ever been in the band. High praise, indeed.

Finding a bass player was a bitch. We had two or three guys we really liked, but we ended up going with Oteil Burbridge, who had played with the Aquarium Rescue Unit with Bruce Hampton and in Butch's band, Frogwings. Oteil is like two clicks away from Stanley Clarke, and he and Jack and are both salt of the earth, so they fit right in.

As good as Jack was, it soon became clear that he couldn't handle the volume level Dickey played at, but Dickey continued to refuse to turn it down. He wouldn't do it for Warren, and he wouldn't do it for Jack; he just didn't give two shits. Finally Jack couldn't take it anymore, so he left after the Beacon in '99. In the years since, Jack has played a lot in my solo band, and I truly enjoy that man's company.

By then, Derek Trucks had kinda come of age, so we brought him on board for the summer tour. Derek brought this new energy with him. Everyone was like, "Oh, boy, who's your new guitar player?" And here come the girls too. God, it was like the old days—only they weren't asking for me!

I think Dickey loved it when Derek came on, because he learned a lot of shit off Derek, though he would never admit it. From where I sat, it would come time for Derek's solo and Dickey would get back, almost drop his hands, and play very little and watch Derek like a hawk. At first I think he tried to outdo him, and then he must have realized—what's that thing about old dog, new tricks?

But not even Derek, talented as he is, could make up for all that Dickey was doing wrong. Finally, I'd had it. Getting clean was like having my windshield washed, and it felt like me, Jaimoe, and Butchie were all too caught up with Dickey's bullshit. In the spring of 2000, we did an eight-show run that ended in Atlanta on May 7; during this stretch, Dickey was drinking a ton of beer, and God only knows what else he was doing. He was in rare form, blowing song after song, and the worse he got, the louder he played. It was a total train wreck, and just embarrassing to the rest of us.

As I walked off the stage, I had it in my mind that I was going to resign from the Allman Brothers Band. As it turns out, Butch was thinking the same thing, and told his wife, Melinda, and our manager, Bert Holman, that he would never play with Dickey Betts again.

Butch and I talked the next day, and I told him, "Man, I cannot take, and will not take, any more of this shit from Dickey. I'm better than this, and I cannot live another day with that son of a bitch trying to lord his bullshit all over us. Fuck this. I'm really pissed at myself for not quitting five years ago."

Butch said, "Well, shit, man—why should we all have to leave, if he's the one who's doing it? Let's just fire the bastard."

"Contractually, can we do that?" I asked. I mean, I hadn't read the contract in a while.

"Man, in the scheme of life, we ain't got no contract," Butch said, and that was it. We both agreed that a line had been crossed and that he had embarrassed us for the very last time.

We got a conference call set up with Jaimoe, and he agreed that Dickey was out of control. The three of us felt he needed to get into rehab and that we should play the summer tour without him, but Jaimoe would not agree to saying he would never play with Dickey again. I remember Jaimoe saying something like "The only way out of the Allman Brothers Band is to quit or die."

It stuck with me, because Jaimoe was right—it was a brotherhood and those were the rules—and it speaks volumes about Jaimoe's character too, after what Dickey had done to him back in 1980. But we agreed that we could not let Dickey's demons take away what we had worked so hard for. We decided to look for another guitar player to play the 2000 summer tour with us.

I wrote a letter to Dickey, and boy, it was a stinger. I faxed it up to Bert Holman, and Bert said, "Well, that's a little harsh. Let's try to ease out of this thing, let's make it as easy as possible and not entice a lawsuit." He said, "Let me try to rewrite it."

That draft was rewritten by Jerry Weiner, the band's lawyer, and we all signed off on it. Then it was eventually faxed to Dickey by Bert. Bert and Jon Podell called Dickey and told him to check his fax machine. And that's when the shit hit the fan.

In the years since then, Dickey has said that we fired him by fax. We never fired him; we said nothing about not working with him ever again. We all had Jaimoe's voice in the back of our heads—"the only way out of the Allman Brothers Band is to quit or die"—and we chose our words carefully. What we told him was this: "Dickey, we've been together a long time—we love you and respect you—but you're getting way off base here, and you're bringing your worldly crap onstage with you. It's been going on so long that we would like to inform you that this next year we're going to be playing with another guitar player, so you can go into rehab, go do whatever you need to do to get yourself fixed. Then hopefully at the end of the year, we can get back together." That is not firing him.

Sure enough, as soon as he got the fax, my phone rang. I knew who it was, and I said, "Dickey, don't even start. I don't want to talk to you."

"What the hell is this?" he asked. "You're firing me out of my own band?"

"Man, this ain't your band no more—you done pissed it away," I said.

He kept going on and on, and I finally said, "Dickey, I don't care to talk to you at all. You can talk to me through my attorney," and that was the last time I spoke to Dickey Betts.

The next thing that happened was not that Dickey got medical help as we had hoped; instead he hired lawyers and sued us. I was afraid it was going to go to court, but it didn't. It went to arbitration, and we had to spend a lot of time in New York in front of an arbitrator named Mark Diamond.

We all met at the hearing, and I have to say, of all the situations we'd been in together since this whole thing began, we'd never been in a setup like that. It's hard to be in a situation like that and not find yourself thinking about the very beginning of it all and how the hell it came to this. When Dickey got there, he brought with him a cassette of every single thing the Allman Brothers had ever recorded. It took up a whole big duffel bag. He unzipped that thing, dumped it out on the floor, pointed to it, and said, "Brilliant."

The arbitrator asked him, "Are you speaking of the Allman Brothers?"

He said, "No—me."

And once he started that shit in there, of all places, I thought, "Well, we don't have to worry about this. He's not going to do himself any favors." We all had to hold back the snickers, and then we started talking about it. We let him know, one by one, that he was not brilliant. We went through this and that, and a whole lot of legal bullshit—it was just a drag. It was kind of embarrassing going around the room telling this guy, this arbitrator, who doesn't even know us, all this real private stuff that we'd been through. I felt like we were kids sitting in front of Mom and Dad, saying "Well, he did this" and "No, he did that to me!" I thought, "Man, is this how it's done?" I couldn't believe the process.

In the end, we were happy with the ruling, but it was all so much energy wasted on such a cold fucking thing. I was so glad when it was finally over. That was when Jaimoe said, "Well, I guess Dickey quit." We did not then, nor have we at any time since then "fired" Dickey. His favorite line that he was "fired by fax" is just bullshit, plain and simple.

Now I don't feel any anger when I think of Dickey. I don't feel much of anything. It's over.

♪

DICKEY WAS FINALLY GONE, BUT WE STILL HAD A TOUR TO DO. WE needed a great player with a thick skin who was willing to deal with the "Where's Dickey?" bullshit and the inevitable comparisons. We found absolutely the right guy in Jimmy Herring. Jimmy had played with Oteil in the Aquarium Rescue Unit and was very good friends with Derek, so that helped a lot. He stepped up to the plate and got us through the summer, but he never wanted to be Dickey's permanent replacement.

Jimmy was happy to be onstage with us, but it was bittersweet for him to get the gig at someone else's expense; he was concerned about the karma of the whole thing. When the summer run was over, so was Jimmy's time with us—but he came through for the Allman Brothers Band, no doubt. I'm tickled pink that he has gone on to such great success with Widespread Panic, and that he's the same friendly, humble guy he's always been.

With Dickey gone and Jimmy Herring not coming back, there was only one person to turn to: Warren Haynes. Sadly, in September 2000, not long after our summer tour ended, Allen Woody died, and that was quite a blow for everyone, especially me. I think about Allen every single day of my life. I don't know what it is, but the boy got under my skin. Obviously, Warren took Woody's death incredibly hard, and given everything that had happened, I thought his returning to the band just made sense.

I picked up the phone, called him, and said, "Brother, it's time to come home." Warren agreed, and we all tore it up at the Beacon in 2001. It was a great run; Warren and Derek had it going on, and Chuck Leavell showed up for four shows, so we gave the New York fans something to remember.

The next logical step was to get this lineup into the studio, which we did in 2003. On that album, Warren and I wrote some songs that I'm so proud of. As a songwriter, Warren makes me feel brand-new. We get on the same wavelength as well as two people can; writing with Warren is kind of like writing with yourself. He's really good at finishing ideas and getting to the end result. When something repeats itself twice, on the third time he'll change the music; it sounds like a whole new thing, but you're still singing the same lines. It's really amazing to watch him do that.

I've never written with anybody else as closely as I've written with Warren. I don't know why that is, but I could just never get it going with someone else. We usually begin with something I've already started. I'll show him where I got stuck, and he'll say, "Okay, let's see," and throw out an idea. Then we'll build on it. We see eye to eye on most everything, and there's total courtesy between us. We both get so into it; it's really intense.

Warren came down to my house in Savannah, and the first thing we did was "Desdemona," which raised the bar for the entire album. We also finished "High Cost of Low Living" and "Old Before My Time," which is a very personal song; I've been through some pretty tough times in my life. "Old Before My Time"—no truer words were ever spoken, man. Butch really loved that song; he felt it was me at my absolute best, which was nice of him to say.

The end result of all this writing was *Hittin' the Note,* and I honestly believe it's the best thing we've cut since my brother was around. We did it in ten days, and it has a lot of spontaneity to it. Everybody was smiling, and there was so much communication— the kind of communication without talking. That good vibe was captured on tape, and it was all because that big dark cloud had been lifted off of us.

For the first time in as long as I could remember we were a group who all liked each other. No more dictators, no more drunks. It was like it had been way back at the start all those years ago, an attitude that Butch, Jaimoe, and I hadn't felt since Macon. On that record, we rekindled something that had been lost for so long—that feeling of what this band was really supposed to be about. The groove was back in the Allman Brothers.

Naming an album is like naming a hound dog—it's not easy. "Spot" and all the other good ones have been used already. We were really floundering, and one day Butch called and said he had come up with "Victory Dance." We all went round and round on that one for a while, and then Butch called again and said, "Dig it man—how about using Oakley's old saying, 'hittin' the note'?"

Back in the old days, I thought that "hittin' the note" was a Chicago phrase that Oakley had picked up on, but I found out that it was actually his own saying. When my brother and Oakley were alive, "hittin' the note" always meant the band was having a great night, with everybody totally on the same page—just right in the pocket, man. It made sense, and *Hittin' the Note* became an easy choice.

That record is just solid, and it brought a whole new breath of life into the band. Since then, we've built on that momentum and chemistry. Right now, the Allman Brothers is as good as we want to be on any given night. The only thing that can stop us is us, and that ain't no lie.

Promo shot for Low Country Blues

CHAPTER EIGHTEEN

Low Country Blues

WHEN I WAS TWENTY OR TWENTY-ONE, I GOT MY FIRST tattoo. There weren't many laws governing tattoos back then. I was in San Francisco, and I went to one of those old houses. I walked up these really steep steps and there was a sign on the door that said, "Welcome, art lovers." I thought I was so grown-up—bullshit.

The guy was sitting there behind an old desk that was turned sideways so he could look out the window. He had two big galvanized buckets, with these long things sticking out of 'em. In one bucket, it was just clear—might have been water, might have been kerosene, who knows? The fluid in the other one was red. I walked in there and he said, "What can I do for ya, son?" I should have said, "Show me the door," but I said, "I'd like a tattoo."

He reached in the red bucket, pulled out two of these things, put 'em in the clear bucket, swished 'em around real hard, and then slung the extra fluid on the wall. I could tell it was blood just by the way it was dripping, but it didn't dawn on me that those were two used needles.

I guess there was something that they loaded into the needles, and they had little covers over them when they were laying in the bucket. He picked them up and *bzzt, bzzt*—"Okay, son, what do you want and what color?" I said I wanted a centaur, for Sagittarius. And that was it.

Nowadays, if the law walks in there, your books had better rhyme with the number of needles you have, since a certain amount of them come in a package. If you don't have a record of each tattoo, you're out of business right there, license taken. But that didn't happen back then.

I think that's where I got hep C. It lay dormant in my liver until the drinking days started. I'd done so much drinking that I had a little cirrhosis, and they'd started watching my liver closely. Around the time I first moved to Savannah in 1999, I went in and got a total physical, and they said I had a spot on my liver.

"Well, what are you gonna do?" I asked.

They said, "We're just gonna watch it."

So we watched it for, like, nine years. In 2006, it had become the size of a dime, but we kept watching. A couple years later it was the size of a quarter, but this time it had real depth to it—it was a tumor. Not only that, but there was another one next to it.

I went to New York, where my manager, Michael Lehman, had gotten me an appointment with Dr. Ira Jacobson—he's a hepatologist and he's like the man to see. He took a biopsy and said what I had was malignant. I'm going, "Oh no, it's the old C word—oh God, I've got cancer."

Between my doctors; my wife, Stacey; and Michael; we all decided I should go on a regimen of interferon. I felt like shit for about six months and we canceled the Beacon shows in 2008, and I didn't play at the Wanee Festival that the Allman Brothers had started organizing in Florida a few years before. I began to feel better for a while, but then it went downhill again, and my viral load shot back up.

By now, there were three visible tumors. Little did they know that on the bottom of my liver, in an area that's nearly impossible to photograph, there was another big one. That motherfucker was older than all the rest of them. It was only later, when they took it out, that they discovered it. Dr. Steve Carpenter in Savannah looked after me real well during this time.

In 2009, Dr. Jonathan Sussman did what they call an ablation. That's when they go in the femoral artery and go up through that, up to the liver, and they shoot it with a big dose of chemotherapy. I felt like dogshit, but at least my hair didn't fall out.

They got that cleared up, and soon after that I went back to Jacobson to get a biopsy, but they couldn't get one. They tried four times, but my liver was too fibrous. I was awake for all this biopsy stuff, and they just kept shooting my liver with lidocaine. He tried and tried until he was getting red in the face and sweating. He couldn't get it, and finally he said, "You ever heard of the Mayo Clinic?"

"Yeah, hasn't everybody?" I said.

"Well, when it comes to transplants, they're one of the best," he said.

"Transplant?" I was confused. This was the first time anybody had mentioned that. I started thinking back to the first heart transplant, which was like a hundred years ago; the guy lived for a week and everybody was all excited.

In early 2010, I went down to the Mayo Clinic in Jacksonville on the recommendation of Dr. Carpenter. Down there, I met Dr. Denise Harnois, who is an incredible doctor and has always had my back. Physically, I still felt good. All the chemo had worn off, so when I showed up, I was in the pink. They examined me, gave me an MRI and a CT scan—the whole shit—and afterwards they said, "Well, because of those tumors, you've qualified for the liver list."

I said, "Yeah, put me on it, for sure," but I asked them, "What if I said I don't want this operation? What would happen then?"

"Well, for about two years, you'll live like you're living now," they told me. "You'll have about two good years, and then you'll start to falter and you'll have a slow, agonizing, painful death—it'll take anywhere from two to five years." So I got on the list at New York Hospital, where Jacobson is associated, and also the Mayo, because I was told they have the shortest waiting list, plus it's only a couple of hours away from home.

While I was waiting, we went on tour—we did the Beacon run and Wanee, and then I did some solo dates—so we contracted with a private jet company. You pay a flat rate, and anywhere you are in the United States, if a liver became available, they would pop over and pick me up within two hours.

It took five months and five days for me to get a liver, and let me tell you it was a tough wait. When I was busy playing gigs it wasn't so bad, but when I came off the road, I spent four or five weeks at home trying not to think about things. I was laying out by the pool one day, and I called my manager and said, "Michael, I'm fucking bored to death. I've ridden all my motorcycles, I've been here, I've been there, I've seen all my friends. When are they gonna fucking call me?"

"Gregory," he said. "People die waiting for a liver."

That hit me real strong. I was on my cell phone, and it took me a minute before I said, "I don't know—I don't wanna die, but all this just seems like bullshit to me."

"Just have another dip in the pool, lay in the sun, have something to eat, and chill," he said.

I hung up, and just a couple of hours later Michael called back all excited. He said that the Mayo had a liver for me.

I was just speechless. "The Mayo has a liver for you." I didn't wanna hear that—but then again, I did! I got in a great mood, and I was real joyous and feeling healed.

I called Judy Lariscy, my house manager, and I said, "Judy, they found me a liver."

She said, "Well, that's great. I already got a bag packed. Throw some stuff together and split."

I got from Savannah to the Mayo in two hours and twenty-two minutes, and it was the twenty-second of the month, so I thought maybe all those twos were a good sign. I got there and they said, "All right, here's your waiting room." We waited and waited and waited—and at four thirty in the morning on the twenty-third they said, "All right, let's get you in your gown."

A guy came in with two shots. I already had the IV in, and he shot them in there. Whew—I was stoned, but I was still conscious. There were television screens all around this one bed in the operating room. A guy came in and he's got a syringe about this long, the plunger's over here, pulled back. The thing was full of what looked like milk. Turned out it was propofol, the stuff that killed Michael Jackson.

"Say hello to your main surgeon," I heard someone say behind me, right as a guy popped into view.

"How are y'all doing today?" he asked.

"I'm okay," I told him. "You ain't gonna hurt me, are you?"

"I'm most certainly going to try not to. You might be a little sore when you wake up, but this too shall pass." You hear that a lot around the hospital.

They hooked up the milk thing, the main doctor tapped his finger, and I went, "Ooohhh." I felt like I weighed nine hundred pounds. And then nothing. No dreams, no nothing. There were about eight people around, all of 'em matched up with the hoods and the gowns; if they had any facial hair, it was all covered. It seemed like I had just dozed off for a few minutes.

I woke up and said, "When are you gonna start?" Then I saw I had a big peace sign on my belly—one big cut down and then two coming off of that. I looked at my fingernails and they'd already started to turn real pink. A little while later, they came in and said, "Man, when we opened the gate, the main artery, that liver just came alive. It turned the most beautiful color red. Usually, we have to give people a few units of blood, but not you."

It went real smooth, it really did. It was great that the first person I saw was my ninety-two-year-old mother, and she had knitted some psychedelic purple booties for me. I was up walking around within twenty-four hours.

This kind of operation is like building a ship inside a bottle: part of the challenge is making more room to work in. They've got one machine that comes down from the ceiling and it goes on either side and spreads your whole rib cage open. Oh, and all the bones back in your spine, they're all in cartilage, right? They need to see back in there, so they pull those, and that's going right down into your backbone, right into your spinal cord, which goes to your brain.

Cutting, suturing, whatever with skin—yeah, that's all painful—but the bone pain was unbearable. I stayed awake for the first four days because the pain was so bad. I got zero sleep for about two weeks, because you just feel it whenever you breathe.

In the end, I stayed in the hospital maybe three or four weeks. It was an ordeal, but it was done.

I GOT THE TRANSPLANT IN JUNE, AND WHILE I WAS HEALING UP, I spent a lot of time thinking about the solo album that I'd finished making the previous December. It had yet to be released, but I knew I had this record in the can, as they say, and that was something to really look forward to. Actually, it was a lifesaver—when things got real bad, real painful, I would just think about this record and it was kind of a life support system. It greatly helped in my healing. As a matter of fact, it might have gotten me mentally ready to start working before I really should have gotten out there and started kicking again.

Before I'd started on the album, it had been a long time since I'd made a record. I had been dodging the words "new album," cringing when they came along, since 2002, when Tommy Dowd passed away. He was the guy, he did it all. After he passed away, I thought, "What are we gonna do when it comes time to record?" I didn't want to meet any new producers, because it felt like going backwards.

In the summer of 2009, I was at the end of a Brothers tour—we were somewhere way north, up around Detroit or Minneapolis—and Michael, my manager, called me and said, "On your way home, I want you to stop by Memphis and meet somebody." Reluctantly I said okay, because this "somebody" turned out to be T Bone Burnett.

I went down there and checked into the old Peabody Hotel. T Bone's reason for being in Memphis was one of the hippest things ever—he was there with a couple of architects and carpenters, and they were looking at the Sun Records studio and measuring it board by board. You wonder what happened to those old rooms—Motown's Hitsville studio had the best rhythm guitar sound in the world, and now they sell T-shirts there, at most. The old movie theater that was the Stax studio, they just let the rent go on that building or something. T Bone's plan was to re-create Sun Records on a piece of land next to his house. I thought that was the coolest thing I ever heard.

Me and T Bone got to talking, and we seemed to have a lot

in common in terms of techniques of recording, our likes and dislikes of music itself. He had some great ideas. He said, "Somebody gave me this modem that has thousands of old old blues songs on it"—old album cuts, like Billie Holiday—old and older; you could see in some of them how swing went into the blues, all done with horns, just amazing. "I'm gonna peel off about twenty-five of these, and I want you to pick out about fifteen that you think we could, not cover—I hate that word, 'cover'—but kind of resurrect."

I took the thing and I listened to them all over about five or six weeks. Basically, what I looked for was something I could do justice to vocally, and also that we could light some real nasty music to. I'd say about half of the songs I hadn't heard before. There were a few songs that just stayed on one chord, like "I Believe I'll Go Back Home" and "Rolling Stone," and I thought, "Well, we just got to make it real interesting hanging on that one chord," and I think we did, I think we got it. I also brought up one that wasn't on the modem, which was "I Can't Be Satisfied," the old Muddy Waters song.

As I was getting ready to do this, T Bone said, "I want you to come to the studio by yourself, don't bring your band," and that almost put a monkey wrench in the whole thing. I had to really think on that one a long time.

I remembered that when we first met Dowd, he had wanted us to come to Miami to record. I thought, "Man, we just got through building this studio at home in Macon," and by this time, in 1970, we had worked 306 nights and I was starting to get a little worn out from the traveling. I thought, "Why go out if you don't have to?"

But my brother said, "This is his trip—he knows what he wants out of us, and I think he knows how to get it. If we go down there, it's his toys and his sandbox. Let's just go on down there and do it." I thought back to my brother saying that and I figured, "What the hell, can't lose, I guess."

About two weeks later, I called T Bone back and said, "All right, I'm on."

Still, he didn't tell me who the band was; I just had to wait and find out for myself. When I got there, there's Mac Rebennack, Dr. John—who'd played on my second record, *Playin' Up a Storm*; we even wrote one together on there called "Let This Be a Lesson to Ya." Then Doyle Bramhall II, who I'd met through Derek Trucks and Eric Clapton. And a guy named Dennis Crouch on upright bass, and Jay Bellerose, who is the most incredible drummer.

Jay only used one stick; the other hand would have a tambourine or a maraca. He tied these things to his leg, hollow like wax grapes, with paper clips, match heads, BBs in 'em, and they put little tiny microphones around his feet. When I first got to the studio, there were drums all over the place. It looked like a drum yard sale—not one drum matched another one. Some of them looked like they were from the Middle East or the Far East. I looked for the mounting on them—no mountings, all wood.

You talk about communication—I could tell these guys something one time and they got it done. The whole band learned all these tunes in nothing flat, and they did them really well. Somehow, the mind-set you get on a song just seems to happen. You look at the tune and right away you hear, is it a quieter song or one with lots of dynamics? That's part of the magic of music, it just creeps in there when you least expect it.

It was so good playing with Mac again. He played some kick-ass piano, and the best part was this time neither of us was looking through the fog. I kept thinking of those early shows in Boston we'd played with him, back when the Brothers were just starting out. I was so joyous inside that he had made it through those days and come out on top. And he felt the same about me. He's so funny, such a character, man—he was definitely the comic relief of the session.

We started playing and it took off like a rocket. I think we got one song and half of another one the first day. After about five hours, I don't really trust myself much. You get to where you can't really tell—your brain gets tired, you get tired all over. Unless we're in a real hot moment, I usually check out around five hours. Then when you come back the next day, it's all nice and fresh. You're rested and you can knock it right out.

T Bone used these old, ancient mics, those old square ones with the holes in them—they look like they should be in front of Groucho Marx. He would set those up all around the room; he had a different way of doing things, no doubt.

About halfway through the session, T Bone said, "I'm sorry, man, you got anything in the writing bag that you want to record?"

"Well," I said, "I don't know, but let me show you this one." I pulled out "Just Another Rider," which was a song Warren and I had written.

He said, "Yeah, that's fine," so I said, "Let it roll." We learned that one inside of a day.

I played a lot of guitar on that album. I can pretty much choose which instrument I need to be playing to suit what I'm doing. If I need to play guitar, then fine, whereas with the Brothers, I usually don't have to since I'm pretty much surrounded by guitars. That was really about the only difference making a solo record—well, that and that if something wasn't working out right, all I had to do to change it was say the word. With the Brothers, everything's a vote, unless it's something really obvious.

I packed enough clothes for about three weeks, and hell, I think we were only there for two. We got fifteen sides in two weeks. I thought, "Man, we're already finished with this thing?" That's the most songs I've ever had on a record, except maybe a double record, but it went down real nice.

When we started *Low Country Blues,* we had blues on our mind. I guess we were into it, because after two or three songs we had the thing named. That was good for me, because until then I didn't have an earthly idea what I was going to call it, and that can mean a lot more than people think. I'm not talking about marketing—it doesn't have to be all catchy or any of those terrible words, it just has to fit. With some albums, the title has nothing whatsoever to do with the record.

This whole thing was like it was meant to be or something, because everything just fell right in its own pattern. Even the cover shot, by Danny Clinch, really caught the right mood. It was really amazing.

Working on *Low Country* was a true highlight of my career. I owe it all to trying to keep an open mind to everything, and I owe so much to Michael Lehman for keeping me focused and making this happen. Just because something isn't the way you thought it should be doesn't mean it's a bad thing.

A FEW MONTHS AFTER MY TRANSPLANT, THE RECORD CAME OUT, and it landed at No. 5—the highest I'd ever been on the charts and the highest debut ever for a blues record, except for one by Eric Clapton, which is pretty good company. We even got a Grammy nomination for Best Blues Album, which was great— the Allman Brothers won a Grammy for a live version of "Jessica" we recorded many years after the fact, and that was still great, even if it was for an instrumental and here I am, the songwriter. To top it off, then they announced they were also going to give the Allman Brothers a Lifetime Achievement Grammy.

It was a little strange that I ended up nominated in the same category as solo albums by Warren and Derek. Some people tried to make it look like it was some kind of contest between us, but it really wasn't—I just feel proud of them, and I was real happy for Derek when he won.

The album's success turned out to be a blessing and a curse. When you have a hit record, you need to go out and work. There were calls coming from everywhere, from Australia and New Zealand, and I always wanted to go to New Zealand. It's the marlin capital of the world.

We were also getting calls from Europe, and I always wanted to build more of a following for the Allman Brothers in Europe. Everybody over there has Allman Brothers records, but in forty-two years the Brothers have only been to Europe three times. The other guys didn't want to do it because they thought we'd make less money there. I still thought it would be worth it, so I did the gigs as Gregg Allman shows in Spain, France, England, Ireland, Scotland, and Holland. Then we jumped down to Germany and we had six stops, and two of them we just burned up. Every gig we played, we just kicked.

After those shows, I caught a serious upper respiratory infection, so I had to tell Vid Sutherland, my tour manager, "Look, I don't think I can do these shows to the quality of what I want, so we're going home."

It was a huge disappointment, but there's nothing I hate more than a subpar performance. I want to give the crowd everything I got. The promoters were real nice about it, and said we could come back anytime and make it up. We came home, but I had to go back out and play three more in America. Then I was off a week. I had to go play one last show in Sturgis, and after that I came home.

The problem didn't go away, though. I kept having water collect underneath my lungs. This had happened maybe four or five times since the transplant, and I'd go down to the Mayo and they took a needle and stuck it in my back, between the ribs. Then they would take it out real quick, stick a catheter in me, and drain it. One time they got 900 ccs of fluid—that's just shy of a liter. You've seen a liter of scotch before or something like that. It's a lot.

They tested it and tested it again and found nothing malignant in there, just water and a little bit of blood. It looked like a little rosé wine. It kept collecting, kept coming, and they said they didn't know where it was coming from. The doctor said, "We need to go in there and suck all the water out, and then stick your right lung to the inside of your chest wall." What started as a relatively straightforward procedure turned into a major operation.

They started in the afternoon, and when I woke up, it was dark. My surgeon came in, and he looked just like Billy Gibbons from ZZ Top, except his beard wasn't as long. He said that because the water had been under my lung, it started to crinkle up on the bottom, and that's why I was short of breath. And I really had been, since Holland. I could still sing—you can make it on one lung—but I was a sick boy.

So I'm sitting in the hospital talking to Judy, and that's when I nodded off and had that dream I mentioned at the start of all this about not going over the bridge. My blood pressure went to zero, but my heart never stopped beating.

The next thing I knew, I woke up with this apparatus around my head and this stuff down in my lungs. I was on a ventilator, and it was breathing for me. It was late morning again, and I thought, "Man, time sure is passing quick!" That scared me so bad, because I couldn't talk and they had my hands tied, like a jailhouse hospital.

"This is just too scary," I thought, and I had this very conscious thought: "I'll go back to sleep, and when I wake up, things will have changed." So I did. I went back to sleep.

When I woke back up, a nurse and a doctor came in and said, "We're going to count to three and then we want you to blow." And when I did, they pulled this thing that looked like a plastic bag for dry cleaning out of my lung.

"What in the hell is going on?" I asked. "What happened while I was asleep?" My foot was bruised; I had bruises all over me where they'd thrown me on the table. In an emergency, they just get you up there fast as they can.

I figured after all that I must be pretty well fixed, but two days later the surgeon and the physician's assistant came back and said, "We are so sorry, Gregory, but we gotta take you downstairs one more time."

I said, "Please, don't tell me—I'm in so much pain already, and you gotta cut again?"

They made a big incision across my back and went in there. They said they had surgical debris down there, blood clots, so they had to get all that shit out of there. When I came to, I was back in my room, and now I was really in pain. They're shooting my IV with Dilaudid, and I couldn't even feel it. But it was mission accomplished.

Your lung is really, really delicate. It's like peeling an orange—you peel an orange with real thick skin and it comes off real easy. But with the ones that are thin-skinned, you can't peel one of those without cutting into it and it dripping all over you. That's the way a lung is. And inside that, you have all these little tiny holes, no bigger than a pin. Each one of these holes had started to drip just a couple of drops of blood every couple of hours. But there's a bazillion of 'em, so it didn't take long for it to add up, and I was pretty much drowning in my own blood.

In the end, though, they fixed what they needed to. When they tried to figure out why this had happened, they realized that a lot of it was related to working too much and too hard. Over time, you realize your limitations, and I know mine, down to how many nights in a row I can play, how many songs in a row I can sing, and which songs need an instrumental on either side of them.

It's time to realize that I'm not a spring chicken anymore. In my mind I'm still twenty-seven, but I have to realize that I'm sixty-four years old. I have to rest.

When I was in the hospital this last time, my daughter Island came to visit me and brought her brand spankin' new baby. My relationship with Island is very good, and I'm telling you, her son really is cute as a button. Just seeing the two of them together made me stronger. I'm about to go to her new home, up on the water in Virginia. She's really caught up in the motherhood thing right now.

Watching my kids grow up has been one hell of a ride. Sometimes I think I'm the worst father in the world, but of course I never had a father, so I don't know what to base it on. You don't get an instruction manual for how to be a father.

One problem with being a heroin addict, even a reformed one, is that when you're going through a divorce and the judge finds out that you're registered in a methadone program, it means that the mother, and the mother alone, will decide when the father gets to see his children. Therefore, I was persona non grata with my kids. Without having had a dad, and legally not being able to see my kids, I really missed out on the father thing.

If there's anything positive to take away from all the health problems I've had recently, it's that I've gotten closer to my children in the last few years, a lot closer. They're good kids. I got four musicians and a nurse. Each one has a different mother, and each one lives in a different part of the country. One lives in San Francisco, one's in St. Louis, one's in Virginia, and Elijah, me and

Cher's kid, travels the world. It would be nice if some of them had grown up down south. Not one of my kids has got a southern accent—ain't that a bitch?

I treat them just like my mother treated me. She told me in my early teens, "Son, be what you want to be, but be the best one on earth—shoot for it, anyway. You may not hit the highest rung, but aim for it." And remember, I did really well in school until I bought that guitar. I was valedictorian two years.

My son Devon Lane Allman is doing quite well. He has a son of his own, Orion Gregory Allman, which made me a grandpa for the first time. Devon's band is called Honeytribe, and he can play the fucking blues. Recently he's teamed up with Cyril Neville, one of the Neville Brothers, and Mean Willie Green playing the drums. They're all from New Orleans.

He comes to visit me on Sundays and Mondays for football. We both love football—but not college football, I can't stand that. The captive audience of all these students and the band and all that shit? The best part about that are the cheerleaders.

Devon's a good kid, and he loves me a lot more now than he used to. One time when I was drunk many years ago, I told him, "Man, you don't want to be in the music business—look what it's done to me. The best thing for you to do is go on to school and do something, but don't bother me." I said some hurtful things to him that he's forgiven me for, which is an age-old story between fathers and sons. The same thing will probably happen between him and his kid, but I hope he learns from my mistakes.

The truth is that I don't know Elijah very well at all. It seems to me that he's not happy, and that he doesn't feel good about things. Elijah was a real happy kid, but because I wasn't welcome in that household, I can't say exactly when he got so down and depressed. The thing is, I don't think Elijah can figure out why he's so down either. He doesn't have much of a family life, and if I was retired, I would get in my car and go and get him. I just wish I could get him turned on to something that he really likes.

The music he makes scares me. They call it gothic, and it's scary-sounding, man. It's like he tries to play as outrageous as he possibly can, and he definitely achieves that! I don't mean that in a bad way. I love him to death, but I don't understand his music; I just don't get it.

My little girl Layla, she's gorgeous, man. She just turned nineteen. She's a singer and a writer, which I think is great. Last year, she started calling me. One time she told me, "Dad, I'm so sick of seeing your picture and your name and hearing your music everywhere. Here I'm trying to get something going, in a completely different genre of music. So what's the big secret?"

I said, "Well, gee, let me write it on the back of a postage stamp and I'll send it to you." Come on—the secret? I guess first you go ask your dad . . .

Having the name has its advantages and its disadvantages. It seems like, unless they're playing the same kind of music that I played with the Brothers, or kind of reminiscent of that music, the name doesn't help. "Now we're gonna bring up Layla Allman—by the way, this little girl's father is you know who, ya da da." Then they're usually scrutinized more. But she went out as Layla Brooklyn, since her name is Layla Brooklyn Allman, and that didn't do it either.

I've tried to put myself in their place, and I think I would have never let people know who I was. In the end, they have to go through all of it—the hard work and carrying amps and all that shit—just like I did. You have to get out there and be seen, and make sure people know they're going to see a kick-ass performance.

This year, the whole family is coming to my house for Christmas. I think we're all really a tight-knit family; it's just that we don't ever see each other, you know? I'm the one that's always gone, so I can't really bitch.

Duane's daughter, Galadrielle, is writing a book about her father, and she's trying to talk to everybody who ever came in contact with him. She's such a sweetheart, and I wish her all the luck in the world on that. It means so much to me to have a connection to her, because I'm the only uncle. At this point, she's more like my third daughter than my niece.

The thing about Galadrielle is that she looks just like my brother. It's not just her appearance—it's everything. She has so many of his mannerisms, I tell you. Sometimes when I haven't seen her for a long time and then I see her, it's just like looking at him.

My family through the years

CHAPTER NINETEEN

Trouble No More

WHEN I WAS A KID IN NASHVILLE, WE WENT TO SUNDAY
school at the Presbyterian church on Green Hills Boulevard. It was a beautiful church, with beautiful grounds.
I enjoyed going there, because I would look at the way the place
was built and I just loved it. I didn't like Sunday school that much,
because we did things that I didn't think pertained to religion. I
thought we should have been over in the big building, listening
to the preacher.

We knew the preacher, and he would come over to the house
every now and then, like they do. It was all well and good, and as
I got a little older, my mother began to give me the option. She
said, "If you want to go to church, I'll take you. If you don't want
to go, you certainly don't have to."

I do believe in God, because somebody had to plan all this—

stuff like this just doesn't happen. I didn't always feel that way, though. For a long time, I didn't really believe in God, but I didn't really not believe in him either. It just wasn't one of my favorite subjects. Where I came from didn't really matter to me: I was here, I was glad I was here, and I hoped to do the best that I could.

Thankfully, by the time everything started going on with my liver, I'd been thinking differently about all that for a while. About fifteen years ago I started wearing a cross, because I finally got some sort of spirituality. Until that point I'd always felt alone, and while sometimes I still get that way because I have a real phobia about being alone, at least now I can do something about it. As long as you have spirituality, you're never alone. It's sort of like my mother said all those years ago: now I have my own kind of faith, just like other people. They take what they want of faith, and they leave the rest alone, and I do the same. That's the way it should be.

A big part of my getting straight with God had to do with sobering up. I've had a life that's gone all different places and directions, and I've missed out on a certain amount of stuff because of the drugs and alcohol. As I got sober, because I was so sick of missing out, I finally reached out and prayed. Before then I'd been praying for a long time, but I never seemed to get any kind of answer. Later on, though, it became clear to me and kinda hit me at once. It was such a revelation, man.

Basically, what I did, in one big fell swoop, was surrender, and with that came all the rest. My life went into something like the spin cycle of a washing machine, and when I came out, I didn't want any more cigarettes, and I damn sure didn't want any more liquor. Now, if I'm having a problem, or a friend of mine is having a problem, or something is keeping me from sleeping, I'll just lay there and not really pray so much as just meditate. I get real still and talk to the Man, and he'll help you if you ask him. The thing is, you have to help too. I don't know where the saying "God helps those who help themselves" came from, but it's so true. If you show a little, God shows a lot. If you just do what you can, he will do the rest.

God is there all the time, and so is my guardian angel, or whatever it is that keeps me from self-destructing, or keeps me out of harm's way. As many bus rides as I have taken, as many planes as I've been on, the law of averages says that somewhere, sometime, something is going to happen. Man, they have watched over me so good—but still, you're the only one who can keep you from lighting a cigarette, or pouring a drink, or loading a needle. It comes down to you having to be the man of decision.

You have to have a real belief in order to deal with life's challenges. My spirituality has allowed me to keep my demons at bay, and the more that happens, the stronger I become. There are times when I've been at the end of my rope, but never once did I seriously consider suicide. I firmly believe that if you take your life, you will go to a place that's mediocre and depressing—which is kind of the way I felt for a great deal of my life, and I don't want to go to a place like that. A lot of people say, "Well, this is your hell, and we're all going to heaven." You know what? This ain't all hell—as a matter of fact, this is miraculous. Life is such a gift.

Since I cleaned up, my faith has continued to pick up over the past few years, and I think it might have something to do with my last wife, Stacey. Of all my wives, I was married to her the longest. We were together for seven out-of-sight years. But when she said, "Let's get married," I said, "Married? Married for what?" I said, "Look, not to bring up my five marriages, but each one of them was fine until we got married, and then it started going downhill." I don't know what it was, but we got married and, once again, it just didn't work.

After it was over, like all my marriages, I really tried to be adult about it and keep some kind of relationship. Here's two people who at one time professed not only to love each other, but to be in love with each other. I still talk to Cher now and then. Cher is really a sweetheart. She has a very broad mind, a very open mind, and we were really in love too. But it's been hard for me to have a relationship like that with my other wives. Nowadays, I talk to maybe two out of six.

Still, one of Stacey's strongest influences on me was to get me thinking about God. All Stacey's people have a certain amount of faith, more than I ever had around me. She got me going to church, even though that got a little bit hinky, because people were asking me for autographs. The preacher was dynamite, and they had a full band, with horns, a killer bass player, and a choir—I loved that part of it. I hadn't been to church in a while, because I didn't believe in the dog-and-pony show—who can outdo who in the collection plate, that stuff bothered me. The church was so crowded, and it became such a thing, a happening, and although I met a lot of nice people, it was too much.

At one point I was going to convert to Catholicism, but they had so many rules. I have to say that the Catholic Church is very much about who has the nicest suit, the valet parking—too much about the money. I don't think you have to dress up or show God a bunch of gold for him to forgive you your sins, love you, and guide you. Then I went to an Episcopal church in Daytona, and it just felt right. The Episcopal Church isn't about gimme, gimme, gimme. The Episcopalians are like enlightened Catholics. They have the faith, but they're a little more open-minded.

Now I sit here in my house in Savannah, look out over the water at the oaks, and know that I have a reason to live. After all I've been through, I can't help but feel I've been redeemed, over and over. Sometimes I scratch my head about why, but the only answer I can come up with is that maybe I deserved it because I've brought a lot of happiness to people's hearts. I get letters by the week from people thanking me for my music, and you can almost see the tears on the paper. Not that this justifies anything I've done, or says that it's okay I got fucked up because I made a lot of people happy—no way. One right doesn't snuff out a wrong. All I'm saying is that maybe God just needed me down here to make some folks happy. Maybe it's that simple.

The only positive that I took from going to all those rehabs is that I kept trying, because I could have stayed out and stayed drunk, and I'd probably be dead now. Eventually, a certain amount of what they tell you in those places rubs off on you. It took me a bunch of times before I realized that I just had to get down to brass tacks. Most people with an addiction problem say, "Well, if you just leave me alone, I can take care of it," and that's wrong—but you don't need somebody standing over you with a stick either. It's like writing songs. There are as many ways to write a song as there are songs, and there are as many ways for people to get healed as there are diseases.

I'm just really thankful that I'm still here, and that I still have all my faculties about me. I'm not quite as quick as I used to be, but who is? Sometimes I'll have an ache or pain, and instead of thinking, "Well, it's just old age," I'll think, "It's probably because I beat myself to death with those fucking drugs."

Fortunately, I've stopped doing that, and I've stopped feeling guilty. I wasn't given any penance, I wasn't told, "You have to do this, this, and this before you're clean and sober, and back right with God." I don't go for none of that shit. I believe that if you're really trying, and you're the little train that could, you're okay.

For me, music and my Maker are related. I think the same of both of them, because they both serve as anchors. If I think that I'm coming apart, I realize that the piano is still here, and it still sounds the same. Sometimes I'll sit down and try to write a song, and nothing will happen. I'll sit and think, "Well, I guess it could be over." Then I'll tell myself, "Just be thankful for the ones that you did write, and if it is over, you damn sure have come out on top."

Music is something to hold on to, and to judge everything else by. It's like a sextant, because it keeps me on track. Music is a means to dig yourself out of the doldrums; it can earn you a living, and it's a friend to have at all times. Whether you're recording or trying to write something, or if you just want to sit and play and think about different things, music is always there. When I play music today, not only can I feel it, I can almost see it. I can close my eyes, and it just takes me away. Music is a very healing thing, it really is.

One time I had a man come up to me, and he was crying. He said, "Thank you for helping me not go crazy from fear in the bush of Vietnam. The worst thing for me was to run out of bullets or batteries for my radio." Boy, it hit me right in the heart, because that's a hell of a compliment. You're getting shot at, but the music gives you something to hold on to.

When you walk up on a stage, ten thousand people are out there. You don't know their names, but they know you and what you can do. What you can do is make them forget their problems for about three hours—and there's a shitload of problems out there, man. Being real easy on them, we'll give each person in that crowd one and a half problems—so there's fifteen thousand problems.

But for three hours, those problems aren't there. It's not that the music puts them to sleep either. We flat-out make them happy. Stomping their feet, clapping their hands, dancing around and smiling, lighting up their cell phones and Bic lighters—that kind of happy. I just love to see that, because it makes me feel like I belong, and everybody needs to belong to something. It makes me feel like I have a purpose, and it's a good purpose. I help make people happy, and I think in the eyes of God, that's pretty damn good. I think he wants his children to be happy—that's why he made music.

MUSICIANS ARE DIFFERENT PEOPLE, MAN. IF YOU TOOK ALL THE people out of Cincinnati and moved them to Louisville, I bet you the musicians would find each other faster than anyone else. I've said this before, and I'll say it again: the only people, besides my mother, who have ever helped me when I was down and out, and did it from the bottom of their heart, were musicians.

You see it with the tsunami or the hurricanes. It never fails—they get a bunch of bands together and raise lots of dough. I just hope and pray that the money gets to where it's rightfully supposed to land. Nothing will get you a first-class ticket to hell faster than stealing money that supposed to go to victims of a disaster. Here's a guy floating around in raw sewage, and you're out at some titty bar, spending his money? Boy, God is watching you, don't you know it!

When you're young and you have all that energy, it's great to have something to channel it into. I was fortunate enough to find music as my one main interest at such an early age. I didn't think I was Elvis, I didn't think I was going to be another Mick Jagger, none of that. I just enjoyed playing music. I couldn't wait to learn something else. Every time I'd learn something new, it would be like a rejuvenation of the whole process, and it built my love for music that much more.

When something wouldn't go my way, I'd have a bad day, or I was plain lonely, I would just go home and play my guitar. Just play and play. It's a shame that everybody doesn't have a teddy bear, like the guitar was for me, something to alleviate their mind of any pain or suffering that they are going through. When you play, you can let it out—it's almost like a good cry.

I'm not saying that it makes the pain go away, but like the old saying, "Music soothes the savage beast," it can be an elixir for your problems. There have been very few times in my life that it's come to that, but when I find myself alone—which is something that I don't care for—I play, and it helps a lot.

My feelings about being alone probably come from when I was just a child, from my father being murdered, from the years of having to stay home while my mother was at work—sometimes it would really get to me, you know? And also when I was in military school in the third and fourth grade, man, you never felt so lonesome in a crowd as attending a military school at the ripe ol' age of eight. You grow up real fast. But it was either that or an orphanage, which would have been intolerable.

I'm a firm believer in everything happening for a reason. Though it might be really questionable in your mind, it had to be done that way. Military school probably instilled a certain strength in me that helped me later. But the solitude, that didn't take. That certainly could have had a lot to do with me getting married all these times. But I've been that way all my life.

When I turned forty, and I didn't have anything to show for the Allman Brothers Band, it was a rude awakening. I had never looked ahead to what was going to happen after it stopped raining gold records and the fans stopped showing up. I don't care about business, I never have. I don't like to go shopping, I don't like to add things, I don't like to worry about money, and I don't think about money. Money doesn't impress me worth a fuck, and it doesn't make me feel good. I've had it both ways—I've been rich and I've been broke. I was blessed that we were able to get it back together, and now that I know I'm going to live comfortably for the rest of my life, it's a very good feeling.

It's easy to pin a lot of our early money troubles on Phil Walden, but that's not entirely fair to him or to us. Phil died in April 2006 after a long, tough battle with cancer. When someone like Phil passes on, someone who had a big impact on your life in both really good and really shitty ways, you have to take a step back and get some perspective on the relationship, and I did just that.

I decided to sit myself down and write a letter to Phil—not about him, but *to* him, directly. I wrote from the heart, and just laid it all out there on the paper. I wasn't able to attend Phil's funeral in Atlanta, but I arranged for my loving niece, Galadrielle, to read the letter on my behalf at the ceremony.

In the letter, I told Phil how I was in awe of him when Duane and I first met him. There stood a man who had managed Otis Redding and Percy Sledge, and now he was managing us. I told Phil that the talent lay within those great artists, but the guidance lay solely in the man standing before me and my brother. I told Phil that at that moment in his office all those years ago, I'd decided to make him and Duane proud of me. I'd decided that I would do my best to never let either one of them down.

I went on to say that just when the rocket was lifting off the ground, God saw fit to throw some undeniable hurdles our way. I admitted to Phil that I truthfully couldn't say that I did the best I could for the band after my brother was gone, because I crawled into a bottle and a syringe. I tried, I showed up, I did what I could for the shape I was in.

It felt good to write that those devils were now gone. I admitted that I wasn't sure if I would have held up at all without the advice and the presence of someone like Phil—actually, not someone *like* Phil, but Phil and Phil only. I tried to pattern my thoughts after what Phil would have done, and most importantly, I would always cherish every moment, good or otherwise, that

I spent with him. I made it clear that I chose to remember the enlightening ones.

I closed the letter by pointing out to Phil that we all had lost a lot through these last thirty-seven years, but that we gained a lot also, and that's where my heart will forever lie. I ended it with these words: "I love you, Phil . . . I always have . . . You're #1 and I know we'll do these things again . . . in a better place. God bless you and your wonderful family. With deepest respect, Gregory LeNoir Allman."

Writing that letter freed my soul, man. I told Phil what needed to be said. I made my peace with him, and it allowed me to close it all out.

It's odd to get to the point where people are starting to look at the legacy of the Allman Brothers. It's a different kind of appreciation, but I couldn't be happier watching it all unfold.

In the last couple of months, I went to Nashville to be honored at a couple of awards shows. At the Americana Awards, I got a Lifetime Achievement Award, which was really nice. It was in the Ryman Auditorium, and it's always neat going in there. They've gone in and refurbished it, but they refurbished it with old stuff, so it's still got the same soul that it always had.

They had an incredible band—a mandolin player, a banjo player, steel guitar. Don Was was playing the bass, and he's an incredible bass player. They said just pick what you want, so I took most of the band, especially the steel player, and we played "Melissa." It was one of the best performances of "Melissa" I've ever done—it was just letter-perfect.

A few weeks later were the Country Music Awards, which were in this huge place called the Bridgestone Arena. They had me come and sing "Georgia On My Mind" with Zac Brown.

It was incredible. I'm sure it might've been a little bit about me coming back to Nashville, where I was born.

On the red carpet on the way in, this lady came up to me and said, "You probably don't know who I am, but I'm Jennifer Nettles, and I'm with Sugarland." I had heard of the band, of course. Then when she won an award that night, she got on the stage and said, "I can think of nothing better than being here except one: I got to meet Mr. Gregg Allman on the way in here." I was backstage when it happened, but they told me what she had said, and then I watched it on YouTube. I was blown away by that.

That's the thing about country music. The people are so gracious, more so than any other kind of music. They're all southern gentlemen and ladies. I know a lot of those folks—Tim McGraw and his wife, Faith Hill, are both dear friends of mine. I feel like I could go to any one of those people and knock on their door and get a real good southern meal.

These days I'm lucky enough that I can count on hospitality from a whole range of folks, including my mother, who actually came to see me just last week. Now she's ninety-four and just fit as a fiddle. She was a CPA all her life, and her brain is so sharp. She makes the best chicken salad in the free world. I told her, "Mama, you could make this chicken salad and sell it in the grocery stores in jars like Maria What's-Her-Face that sells all that stuff, or Ken that sells all the salad dressing—you should have Geraldine's chicken salad." Like it ought to be, you know? It's dynamite.

My mother used to be a heavy drinker, and if you ask her about it, she'll say, "I drank till I didn't wanna drink no more, then I stopped." But she has the Serenity Prayer tacked right over her bed. The moment she saw me having trouble with alcohol, she just quit. A quart of Canadian Club a day and a pack of Chesterfields, and she just quit—not a shake, not a shimmy.

Whenever she and I get together, we have the best time. Even after all these years, the two of us, we've been through it all and then some. She's so afraid that I'm gonna die before her. That would just crush her, to lose two sons and a husband. Since October 29, 1971, it's just been me and her. I'm just gonna keep doing my best to stay strong for her and for the band.

As for the future of the Allman Brothers, one thing I know for sure is that we've got the Beacon Theatre for as long as we want it. In 2010, they bounced us out, but they gave us a big public apology about that. I wasn't expecting that—just let us back in and we'll be fine—but the best part is that now we got a deal with them where nothing can stop us coming every March, until further notice. It's so good to have a thing like that, which keeps recurring every year. I never dreamed that I would be so fortunate as to have something like that happen to me in life. And the crowd keeps coming back, and that just amazes me. It's a blessing, it really is.

I think I'm proudest of the way the Brothers hung in there during the hard times. We always did have staying power, as long as no crap started within the band. As long as we could hang together, we could deal with the slings and arrows from the outside, because we were impenetrable. We've always done our very best musically, we've never taken any shortcuts. We prove that where it matters the most—on the stage. The Allman Brothers have always given the people their money's worth, every night. We do our best to send the fans home happy.

It's an exceptional feeling to see all those young folks at the shows. When I was a kid, I didn't listen to Tommy Dorsey. There was a generational line drawn when it came to music. Kids today love Jimi Hendrix and the Grateful Dead—all kinds of good music. They love the Allman Brothers. There's that old saying, "Fun for ages six to sixty," and by God, that's what our audience is.

It's strange, because it used to be, "Hey, man, could you sign this for my kid?" Now it's, "Could you sign this for my mom? She named me after one of your tunes." A lot of times, the whole family comes to a show. Sometimes it's just a mom or dad, because one of them will feel like, "I can't go to a concert anymore, that's crazy—we're not old hippies." Well, once an old hippie, always an old hippie! And when they show up, they have a ball. It takes them back, and I love to see that.

We've had one hell of a run over the last few years, and we're very blessed to have such excellent musicians, with really good hearts. Warren Haynes, Derek Trucks, Marc Quiñones, and Oteil Burbridge have meant the world to me, Butch, and Jaimoe. They've played a huge part in this band, and they've added some good comic relief over the years. Those guys have genuine love for the Allman Brothers, and they give it 100 percent. Derek gets better every year, Oteil gets better every year, and Warren, of course, gets better every year.

It means so much to still be standing up onstage with those two warriors on the drums, Butch and Jaimoe. They both have so much pride in the Allman Brothers Band, and so do I. And why not? Over the years, what we've accomplished has finally sunk in. When we started out, we were a great cover band, but I didn't see any longevity in it. So I never expected anything like this, not in my wildest dreams. It is a sensational feeling—like "Man, we did all that?" Sometimes I just revel at the accomplishments of the six of us and what it's led into. I'm so thankful that we could bring happiness into so many hearts.

Now we even have a museum of the Brothers' history set up at the Big House in Macon, which I think is wonderful. One of our longtime tour personnel came up with the idea of turning the house into a museum. All the guys in the band got behind it, and we reached out to some of our friends and fans and asked them to help fund it, because it takes a lot of money to keep that thing up—to keep it clean, keep all the photos. We had to put an air system in there so that things wouldn't wrinkle up. You don't want the stuff to look shopworn and all yellowed out. Of course, you need a good sound system, all that stuff. And I'll be damned if it didn't work. The museum makes me real, real proud, and I try to get down there as much as I can.

I want to make sure to thank the doctors and nurses at the Mayo Clinic for all the great care they gave me, and let everyone know how much I appreciate the gift of life I received from my donor. Because of that unselfish act, I was able to return to my music.

For now, I'm taking it real easy, because they said, "If you go back out on the road like you did after your transplant, you're gonna have problems." But a player has got to play. I'm gonna try my damnedest to go as light as I can, but if traveling and making music is what takes me, I can't think of a better way to go.

Music is my life's blood. I love music, I love to play good music, and I love to play music for people who appreciate it. And when it's all said and done, I'll go to my grave and my brother will greet me, saying, "Nice work, little brother—you did all right."

I must have said this a million times, but if I died today, I have had me a blast. I really mean that—if I fell over dead right now, I have led some kind of life. I wouldn't trade it for nobody's, but I don't know if I'd do it again. If somebody offered me a second round, I think I'd have to pass on it.

ACKNOWLEDGMENTS

Thanks to my children, Devon, Elijah Blue, Island, Layla, and Michael; my niece, Galadrielle; and everyone else who makes my life so full.

To my dear friends, Chank Middleton and Floyd Miles, who have been with me since the beginning. I love you guys.

Thanks to all of the Allman Brothers Band members for making music with me over the last forty-three years, and to the Allman Brothers management, production, and road crews for helping to keep it together. To the Gregg Allman Band and crew for continuing to play killer music night after night.

To EJ Devokaitis for his invaluable efforts in pulling together all of the photos as well as for taking good care of the Big House Museum.

I need to thank Lisa Sharkey for her enthusiasm about this book, and my editor, Matt Harper, for all his hard work. Also my thanks to Liate Stehlik, Lynn Grady, Sharyn Rosenblum, Tavia Kowalchuk, Shawn Nicholls, Ana Maria Allessi, Marisa Benedetto, and all the HarperCollins/William Morrow team. And to Frank Weimann and Jeff Silberman at the Literary Group.

To the fans around the world who have loved me and my music and have always been there. You guys are the best.

Finally, I must thank my manager, Michael Lehman, for making me feel that there's a lot more successes coming down the road, and for believing that I had a story worth telling and turning that belief into this book. Thanks, bro.

CREDITS

Pages v, 28: Allman Family Archives; page 8: courtesy Brenda All-man, Allman Family Archives; pages 53, 54: courtesy SATV; page 78: Bernd Billmayer; pages 103, 206: ABB Archives; pages 104, 130, 158: Twiggs Lyndon; page 178: © Jim Marshall Photography LLC; page 194: © Stephen Paley; page 205: courtesy Wolfgang's Vault; page 223: courtesy Jerry Weintraub; page 224: www.SidneySmith Photos.com; page 239: "Please Call Home," written by Gregg Allman, courtesy of Elijah Blue Music/Unichappell Music; page 240: © 1996 Gilbert Lee, glee@gilbertlee.com; page 260: Michael Ochs Archives/Stringer/Getty Images; page 276: Herb Koss-over; page 293: courtesy Big House Museum Archives; page 294: Brian Hagiwara; page 312: Kirk West/ABB Archives; page 333: R. J. Capak; pages 334, 344, 363: Danny Clinch; page 364: Mama A and Gregg: W. Robert Johnson; Gregg and Galadrielle: Toby Can-ham/Getty Images Entertainment/Getty Images; the two others are Allman Family Archives

First Insert

Pages 1 (*top left and right*), 2 (*top left, bottom left and right*), 3 (*bottom right*): Allman Family Archives; pages 1 (*bottom left and bottom right*), 2 (*top right*): courtesy Brenda Allman, Allman Family Archives; page 3 (*top*): courtesy Ann Williams Bacon & Matthew D. Godwin; page 3 (*bottom left*): courtesy Lee Hazen & Joe Bell; pages 4, 7 (*bottom left*): ABB Archives; pages 5, 9 (*bottom*): © Stephen Paley; page 6 (*top*): Baron Wolman; page 6 (*bottom*): Albert J. Sullivan; pages 7 (*top right and bottom right)*, 8, 9 (*top*), 13 (*bottom*): Twiggs Lyndon; page 7 (*top left*): W. Robert Johnson; pages 10 (*bottom*), 11: © Jim Marshall Photography LLC; pages 10 (*top right*), 14, 16 (*top left*): www .SidneySmithPhotos.com; pages 12 (*top*), 15 (*top*): © Bob Gruen/ www.bobgruen.com; page 12 (*bottom*): Peter Tarnoff/Retna; page 13 (*top*): Annie Leibovitz/Press Images; pages 15 (*bottom*), 16 (*top right and bottom*): Herb Kossover

Second Insert

Pages 1, 2, 6 (*top*), 7 (*top left and right*), 8 (*top and bottom left*): www .SidneySmithPhotos.com; page 3: Jeffrey Mayer/JTMPhotos, Int'l; page 4 (*top*): © 1996 Gilbert Lee, glee@gilbertlee.com; page 4 (*bottom*): courtesy Chank Middleton and Mama Louise Hudson; pages 5 (*top*), 6 (*bottom*), 9 (*top*): Herb Kossover; page 5 (*bottom*): Steve Morley/Redferns Collection/Getty Images; page 7 (*bottom*): Michael Ochs Archives/Stringer/Getty Images; page 8 (*bottom right*): © Bob Gruen/www.bobgruen.com; page 9 (*bottom*), 10: Kirk West/Big House Museum Archives; page 11 (*top*): Brian Hagiwara; page 11 (*bottom left*): Alan Schwartz; page 11 (*bottom right*), 12 (*bottom left*), 13 (*bottom right*): Kirk West/ABB Archives; page 12 (*top*): Toni Brown; page 12 (*bottom right*), 13 (*bottom left*): Danny Clinch; page 13 (*top*): © Jay Blakesberg; page 14 (*top*): Michael Weintrob 2012; page 14 (*bottom*): © Derek McCabe; page 15 (*top*): © Dino Perrucci; page 15 (*bottom*): © Joshua Timmermans/Noble Visions; page 16 (*top*): WireImage/Rick Diamond/Getty Images; page 16 (*middle and bottom*): David Plakke Media, NYC

INDEX

Note: Page numbers in italics refer to photos.

INDEX

INDEX